THE SWORD IS NOT ENOUGH

Manchester University Press

THE SWORD IS NOT ENOUGH

Arabs, Israelis, and the limits of military force

Jeremy Pressman

Manchester University Press

Copyright © Jeremy Pressman 2020

The right of Jeremy Pressman to be identified as the author of this work has been asserted by him in accordance with the Copyright, Designs and Patents Act 1988.

Published by Manchester University Press
Altrincham Street, Manchester M1 7JA
www.manchesteruniversitypress.co.uk

British Library Cataloguing-in-Publication Data
A catalogue record for this book is available from the British Library

ISBN 978 1 5261 4617 5 hardback

First published 2020

The publisher has no responsibility for the persistence or accuracy of URLs for any external or third-party internet websites referred to in this book, and does not guarantee that any content on such websites is, or will remain, accurate or appropriate.

Typeset in Arno Pro and Univers
by R. J. Footring Ltd, Derby, UK
Printed in Great Britain by TJ International Ltd, Padstow

CONTENTS

Acknowledgements vi

1 The Arab–Israeli fight 1
2 Force as the dominant policy 20
3 Peace cannot be forced 68
4 Force, insecurity, and failure 99
5 Missed diplomatic opportunities 133
6 Changing the dominant idea 172
   Conclusion 189

Notes 212
References 244
Index 281

ACKNOWLEDGEMENTS

I greatly appreciate the many colleagues, friends, and family who offered thoughtful feedback and commentary. I offer great thanks to the many librarians who helped with this research. I appreciate that the University of Connecticut Humanities Institute, the University of Haifa, the University of Jordan, the Norwegian Nobel Institute, and several conferences gave me the opportunity to present and/or reflect upon parts of this project. Thank you to Manchester University Press for the opportunity to make my argument public. As I have worked on this book, the Department of Political Science at the University of Connecticut has been an excellent home.

The opinions, arguments, and any remaining errors in this book are my own.

This book is dedicated to Audrey, whose passion for a better world inspires me. Her unending love and support helped make this book possible.

Chapter 1

THE ARAB–ISRAELI FIGHT

In the wartime environment of 1948, the Khairi family was expelled from their home in what is today Ramle, Israel. The Khairis, a Palestinian family, ended up in the West Bank. After the 1967 war, which brought the West Bank under Israeli rule, Bashir Khairi, a young boy in 1948, visited his former home in Ramle. But he was never able to regain control of the home or move back to it. Khairi, later a leader in the Popular Front for the Liberation of Palestine, drew a very clear lesson from the experience: 'Force expelled us from our land, he reasoned, and only force will get it back'.[1]

In 1956, Moshe Dayan, then the chief of staff of the Israel Defense Forces, delivered the eulogy at the funeral of Roi Rutenberg, a Jewish resident of Nahal Oz, a kibbutz near the Gaza Strip. Rutenberg had been killed in an ambush. Dayan mentioned the temptation to despair and to fail to face up to the meaning of Rutenberg's death. But in the end, Israelis could not look away from the hard meaning of the loss: 'This is our life's choice – to be prepared and armed, strong and determined, lest the sword be stricken from our fist and our lives cut down'.[2]

This book illustrates and critiques the beliefs that Arabs and Israelis hold about how best to achieve their fundamental political and security goals. What is the best way to get what one wants in international affairs? In the Arab–Israeli context, the dominant belief has been that (1) military *force* is the best way to achieve one's goals and (2) negotiations and concessions are a sign of weakness that only invite further demands and military attacks.[3] In contrast, the major *alternative* belief is the reverse, meaning that (1) *negotiations* and concessions are the only way to secure a stable and peaceful future and (2) a reliance on military force is often counter-productive. This book's primary focus is on assessing and understanding the effectiveness of force, the dominant belief. Of course, because these two beliefs are inter-related, many of the judgements about the success or failure of using military force have implications for the success or failure of negotiations as well.

To be clear, my interest is in analysing and evaluating what political actors believe about the policies or means that they may pursue. I am not evaluating their beliefs about the ends, goals or interests. Instead, I take as given that the Arab states, Israel, and the fragmented Palestinian national movement have the standard array of ends and national interests such as the desire for security, for maintaining independence, for ensuring state survival, and for protecting the integrity of their borders and territory.

I provide evidence that the dominant belief is that using force is the best way to get what you want. I also note evidence of the main alternative belief, the efficacy of negotiations. The dominance of the belief in military force has meant that war and confrontation characterize much of the Arab–Israeli relationship. That said, there are examples of where the alternative idea broke through and negotiations were the favoured means, whether with a successful result (an Egypt–Israel treaty in 1979 and an Israel–Jordan treaty in 1994) or not (the Oslo diplomatic process, 1993–2001; the Annapolis diplomatic process, 2007–2008).

Despite the continued dominance in policymaking circles of the idea that force is the best foreign-policy tool, that very emphasis on force has three major shortcomings. First, negotiations – not force – are the only means by which to conclude a peace agreement. Military means fall short, so a continued policymaking commitment to force precludes moves toward ending the conflict. Second, the use of force has often led to greater insecurity, the exact opposite of what its proponents desired. In short, the belief in the success of military force often has proved counter-productive. Third, this same belief in force has resulted in missed diplomatic opportunities.

I do not mean to suggest that military force and diplomatic negotiations are wholly separate. Governments may be pursuing both pathways simultaneously. Some overlap between different tactics is inevitable. Rather, my concern is about the emphasis. Which one is primary in their thinking? Which one do officials view as more likely to produce national security and other important outcomes they seek?

There are already many excellent histories of the Arab–Israeli conflict, and I do not seek to replicate them here.[4] Most of them take a detailed, chronological approach. Instead, this book is a work of historical explanation. It draws on existing theoretical and historical work and uses brief case studies to illustrate different understandings of force, negotiations, and their interactions in the Arab–Israeli conflict. I cannot describe what I hope to do better than in the words of Theda Skocpol, a professor at Harvard University: 'Some books present fresh evidence; others make arguments that urge the reader to see old problems in a new light. This work is decidedly of the latter sort.'[5] This is neither a comprehensive history nor a theory-generating work. Rather, it is a stylized, selective history that, I hope, will deepen the reader's understanding of the Arab–Israeli relationship.

Ideas and methods

I use the terms 'beliefs' and 'ideas' interchangeably. Either way, I am interested in how Arabs and Israelis, and especially their leaders, *think* and *talk* about the usefulness of military force and negotiations. The last few decades have seen a lot of scholarly attention devoted to ideas, especially with the introduction and growth of 'constructivist' thinking in the study of international relations.[6] Professor Jeffrey Legro's definition of 'beliefs on instrumentality' accurately captures the object of my interest in Arab–Israeli relations. In Legro's words, I study 'beliefs about effective means for achieving interests or how states think about achieving their ends ("instrumentality")'.[7] Like Legro, I describe each belief and its specific content. However, whereas he was most interested in explaining why such beliefs change, I am more interested in the negative consequences that have resulted from the specific dominant belief that I study. What is the impact of the ideas?[8]

To assess the Arab and Israeli beliefs about the usefulness of force and negotiations, I look closely at speeches, statements, and foundational documents. I evaluate what policymakers said. The tradition of analysing speech, discourse, rhetoric, and narratives has been widely used in the study of politics.[9] As Alan Finlayson and J. Martin explained, 'The political speech can provide a glimpse into the process by which ideas and beliefs are manifested in argumentative contexts'. Speeches, they added, seek to get others 'to see situations in a certain light'.[10] I looked for details and themes that were repeated across several speeches, with the idea that repetition means an idea or belief is more important than a one-off point.[11] While I rely on a wider set of statements, scholars have sometimes based a political argument on a close textual reading of a single important speech or important document.[12]

In addition to looking at speeches and statements, the other main method in this book is the historical case study.[13] Such studies are especially important for allowing me to flesh out in chapters 3, 4, and 5 the shortcomings of the belief in the success of using force. In other words, historical case studies help illustrate what can result from a deep, abiding belief in the power of military force to get one's way in international affairs. By providing multiple historical examples, I seek to rebut in advance the idea that one can come up with one example for just about anything. Rather, these short cases illustrate a continuing tendency in the conflict's history. Because I aim to give multiple examples in each chapter, the cases do not have the depth of a full-blown case study, but they still provide some convincing evidence and demonstrate a little bit wider applicability of the thesis or claim.[14]

Historical case studies also shed some light on events that confirm or disconfirm either the advantages of force or the advantages of negotiations. As Legro noted, events can undermine or reinforce a dominant or an alternative idea. If the new idea can 'generate desirable results', it may stick.[15] Yet events that should bolster or undermine a belief do not automatically do so. Existing beliefs may be resilient in the face of recent events and episodes.

Overall, though, what also becomes apparent is that the belief in the success of relying upon military force as the primary policy often has been resistant to events that seem to challenge its central tenets. The idea of using force is resilient. In contrast, the belief in the success of negotiations has been more quickly undermined by events that challenge its central tenets.

I should note that the cases here are not selected to test certain theories or to develop new theories or one new grand theory. Instead, the cases are illustrative, meant to exemplify my probing of the dominant idea that the other side understands only force. Overall, I want to *evaluate* a common, central belief (that force is the best tool in the foreign-policy toolbox) that is often held by people, both inside and outside the Arab–Israeli conflict, regarding that conflict. I demonstrate that that belief creates certain problems. In order to do so, I highlight some historical episodes that *illustrate* those problems. I aim to help people better *understand* the Arab–Israeli conflict, and thereby affect the *meaning* of the conflict in people's minds, rather than test political science theories or build a new grand theory.

Rival beliefs: military force versus negotiations

States have the choice of at least two different beliefs about the use of force and negotiations in international affairs. On the one hand, international actors may believe that military force is more likely to lead to success in foreign policy. On the other hand, they may prefer negotiations.

The dominant idea: force

A belief in armed force as the preferred policy instrument means that countries, or the Palestinian national movement and its constituent elements, and their leaders assume that things like threats to use force, arms buildups, strong and militant rhetoric, high spending on national security, deterrence, coercive diplomacy, and, when necessary, violence, conflict, and war are the key elements in a country's or organization's foreign-policy toolbox.[16] At the same time, actors may recognize that there are other diplomatic and cultural approaches – I am especially thinking of negotiations – but they nevertheless hold that such efforts are secondary to military strength, force, and coercion. If I threaten or use military force, my adversary will capitulate and concede, and I'll get what I want.

The different ways that states or organizations may use force in this way are as follows:

(1) internal military buildup (internal balancing)
(2) formation of military alliance (external balancing)
(3) supply of military aid (may include arms)
(4) exhibiting a military posture (e.g. alert, mobilization) – military moves that fall short of the actual use of military force
(5) language of force (rhetoric that includes threats to use force or doctrinal or ideological support for force)
(6) civilian direct action (violent demonstrations)
(7) structural violence against people or property (may include arrest, detention, expulsion, sexual assault, torture) – repression or violence against civilians by the state's military establishment, including counter-terror activity
(8) unconventional violence, that is, not by the state's military establishment and indeed often *against* the state's military establishment, such as terrorism and political assassination, using –
   (a) knives, stones (weapons short of guns)
   (b) small arms (guns)
   (c) suicide or car bombings, IED (bombs)
   (d) sexual assault, abduction, torture
(9) conventional force used by armed actors (state or non-state), often called 'war' –
   (a) closure, blockade
   (b) occupation of territory
   (c) small-arms attack (i.e. with a weapon that can be carried)
   (d) artillery and ground attack, rocket fire (usually if both, then 9d subsumes 9c)
   (e) aerial attack

(10) use of massive unconventional force – chemical, biological, radiological, nuclear.[17]

Better understanding how military force has affected the Arab–Israeli conflict contributes to a broader debate in international relations. Military force has long been central to the discipline. As Kenneth Waltz, the most prominent realist scholar, explained, 'The daily presence of force and recurrent reliance on it mark the affairs of nations. Since Thucydides in Greece and Kautilya in India, the use of force and the possibility of controlling it have been the preoccupations of international-political studies.'[18] Around the same time, Robert Keohane and Joseph Nye argued that 'realists assume that force is a usable and effective instrument of policy. Other instruments may also be employed, but using or threatening force is the most effective means of wielding power.'[19] As Paul Gordon Lauren, Gordon Craig, and Alexander George explain, armed force 'carries a seductive appeal to those who believe that military might will enable them to act as they wish and get what they want'.[20]

In the Arab–Israeli arena, the most common belief is that a repeated reliance on military force will help achieve central goals such as independence and survival. Defeat and destroy the other side, or at least repeatedly hit them hard enough so that eventually they concede.[21] Another way to think about it is that states seek a massive and increasing advantage in military capabilities; a large and growing imbalance will force the weaker party to accept a resolution, probably one dictated by the stronger rival.[22] For example, in a call for a more forceful US policy, Robert Kagan warned of enemies who 'still believe in the old-fashioned verities of hard power, at home and abroad. And if they are not met by a sufficient hard-power response, they will prove that, yes, there is such a thing as a military solution.'[23] Or, perhaps even a party that appears weaker when judged by traditional measures of power may be able to inflict enough constant pain – loss of life, fiscal costs, uncertainty, instability – that the seemingly more powerful side says enough is enough and backs down.[24] There are some examples of when the idea that force produces concessions has succeeded in the Arab–Israeli conflict.

One important version of this idea revolves around the notion of deterrence.[25] By threatening the use of force, the rival will be *deterred* from acting aggressively or seeking to realize its territorial or political ambitions. Or, to think of it using a common term from the discipline of international relations, a less powerful state will 'bandwagon' with a more powerful state.[26] The less powerful state will think it better to join or appease this powerful, angry state than to risk a destructive confrontation. In the real world, in 2002–2003 the George W. Bush administration's arguments for invading Iraq were often based on this kind of logic; neo-conservative thinkers embraced the concept of a powerful United States deterring and cowing its enemies.[27] What would happen if the United States used force to topple Saddam Hussein? Former US vice-president Dick Cheney explained: 'Extremists in the region would have to rethink their strategy of Jihad. Moderates throughout the region would take heart.'[28]

As a further example, Amir Lupovici of Tel Aviv University offers powerful support for the notion of seeing Israel's recurring policy of deterrence as an idea. He further argues that Israel's commitment to deterrence – an idea – also constitutes its identity. This is not automatically the case in every country, and he offers Spain as a counter-example. Citing other scholars, he embraces the centrality in Israeli thinking of the idea of military force's usefulness: 'As Yaniv suggests, the use of force has "become almost an instinct with the Israelis"'. Lupovici noted 'A dominant Israeli view is that the Arabs only understand force'.[29]

Although Lupovici is focused on ideas and identity and I am focused only on ideas or beliefs, I think the general consistency of the two works reinforces my claim that the efficacy of force is the dominant belief.[30]

The idea is not only that force is the superior tactic but also that offering to negotiate and to put concessions on the table is a sign of weakness. The Middle East is a rough neighbourhood. Keep your guard up, lest you open yourself up to exploitation. Negotiations create vulnerability and other actors will use the diplomatic opportunity to take advantage. They may simply pocket concessions that are offered without making any concessions of their own. They may use negotiations as a deceptive ploy to prepare for or execute a military attack. In any case, negotiations may very well lead to insecurity and could even jeopardize a country's core needs, like independence, survival, and territorial integrity.

The secondary idea: negotiations

Having outlined the dominant idea in the Arab–Israeli conflict, let me now turn to the secondary idea. That secondary belief is the inverse of the first idea (that force and military strength are the best approach). Instead, it is the idea that negotiations and concessions will lead to the achievement of core national objectives. By reliance on negotiations, I mean that countries, national movements (in particular the Palestinian national movement), and their leaders assume that things like concessions, cooperation, mediation, negotiations, treaties, and some types of diplomacy are the key elements in a country's or organization's foreign-policy toolbox.

Negotiations make room for nuance and clever solutions, whereas force is often a blunt, winner-takes-all instrument. In negotiations, the parties set priorities and start to think more deeply both about what they must have and about what they might be willing to concede in the name of stability or peace. Negotiations may also lead to greater interactions between leaders, who then learn about the leaders on the other side and, gradually, begin to better understand the other's needs. They start to see the possibility of coexisting and minimizing, if not eliminating, the human losses.

The other component of this second belief is that the threat and use of force are often counter-productive. Force can backfire, leading to greater insecurity as it emboldens adversaries, sparks arms races, and invites forceful and violent responses. It obscures diplomatic openings that might lead to a pause in or end of the conflict. It causes great human suffering, including countless casualties. It has a self-perpetuating quality that creates lose–lose situations.

Let me be clear that this second, alternative idea (that favours negotiations) is not defined as total capitulation or surrender to the other side. It is neither a pacifist belief nor a renunciation of the threat or use of force. Actors do not simply demilitarize and then peace emerges. For the person who says 'but military force has a time and a place', yes, there *are* historical cases where the reliance on force has helped Arab or Israeli actors achieve national objectives.[31] Instead, this second belief is about a balance between force and negotiations and avoiding constant, exaggerated appeals to military force.

Although this idea emphasizing conciliatory means has been the secondary one for much of the conflict, negotiations have played a continuing role. They have not been wholly absent and, moreover, have resulted in two triumphs for the idea that fundamental ends can be secured through the means of negotiations: the 1979 Egypt–Israel peace treaty and the 1994 Israel–Jordan treaty. Since 1967, Arab states, Israel, and the Palestinian national movement have sometimes rejected but sometimes accepted the idea of sitting down at a table to settle their differences. At these moments, we see leaders turn away from an emphasis on military force. At the 1979 treaty signing, Egypt's president, Anwar Sadat, drew on the biblical prophet Isaiah: 'Let us work together until the day comes when they beat their swords into plowshares and their spears into pruning hooks'. Menachem Begin, the Israeli prime minister, spoke in similar terms: 'Now we make peace, the cornerstone of cooperation and friendship'. Years later, at the White House signing of the first Oslo agreement in September 1993, Israel's prime minister, Yitzhak Rabin, embraced a future that moved away from the reliance on military force: 'We wish to open a new chapter in the sad book of our lives together, a chapter of mutual recognition, of good neighborliness, of mutual respect, of understanding'. Moments later, Yasser Arafat, chairman of the Palestine Liberation Organization, expressed the same hope: 'My people are hoping that this agreement which we are signing today will usher in an age of peace, coexistence and equal rights'.[32] In short, sprinkled among the many forceful statements and actions is the idea that negotiation and reconciliation are pathways by which to advance a state's national objectives.[33]

Ultimately, I agree with Jennifer Milliken that different ideas make possible or impossible different foreign policies.[34] In her example using the first Gulf War, she notes how 'an elite's "regime of truth"' made military intervention possible but excluded other policies 'as unintelligible or unworkable or improper'. What policies were excluded? What policies did the George H. W. Bush administration deem as unworkable or improper in 1991? Milliken says that Bush officials did not commit to policies of either 'doing nothing' or 'seeking a diplomatic settlement'.[35] What she calls the elite's regime of truth is, to me, another version of thinking about the ideas that make certain policies more likely and others less likely. They had ideas about how beneficial military force would be in international affairs and that predisposed them to use it in the Iraqi case.

The shortcomings of relying on force

If I am correct about the over-reliance on military force in the Arab–Israeli conflict, what are the negative ramifications of that idea?[36] I answer that question in three parts – chapters 3, 4, and 5 – but the overarching point is clear: we do not often appreciate enough how the use of military force becomes a self-fulfilling prophecy, helping to bring about the very dangers we are seeking to avoid.

First, while reliance on force can bring adversaries to a state of non-belligerency (they are not actively fighting each other), *force cannot compel either party to sign a peace treaty, engage in normal diplomatic relations, or warmly embrace the other*.[37] Instead, things like normal diplomatic relations and warm interactions can come only through negotiations and post-war reconciliation. If the desired outcome is peaceful relations, forceful interactions at best can get the belligerent parties only halfway to their ultimate goal. The Camp David Accords (1978) and the Egypt–Israel peace treaty (1979), key parts of a process that transformed relations from war to peace, exemplify this argument. I also consider a case when force was not enough to seal a peace deal, the Israeli–Syrian interactions of the 1990s and 2000s. Military force cannot compel states to embrace the other side, to normalize, and to develop deep economic and cultural relations.

Second, *reliance on force can cause greater insecurity* rather than bringing the desired improvement in the security and military standing of a country or organization. The emphasis on military force can lead to a range of unintended outcomes that harm national security. Such outcomes might include suffering casualties; losing resources and/or territory; fuelling counter-attacks; generating or exacerbating an arms race; improving a rival's international political standing; undermining support at home for negotiations; strengthening a rival's view that one is hostile or hawkish; creating a new enemy or rival at both the individual and the organizational level; and causing other detrimental policies (e.g. expansionism). I illustrate these negative outcomes by looking at: the Gaza Raid and Suez war (1955–1956), a war between Egypt and Israel/Britain/France; the 1967 Arab–Israeli war, in which Israel both defeated Egypt, Jordan, and Syria, and occupied extensive new territory; the 1982 Israeli invasion of Lebanon; and the second Palestinian intifada (uprising) in the West Bank and Gaza Strip, which lasted from 2000 to 2005.

The same examples that show how military force can create greater insecurity also illustrate the kinds of things proponents of negotiations point toward to support their idea that negotiation is the best means and military force is not, because of all the damage it can do. To state the obvious, these two ideas are mirror images, so support for one generally undermines the other, and vice versa.

In general, it is worth noting, too, that the claim that force and strength provoke an even more damaging backlash echoes one of the grand claims in international relations, that balancing behaviour is the norm of international affairs.[38] Balancing is the idea that concentrations of power spark counter-concentrations of power. If one country gets too powerful, others form a counter-coalition to confront it. In other words, the assertion of military might does not lead rivals to back down or join with the powerful state. Instead, it prompts them to try to out-muscle the state that initially emphasized military strength and force.

Also, the belief that efforts to improve national security might actually backfire hearkens back to the security dilemma – the

The Arab–Israeli fight

idea that efforts to improve one's own national security may provoke one's adversaries to take forceful counter-measures. I do not think these Arab–Israeli cases are a smooth fit with the security dilemma. One type of security dilemma assumes that both sides use defensive tactics to advance defensive aims.[39] The dilemma is that they might misperceive the other's moves and ascribe offensive content to what was intended as a defensive move. Due to this misperception, escalation and confrontation may result where nobody wanted them. In the cases here, however, Arab and Israeli actors often take offensive action. Egypt's moves in May 1967 or the 1982 Israeli invasion of Lebanon should not be categorized as misunderstood defensive tactics. In terms of the goals of military action, whether the aims were defensive and oriented to the status quo is ambiguous in some examples and simply not the case in other examples.

A less common definition of the security dilemma considers cases where one state can protect itself only by undermining the security of its rival.[40] It still has defensive aims but it might use offensive or aggressive tactics to try to achieve those aims. But this definition of the security dilemma faces a similar challenge when looking at historical cases. The defensive nature of the objectives is hotly contested. Egypt could argue that it was defending its allies such as Syria when it escalated the situation on its frontier with Israel in May 1967, especially given that the Soviet Union had inaccurately told Egypt that Israeli forces were massing on the border of Egypt's ally, Syria. But Egypt's policies were provocative and challenged Israeli security. Israel could say that it invaded Lebanon in 1982 to defend itself from the Palestine Liberation Organization (PLO), which was then headquartered in Lebanon, but the invasion of another country all the way to its capital (Beirut) and the desire to engineer the establishment of a friendly Lebanese government that would formally ally with Israel were goals beyond the defensive realm.

Neither Egypt in 1967 nor Israel in 1982 was content with the status quo.

The Palestinian national movement, like any national liberation movement, is challenging in this light as well. It is a non-state actor, not an independent country like the other actors in this book, and it is seeking to achieve Palestinian self-determination. By definition, the PLO did not accept the status quo because there was no state of Palestine in the status quo. It was not seeking to defend something it already had, as one could at least plausibly argue for a nation-state. Since it sought to revise the existing state of affairs, its aims hardly qualify as defensive (even if what it ultimately sought was security for the Palestinian people).

Whatever one decides about the utility of the security dilemma, the broader argument of chapter 4 stands independently: the threat and use of military force sometimes makes a state's national security situation worse, not better.

Third, *the belief in the effectiveness of military force can result in missed diplomatic opportunities.* The belief in force makes leaders predisposed to express scepticism about potential diplomatic openings. Negotiations are thought of as a sign of weakness. Entertaining negotiations and concessions only invites further challenges by one's adversary. If one gives an inch, one's rival will take a mile. Diplomacy is derided as mere appeasement and diplomatic offers are often a treated as if they are a ruse. I use short case studies to characterize how the diplomatic opportunities are missed or dismissed. When I come to historical case studies of missed opportunities, I analyse: the PLO's plan of 1974, when it said it would establish Palestine on any part of liberated land rather than waiting for total territorial control; the Arab League's Arab Peace Initiative (2002), a blueprint for two states next to each other, Israel and Palestine; and Israel's 'disengagement plan' (2005), when Israel closed down its settlements in the Gaza Strip and withdrew about 8,000 Israeli settlers.

The Arab–Israeli fight

The point of this book is not that force and coercion have no value in international affairs. Sometimes Arab and Israeli actors have relied on force and coercion and still achieved some important objectives. The Egypt–Israel peace process on which I later build the case that force is insufficient to move past non-belligerency is itself also an example of the impact of military force. For had Israel not triumphed in the 1967 Arab–Israeli war in the way that it did and had Egypt not triumphed in the 1973 Arab–Israeli war in the way that it did, Egypt and Israel post-1973 would not have welcomed non-belligerency and then more conciliatory relations.[41]

In short, the *interplay* between force and diplomatic negotiations is crucial. One problem for states and organizations, though, is that they are not finely calibrated machines that can adjust the exact dosage of force and diplomacy in an instant in any given situation. In the Arab–Israeli arena, the balance has tilted toward strength, force, and coercion. Many of the participants have focused on the benefits of military force, to the detriment of other options.

I also want to acknowledge up front that this conflict includes two different types of entity: countries and non-state actors. The countries – or 'states' as scholars often call them – are in a different and fundamentally more powerful position in terms of material capabilities. So to say, for example, that many in Israel and in the Palestinian national movement believe in the likely success of relying upon military force is not to say that the types of military force (and economic resources) that they have at their disposal are equal or equally powerful. Israel, and other states like Egypt and Syria, have a distinct advantage over non-state actors when measuring how much force they can muster. That does not guarantee the states will use force efficiently and translate force into the desired influence, but it does highlight an important distinction to keep in mind. One result is that when threatening or using force, non-state actors, such as the Palestinian national movement, may to a greater degree also need to generate some symbolic or political impacts from the threat or use of force, since actual military defeat of the other side is unlikely.

Summarizing the argument

The conventional position is the Arab and the Israeli belief in the power of military force. But this belief in military force cannot lead states all the way to treaties and peace; it can get them only part way to the final destination, as can been seen in the Egypt–Israel and Israel–Syria case studies. Moreover, many force-dependent policies result in counter-productive national security outcomes. The threat and use of military force often backfire: states end up with less security, not more. As examples, I consider Israel and its role in the Gaza Raid and Suez war (1955–1956), Egypt and other actors in the 1967 war, the Israeli invasion of Lebanon in 1982, and the Palestinian side in the second intifada, which started in 2000 and ended in 2005. The idea that policies based upon force and strength, not negotiations and concessions, are the best policies can lead to missed diplomatic opportunities. In order to illustrate this point, I delve into three missed opportunities: in 1974 (the PLO's ten-point programme), 2002 (the Arab peace initiative), and 2005 (the Gaza disengagement).

To better achieve national security and other core objectives, the Arab states, Israel, and the Palestinian national movement need to turn toward greater reliance on negotiations and making mutual concessions. Charles Freilich, a scholar and former Israeli official, and I look at many aspects of the situation differently. But one of his conclusions summarizes my thoughts about Israel and the Arab parties, who are 'likely to find diplomatic tools to be both increasingly necessary and often more effective than military means'.[42]

How has the belief in military force remained in the dominant position? At the same time, what pathways allow a secondary belief, such as the importance of negotiations, to sometimes ascend and shape actors' actions? These are important questions as well. Military force is often dominant for three reasons: (1) because the structure of global politics is dangerous and competitive (or 'realist'); (2) because there are many conflicting voices speaking for each government, organization, or people, and thus it is hard to project a consistent, welcoming message; and (3) because the emotional impact of fear can make policy-makers seek military solutions, rather than negotiating. As for change, and the rise of an alternative idea based on negotiations and concessions, the key factors might include leaders who advance the idea of negotiations as a more effective policy tool; the actions of external mediators; an unexpected event that shakes up the status quo; positive back-and-forth or tit-for-tat interactions that build toward full-blown negotiations; and changing threat environments that create breathing space for more conciliatory policies. In short, the impact of a dominant idea is at the heart of this book, but we should not assume the same idea will always hold sway. Ideas about the best means for advancing one's foreign-policy objectives can change.

Chapter 2
FORCE AS THE DOMINANT POLICY

Our people must choose the path of holy war because, if we do not fight, our people will die. This world only understands the language of force.¹ (Ahmed Yassin, Hamas founder)

This is a tough neighborhood and there is no compassion for the weak.² (Ehud Barak, Israeli prime minister)

We aren't North America or Western Europe, we live in the Middle East, in a place where there is no mercy for the weak. (Ehud Barak)

In a fictitious account of the Israeli–Palestinian conflict, a Palestinian character imagines himself on an Israeli talk show. Asked about the Israelis, he contends, 'Blood. That's what they understand.' Earlier, after a bombing in Tel Aviv where the Palestinian bomber was suspected to be from the West Bank city of Nablus, an Israeli soldier proposes a solution along the same lines: 'They ought to wipe out the whole of Nablus'. 'Would that help?' asks one of the protagonists. 'The only way to teach them. They came from Nablus? Tomorrow there's no Nablus. Day after that the guy from Hebron will think twice before going on his mission', the soldier explains.⁴

Many Arabs and Israelis believe that the use of force is the most effective instrument for achieving their national security and territorial goals. Everyone only understands the language of force. To put it in historical terms, major shifts in the conflict such as moves toward non-belligerency and the offering of territorial or other concessions are a result of the use of force and violence by one party or another.

The idea of looking strong, buying arms, and forming alliances is meant to deter or compel other actors to respond even without having to engage in actual conflict. If I have big muscles and look like I am willing to hit you hard at the slightest provocation, you will not even think of testing me and risking physical punishment. While that might sound logical, the changes in the Arab–Israeli conflict have not emerged from threats or the potential of force but rather from actual confrontations and wars. The 1967 war, the 1973 war, and the first intifada (Palestinian uprising) from 1987 onwards all affected how one or more parties viewed their adversary on the fundamental question of war and peace. Some examples: As a result of Arab–Israeli wars in 1967 and 1973, Egypt moved toward a negotiated end of its conflict with Israel. These same wars, Israel's general conventional military advantage, and the decline of the Soviet Union combined to reshape Syrian thinking toward Israel. The first intifada pushed some additional Israelis to consider a negotiated resolution of the Israeli–Palestinian conflict.

What these examples also suggest is that just because Israel has the most advanced weaponry and has demonstrated its success on the conventional battlefield does not mean that other actors lack the ability to effectively use force *against* Israel. Since 1967, it has been increasingly clear that Israel is the most powerful conventional military entity in the region. Israel has used that to its advantage, as some of the historical examples indicate. Yet not only have Arab states and non-state actors (the Palestine Liberation Organization; Lebanon's Hezbollah; and Hamas, a group of Palestinian Islamists) still used force against Israel since then, but on occasion they have also used force to change Israeli policy. Thus, despite the imbalance of military power, the impact of force on policy has gone in both directions.

The first section of this chapter highlights several prominent examples of Arabs and Israelis touting the effectiveness of using force for advancing the goals set out in their documents and statements. It provides evidence that the belief in the likely success of force is usually the dominant belief in the Arab–Israeli conflict. This evidence is presented so as to substantiate an empirical claim. Force is seen as a necessary part of operating in the region. The second section looks at rhetoric from the battle between Israel and Hamas in 2008–2009, further evidence of the power of this idea that force is the best means for accomplishing major state objectives. The third section illustrates historical cases where the threat or use of military force helped a state or non-state actor advance its political and military aims. Unlike the chapter's first two sections, this section is not meant to prove that Israelis and Arabs hold this dominant belief but rather is an effort to show that people who hold the belief can point to historical moments that seem to buttress the idea. They have witnessed or studied episodes in history that seem to substantiate this belief in the efficacy of military force. The brief cases include: the 1967 Arab–Israeli war, also called the Six-Day War or June War, and how it shifted Egyptian and Syrian policy toward Israel; Israel's strength in the late 1960s and early 1970s as a factor undermining the Palestinian national movement's military approach; the first intifada, which pushed Israel toward a negotiated resolution of the Palestinian question; and two Israeli unilateral territorial withdrawals that emboldened the 'force works' narrative, from Lebanon (2000) and from Gaza (2005). These are questions of degree, where slight shifts in one direction or another might be consequential. That said, the argument is that force was an important cause but not the only one, as I will address in each case.

This chapter, then, sets the stage for the rest of the book. Yes, many Arabs and Israelis see military force as the best means. And, yes, sometimes they even can point to some history that seems to back up that idea. But, as subsequent chapters will make clear, the idea is not as beneficial as it is sometimes portrayed; instead, reliance on military force exacts significant costs and is associated with important shortcomings.

Arab and Israeli claims about the use of force

In both elite statements and foundational documents, Arabs and Israelis often express belief in the idea that the use of force is the best means to achieve one's goals. In doing so, the usually unstated implication is that the other side will either concede or be defeated. Concessions could result directly or there could be an intermediate detour through escalation. But the underlying principle is the same either way, a belief that force will help one's own side achieve its security and territorial goals. The examples that follow are typical ones from the history of the Arab–Israeli confrontation: Vladimir Jabotinsky's 'The iron wall'; the charter of the Palestine Liberation Organization (PLO) (1968); and the Hamas charter (1988).

Although no single foundational document explains the Israeli reliance on force, strength, and military power to deter and undermine its adversaries, some of the contemporary explanations turn to Vladimir Ze'ev Jabotinsky's concept of the iron wall to explain Israel's national security doctrine.[5] Jabotinsky was the leader, until his death in 1940, of the then smaller branch of Zionism, Revisionist Zionism. The Revisionists were more open to the use of force to achieve Zionist aims against the Arabs and the British, the great power that was then in charge of Palestine. They were also less sympathetic to leftist-socialist economic principles, and perennially playing second fiddle to the dominant Labor Zionists in the Yishuv, the Zionist project and quasi-government prior to Israel's establishment in 1948. They advocated Jewish settlement on the east bank – what is today Jordan – as well as the west bank of the Jordan River. In 1923, Jabotinsky published 'The iron wall'. The importance today attributed to Jabotinsky's essay is especially striking given his original location outside the Zionist mainstream.

In Jabotinsky's relatively short work, he argued that only Zionist strength would act as the guarantee of the Jewish national project. Zionism could 'proceed and develop only under the protection of a power that is independent of the native [Arab] population – behind an iron wall, which the native population cannot breach'. The Arab side would repeatedly crash into the wall until, exhausted, they would recognize the futility of the exercise: '[W]hen a living people yields in matters of such a vital character it is only when there is no longer any hope of getting rid of us, because they can make no breach in the iron wall'. Having failed many times, the Arab side would sue for peace. But first, the Arabs would need to push aside extremist leaders (who say 'Never!' to making peace) and adopt more moderate leaders 'who will approach us with a proposal that we should both agree to mutual concessions'. In short, Jabotinsky wrote, 'the only way to reach an agreement in the future is to abandon all idea of seeking an agreement at present'.[6]

One might object to the emphasis on Jabotinsky since his revisionist stream was secondary to Labor Zionism during the entire pre-state period and for the first twenty-nine years after Israeli statehood in 1948, until Likud's victory in the 1977 election. That said, Labor's activists had similar views about the value of force, as the disagreements between David Ben-Gurion and Moshe Sharett, Israel's first two prime ministers, demonstrate. With the impact of the Arab revolt (1936–1939), an Arab backlash against both Zionist expansion and the British mandate, historian Gideon Shimoni argues that Ben-Gurion 'formed the increasingly firmer conviction that only the creation of accomplished facts and the gaining of deterrent strength would drive the Arabs to some form of understanding'.[7] This wording starts to sound consistent with Jabotinsky's thoughts.[8]

Israeli discussions around the 1967 war offer many illustrations of the Israeli belief in the advantages of military force and strength. Major-General Yitzhak Rabin, as military chief of staff prior to the 1967 war, said: 'Israel must be strong enough to deter aggression. Pacts and treaties are not enough to ensure peace; we must go on buying the arms we need and which we cannot produce for ourselves.'[9] Rabin does not outline a pathway from force to treaties, but he does favour strength as a core element of Israeli policy. Israeli military doctrine had relied on strength to deter Arab attack. Israeli military leaders did not want to undermine that approach in response to Egyptian president Gamal Abdel Nasser's tests of May/June 1967.

On 25 May 1967, Israeli prime minister Levi Eshkol travelled to the southern command and heard a similar message. General Ariel Sharon, himself later an Israeli prime minister, spoke out about the need to destroy the 'whole Egyptian army'. His view was the 'consensus' view of the military commanders at southern command: 'Unequivocally, they considered the restoration of Israel's deterrent capability to be the central issue and urged the choice of military action as the only relevant response'. Ezer Weizman, the deputy chief of staff of the Israel Defense Forces (IDF), said the 'situation was a dangerous one and of far-reaching consequences to the credibility of Israel's deterrent capacity'.[10]

The Israeli emphasis on deterrence has been an enduring feature of Israeli strategic thinking. Declassified Israeli documents demonstrate that Israeli military leaders were often thinking in such terms. In January 1967, for example, Eshkol met with Rabin and other military leaders to discuss Syria and Palestinian attacks. Uzi Narkiss, head of Israel's Central Command, stated it succinctly: when the Arabs are hit, 'they retreat'. Rehavam Ze'evi, deputy head of the IDF operations branch, also supported the use of force to stop Syria and to deter other countries. Rabin argued that solving the terrorist problem might require a military 'blow'. Striking Egypt in the 1956 war, Rabin noted, had led to 'ten years of quiet'.[11] Deterrence has been a core component of Israeli policy.

Various Israeli leaders and observers have repeatedly expressed similar sentiments. In 1953, for example, Moshe Dayan highlighted the sword while delivering a eulogy: 'This is the fate of our generation, the choice of our life – to be prepared and armed, strong and tough – or otherwise, the sword will slip from our fist, and our life will be snuffed out'.[12] In a 2012 lecture, former Israeli prime minister Ehud Barak favourably quoted Dayan.[13] Early in the conflict, Moshe Brilliant, an Israeli journalist, argued that, since 1948, 'each reluctant step the Arabs took from hot war toward peace was taken when they were held by the throat'.[14] In 2002, Assaf Oron, an Israeli who refused to carry out his military service for political reasons, reflected on his upbringing:

> As a little child growing up in Israel under Golda Meir and Moshe Dayan, all I heard was that the Arabs are inhuman monsters who want to throw us into the sea, they understand only force, and since our wonderful IDF has won the Six Day War they know not to mess with us anymore – or else.[15]

As prime minister, Ariel Sharon said 'If the Palestinians are not being beaten, there will be no negotiations.... Only after they've been battered will we be able to conduct talks.'[16] During the Israel–Gaza war of 2012, Gilad Sharon, son of former prime minister Ariel Sharon, wrote that Israel should flatten Gaza and made reference to what the United States did in Hiroshima and Nagasaki at the end of World War II, the ultimate example of the use of military force.[17] At Ariel Sharon's funeral in early 2014, Benjamin Netanyahu, Israel's prime minister, said Sharon 'understood that in matters of our existence and security, we must stand firm'. Sharon, some commentators noted, was the archetype of 'Gun Zionism'. One critic argued that Sharon 'displayed a consistent preference for force over diplomacy in dealing with the Arabs'.[18] Ari Shavit, an Israeli journalist and military reservist, reflecting on his military service at a detention camp in Gaza during the first intifada, contended that 'Only the willingness to use force is what keeps us alive here'.[19] During the Israel–Gaza war of 2014, Avi Shilon, an Israeli historian, observed 'history has proven that the way to make [peace] happen is through the use of force'.[20] An Egyptian analyst, Aymin El-Amir, summed it up this way: 'Israel, however, has never abandoned the belief that military hegemony is more rewarding for its expansionist ambitions than to settle for a just peace'.[21]

In 2015, when the IDF publicly released a strategy document for the first time, it not surprisingly highlighted the centrality of military force. It spelled out Israel's commitment to deterrence. Moreover, for deterrence to work, it was important that Israel was '**Building a force** that is partially visible to the enemy, which shows our capability and readiness to cause it damage'.[22]

The idea that force provides the answer is often coupled with a belief in the inefficacy of negotiations and concessions as a means for achieving foreign-policy objectives. Negotiations and, in the Israeli–Palestinian case, territorial withdrawal are signs of weakness and only invite further depredations.

The track record of Benjamin Netanyahu, Israel's longest-serving prime minister, illustrates this tendency with regard to both the Palestinians and Iran. (He is also a believer in the value of force: 'We will live by the sword forever'.²³) In the mid-1990s, he led right-wing Israeli opposition to the biggest Israeli–Palestinian negotiating breakthrough in history, the Oslo process and its implementation. In his first stint as prime minister, spanning 1996–1999, he dragged his heels regarding Oslo and forced re-negotiations of already negotiated issues (e.g. Israeli military redeployments) rather than building co-operation and trust through further agreements on additional issues. His vision did not seem to allow for genuine Palestinian sovereignty as part of a two-state solution but rather Palestinian autonomy in small, non-contiguous chunks of the West Bank. Years later, during the election of 2015, he explicitly ruled out a Palestinian state: 'Whoever moves to establish a Palestinian state or intends to withdraw from territory is simply yielding territory for radical Islamic terrorist attacks against Israel'.²⁴ A negotiated, two-state solution is, in his words, turned into appeasement of radical, Islamic terrorism. The claim is not just that negotiations would not ensure desired state objectives like security but that talks and concessions would greatly *worsen* Israel's national security position.

In June 2009, Netanyahu gave a speech that did suggest openness to a negotiated solution, but putting too much weight on that speech misses many of his standard, anti-negotiations arguments he made in the very same speech. If several conditions were met, he said, 'we [Israel] are ready to agree to a real peace agreement, a demilitarized Palestinian state side by side with the Jewish state'.²⁵ Is it possible that he wavered from his long belief in the need for military force and the avoidance of mutual concessions, and instead embraced the idea that negotiations could lead to the achievement of fundamental national objectives? Perhaps, but that the speech came early in his second tenure as prime minister and just months after US president Barack Obama took office and called for a renewed US push to secure a negotiated two-state solution is important as well. If one were to see this speech as Netanyahu breaking with his dominant idea (force plus no negotiations or concessions) and turning to a different idea (supporting negotiations and concessions), the speech could illustrate a pathway for ideational change, the role of third-party mediators in effecting such change in beliefs.

Yet I think a full reading of the language of the speech, not to mention subsequent events and Netanyahu statements, reveals many of his usual arguments and deep scepticism about negotiations and mutual concessions. In that same 2009 speech, he extensively criticized the core principle of a two-state solution, territorial withdrawal: 'all our withdrawals were met by huge waves of suicide bombers... The argument that withdrawal would bring peace closer did not stand up to the test of reality.' A rejection of territorial withdrawal is tantamount to a rejection of the idea of a negotiated two-state solution. The formula is based on the idea of land for peace, with Israel trading land it won in the 1967 war for peace treaties with Arab parties. No territorial withdrawal, no land-for-peace formula. He put other conditions too: that Palestinian refugees would not exercise their right of return to what is now Israel; that the Palestinian state must be demilitarized; that Jerusalem will remain Israel's united capital, a claim at odds with the notion of Jerusalem serving as the capital of a State of Israel and a State of Palestine; that Israel would not talk to Hamas; and that the Palestinians must recognize Israel 'as the national homeland of the Jewish People' or, elsewhere in the speech, 'as the state of the Jewish people'. On the three major contested issues of land, refugees, and Jerusalem, Netanyahu ruled out all substantive concessions.[26] So though he said the words 'a demilitarized Palestinian state', he ruled out all the negotiating components that would make possible such a state alongside Israel. One could certainly read his speech as consistent with his earlier notions of Palestinian autonomy, not independence. But autonomy is essentially a policy to avoid a framework of mutual concessions.[27]

I would further note what he did *not* say in the 2009 speech, because that also tells us how he views the idea of negotiations and concessions to the other, Palestinian side as a means to achieve national goals. He never said 'two-state solution'. The word 'negotiations' appeared only once in the entire speech. He never said the Palestinians had a legitimate right to national self-determination. He did not say the Palestinians had the right to establish a sovereign state.

In his second stint as prime minister, starting in 2009, Netanyahu worked continuously to undermine multilateral negotiations with Iran over its nuclear capabilities. His government vehemently objected to the interim agreement (2013) and to the final agreement with Iran, the Joint Comprehensive Plan of Action (JCPOA), in 2015. In defiance of the Obama administration, he came to Washington in 2015; spoke directly to the US Congress; and attacked the idea of negotiating with Iran on nuclear matters. In 2018, when the Trump administration discussed withdrawing from the JCPOA, Netanyahu weighed in on 30 April with a speech recycling past charges against Iran for its pursuit of nuclear weapons. Though I would guess Donald Trump was already intent on withdrawing whether Netanyahu spoke publicly or not, the speech appeared to support that idea. Trump announced the US withdrawal on 8 May 2018.

In chapter 1, I noted that Amir Lupovici's book on Israeli deterrence thinking is broadly consistent with my argument. Another example is Raffaella Del Sarto's scholarly work, *Israel Under Siege*, where she argued that the Israeli commitment to military force has only grown stronger in recent decades. She agrees that Israel has long relied on deterrence and the use of force, but 'these notions were usually also the subject of fierce domestic contestation'.[28] Post-Oslo, the debate or contestation has faded, making the role of force in Israeli policy even more prominent.

In sum, one way to look at Israel, then, is as a country building up its strength through the development of its own military and through the formation of alliances with both regional actors and great powers. Israel has often looked beyond the Arab world, forming an alliance, for example, with the Shah's Iran (until his fall in the 1979 Islamic Revolution) and Turkey (until Israel's fallout with the government of Recep Tayyip Erdogan). Israel built a powerful economy with heavy investments in defence and research and development.[29] France provided major conventional and non-conventional military support in the decade leading up to the 1967 war. By the early 1970s, the United States had fully taken over the role of Israel's military and political patron. Israel fully embraced the idea that its survival depended on having the best military in the region. It is not the only belief in Israel, as I will come to in later chapters, but it has been the dominant one.

Turning to foundational Palestinian documents, the Palestine Liberation Organization (PLO), founded in 1964 at the behest of Egypt under Gamal Abdel Nasser, is another example of the belief in military force as the primary means for accomplishing major aims. While Nasser hoped to use the PLO as a tool to control or harness Palestinian nationalism, the conduct and outcome of the 1967 war transformed the PLO. After the war, the PLO moved away from Egyptian tutelage and toward taking the leading role in the fight with Israel and in the effort to establish an independent Palestinian home. In terms of personnel, Yasser Arafat and a new cadre of Palestinians took over the PLO. Among other changes, they revised the PLO charter in 1968 to highlight the aggressive, militant approach they would take to defeat Israel.[30] Other Arab actors favoured force as well; *al-Baath*, a Syrian newspaper, explained on 31 August 1967, 'The occupied Arab territories will be evacuated by the enemy only through armed struggle. The Israeli enemy will be liquidated only by means of force.'[31]

The PLO charter of 1968 relied on armed struggle to bring about the liberation of Palestine. The presumption in 1968 was that this meant the liberation of all of Palestine, from the Jordan River to the Mediterranean Sea, and thus the elimination of Israel as the Jewish state. The United Nations' 1947 call for the partition of Palestine was 'illegal' (article 19 of the PLO charter). Only force could achieve Palestinian objectives: 'Armed struggle is the only way to liberate Palestine. Thus it is the overall strategy, not merely a tactical phase' (Article 9). The PLO would achieve its territorial aims through 'armed Palestinian revolution'. Force might provoke escalation, but this would be a welcome development because it would move the PLO closer to the liberation of Palestine. The PLO did not oppose Israeli concessions in response to the Palestinian use of force but was prepared for an intermediate violent escalation as a likely precursor to Israeli concessions. The PLO's approach was consistent with common beliefs in the 1960s about people's revolutions and guerrilla warfare (article 10). The 'primary condition' for peace, according to Fayez Sayegh, a Palestinian spokesperson in the United States, was the liberation of Palestine.[32]

Fatah – the Palestinian National Liberation Movement and largest member of the PLO – made other pronouncements in the 1960s that express the idea that force is a powerful means to achieve Palestinian national independence: 'Our people, the people of the Catastrophe, know by instinct that Israel will not disappear by a natural disaster, not by persuasion, not by the decisions of Arab or international bodies, or vain and sterile politics'.[33] In a similar vein: 'Israel says, "I am here by the sword." We must complete the saying – "and only by the sword shall Israel be driven out".'[34] The People's Front for the Liberation of

Force as the dominant policy

Palestine (PFLP), a smaller organizational member of the PLO, was straightforward in December 1967: 'The only language which the enemy understands is that of revolutionary violence'.[35] Much later, in 2001, Marwan Barghouti, a top Fatah leader, though aiming for a negotiated resolution, still extolled the virtues of force: 'I reached a simple conclusion. You don't want to end the occupation and you don't want to stop the settlements, so the only way to convince you is by force.... This [second] Intifada will lead to peace in the end. We need to escalate the conflict.'[36]

In practice, the PLO tried to realize the armed struggle and advance the Palestinian cause through fighting Israel inside the occupied territories – a brief phase – and then, increasingly in the 1970s, through the use of terrorist attacks against Israeli and other targets. The PLO enlisted thousands of soldiers to the Palestine Liberation Army and received weapons, training, and financial support from many Arab states and from the Soviet-led Eastern bloc.

Twenty years later, a different Palestinian charter also made a statement about the centrality of military force for the achievement of Palestinian national aims. Palestinian politics were not immune to the rising tide of political Islam in the 1970s and 1980s. A few months after the outbreak of the first intifada in 1987, Islamist elements in Palestinian society formed a new organization to confront Israel, rejuvenate Palestinian society, and promote individual Muslim piety: the Islamic Resistance Movement (Hamas). When the PLO signed the Oslo agreement with Israel in 1993, the relatively new organization Hamas became the focal point for continued Palestinian confrontation with Israel. Hamas 'had come to stand for all that Arafat had abandoned as he came in from the diplomatic cold. Principally, Hamas reserved the right to use violence and terror as legitimate weapons of struggle, and it laid claim to *all* of historic Palestine as a homeland for their people.'[37]

The Hamas charter (1988) is even more explicit than the PLO charter about the role of force in recapturing Palestine.[38] The charter opens with several quotations, including this one, attributed to Imam Hassan al-Banna: 'Israel will exist and will continue to exist until Islam will obliterate it, just as it obliterated others before it'. In articulating a view of history, the charter turns to the role that force played in defeating the Crusaders. The lesson is clear: 'This is the only way to liberate Palestine. There is no doubt about the testimony of history. It is one of the laws of the universe and one of the rules of existence. Nothing can overcome iron except iron' (article 34). The charter also explicitly rejected reliance on negotiations: 'There is no solution for the Palestinian question except through Jihad. Initiatives, proposals and international conferences are all a waste of time and vain endeavors' (article 13). Such conferences serve only as cover for the 'infidels' to control Islamic land such as Palestine.

In practice, Hamas pursued the armed struggle through its military wing, the al-Qassam brigades. Hamas also used terrorist attacks, including many suicide bombings. Hamas sought to undermine the Oslo peace process and participated in the violent confrontations with Israel during the second intifada (2000–2005) and thereafter.

Hamas leaders concurred with the earlier Fatah belief in the power of military force for accomplishing Palestinian objectives: 'It is not a coincidence that Zionists' willingness to negotiate was evident when the first Intifada started taking a heavy toll on the occupation, and when [the] Al-Aqsa Intifada placed unprecedented pressure on the Zionist military, economy, and society as a whole.'[39] Note the reference to historical events, the two intifadas of 1987–1993 and 2000–2005, as proof that the idea of using military force is a viable one. This contention reflects the interplay between ideas and historical events I mentioned earlier. In another example of the idea of the commitment to

Force as the dominant policy

force, Khalid Mishal, then head of the Hamas political bureau, was concise, saying that 'Israel, like any occupier, only respects the logic of force' (2006) and 'Land is only liberated by the gun' (2007). Yet he, like Barghouti, saw force as linked to a resolution, or in Mishal's case a long-term truce or *hudna*: '[But] history confirms that if a party opts for the political solution and has no [force] to back it, it'll make no progress, it will regain nothing'.[40] Negotiations did not exist independent of force; force appears to be the dominant idea.

On the Arab side, parallel sentiments have been expressed in Egypt as well. For example, in 1954, Saleh Salem, an Egyptian official, said, 'Palestine can only be recaptured by the sword and Arab unity'.[41] In July 1959, Gamal Abdel Nasser, Egypt's then president and leader of the pan-Arab movement, told a Cairo rally that 'We are awaiting aggression by Israel and any supporters of Israel. We will make it a decisive battle and get rid of Israel once and for all. This is the dream of every Arab.' Nasser went on to emphasize Egyptian power: 'We are today stronger than in 1956 when we defeated Britain, France and Israel'.[42] In 1965, after the establishment of the PLO and the Arab summit system, some observers suggested Nasser was changing tactics by trying to stoke a war of liberation against Israel, rather than resorting to a frontal, conventional attack.[43] Speaking to a crowd in Asyut, Egypt, in March 1965, Nasser called for the return of the Palestinian people to their homeland, saying, 'we must remember we will not enter Palestine on paths strewn with roses or spread with red carpet but on ground soaked with blood'.[44] After the 1967 war, during which Israel had captured extensive Arab land, including Egypt's Sinai Peninsula, Nasser was quoted as saying, 'what was taken by force can only be regained by force'.[45]

When taken together, these documents, speeches, and other expressions help paint a picture of a widespread belief that force, strength, violence, and might are the most effective instrument or approach to one's foes in the Arab–Israeli conflict. How to ensure survival, win wars, produce territorial concessions and the like? Be strong. Threaten or use force. Avoid negotiations and concessions.

In the next section, I demonstrate that both the Arab and the Israeli belief in the effectiveness of military force and the dangers of negotiations and concessions is firmly rooted in more recent events, not just in the past. Looking at the Israel–Hamas military confrontation in 2008–2009 illustrates the centrality of this idea and the policies that follow from it. In this 2008–2009 case, we see the exact kind of language or characterization of the fight that we would expect to see if the dominant belief were a commitment to military force rather than a preference for negotiations and mutual concessions.

Israel–Hamas, 2008–2009

In the Israel–Hamas fight of December 2008–January 2009, one can see countless examples and expressions of the belief in the primacy of military force. 'The only way to deal with occupation is with a rifle', said an unnamed Hamas leader.[46] On the Israeli side, Tizpi Livni, minister of foreign affairs, made a parallel claim about force: 'We have made a change in the equation, gone are the days in which Hamas fired at us and we kept quiet. They erred in thinking that when Israel restrained itself, it would not respond.'[47] The war highlighted the common belief in the role that force would play in causing the other side to back down as well as the danger of appearing weak or unwilling to fight. In general, the war demonstrated that these recurring beliefs deeply inform the rhetoric and decisionmaking of Palestinians and Israelis. This section reviews the arguments made by Israel, Hamas, and many observers.

What is striking about this Gaza war and Israel–Hamas relations in general is that both might be attempting to learn from the Israel–PLO relationship. Israel held strong until the PLO capitulated on favourable terms at Oslo in 1993. Meanwhile, Hamas fears falling into the same trap as the PLO and while it might entertain notions of accommodation and negotiations with Israel, it will do so only if it can avoid submitting as the PLO did earlier. But if both view the PLO that way, it makes for a long-term butting of heads, with Israel intent on forcing change and Hamas intent on avoiding being forced to change policy to anything like the degree the PLO changed in the late 1980s and early 1990s.

Before delving into the details of the war, it is important to note the larger context in which the Israel–Hamas skirmish took place. Though supporters of the Muslim Brotherhood had been active in Mandatory Palestine and then Gaza and the West Bank, Hamas, an offshoot of the Muslim Brotherhood, had formally come into being in late 1987 for a variety of reasons, including the growth of political Islam throughout the region and world.[48] In the 1960s, the Brotherhood members in Gaza argued that winning over more adherents to Islam was a precursor to Palestinian national liberation, unlike Fatah, which focused on immediate liberation. Israel looked the other way as Palestinian Islamists started to challenge the PLO's secular nationalists in the 1970s and early 1980s.[49] Israel officially recognized Sheikh Ahmed Yassin's group, Mujama al-Islamiya, as a charity and then as an association in 1979.[50]

But then the Islamists' primary aim started to shift. In the early 1980s, in part in reaction to the formation of a militant splinter group, Islamic Jihad, the Brothers embraced the armed struggle in addition to a continuing commitment to social change and the Islamicization of the Palestinian populace.[51] After the PLO signed the Oslo accords with Israel in 1993, Hamas fully took on the mantle of Palestinian resistance to Israel. In 1992, Israel had expelled over 400 Hamas officials to Lebanon, unintentionally helping Hamas deepen ties with Lebanon's Hezbollah. Just as the long-time engine of Palestinian nationalism, Fatah and the PLO, opted for acceptance of Israel, Hamas waved the banner for continued military confrontation.

Hamas drew some support from the failings of Oslo, both in the years when the Oslo diplomatic process was ongoing (1993–2001) and in its aftermath. Had the Oslo agreement worked out as its originators had hoped, Hamas might never have had enough political support to play such a central role in Israeli–Palestinian relations as it did in the early 2000s. The larger point is that Israel's and the PLO's failure to lock in the shift toward diplomacy, negotiations, recognition, and peace left the door wide open for the rejuvenation of confrontation.

Israel and the Palestinian Authority (PA), the governing entity created by the Oslo agreements, themselves were not doing all they could do to slam that door shut, given that they still had many forceful interactions in the 1990s and 2000, and Israel's settlements only grew larger and more deeply entrenched in the West Bank.[52] The Israeli and PLO institutions that were instruments of force did not go away. Even if one were to assume they no longer believed force was the primary means to interact with the other in the Israel–PLO dimension – and that is a questionable assumption – at a minimum both of them relied on force at least in part to meet the challenge of Hamas. Diplomacy becomes harder when multiple players are pursuing force and negotiations at the same time.

At times, too, the assumption that Israel and the PLO did not use force against each other was not valid. In 1996 and 2000, for example, Israeli and PLO/PA forces clashed directly. More generally, Israeli critics of Oslo charged that Arafat never let go of the PLO's key instrument of force: the tie to anti-Israeli terrorism. Palestinian critics questioned the continued intensity of Israeli settlement, occupation, and coercion. Hoping negotiations will spur cooperation is a challenging idea when forceful actions are occurring simultaneously.

The Israeli–Hamas relationship has been a violent one. In the 1990s and 2000s, Israel wanted to crush Hamas either directly or by delegating the task to the PA. Israel assassinated top Hamas leaders, including Sheikh Ahmed Yassin, Abdel Aziz al-Rantissi, Salah Shahade, and Ismail Abu Shanab. Israel created an international incident in its failed assassination of Khalid Mishal in Jordan in 1997. The 2010 killing of Mahmoud al-Mabhouh in Dubai was a lesser controversy. This approach mirrored Israeli assassinations in earlier decades of top PLO officials such as Abu Jihad. Many other Hamas leaders were arrested. As Hamas won the 2006 Palestinian parliamentary elections and took control of Gaza in 2007, Israel, with international support, demanded Hamas meet three conditions (renounce violence, accept past Israeli–Palestinian agreements, and recognize the State of Israel). This use of conditions again echoed the Israeli and US approach to the PLO in the 1970s and 1980s. Both during the second intifada and in the 2008–2009 clash, Israel attacked Hamas's institutions and lower-ranking personnel. It killed and wounded many Palestinian fighters and civilians.

Hamas relied on force as well. Starting in the 1990s, Hamas worked to undermine the Oslo process by blowing up Israelis, most famously with suicide bombings of buses and restaurants. In the 2000s, Hamas began using rockets and tunnels to attack Israel from Gaza. Rockets could overcome the fence Israel had built in the mid-1990s, and rebuilt in 2000–2001, to contain the Gaza Strip.[53] Sometimes Hamas loyalists fired them while on other occasions different Palestinian groups inside Gaza, such as Islamic Jihad, used them. Though the rockets caused only limited damage and casualties, they inspired fear among the

Israeli population. The point here is not that the two sides were able to inflict a similar amount of damage; their capabilities differ greatly and thus the impact has been uneven. The Israeli military is much more powerful. But both believed force was the crucial tool in dealing with the other. For Hamas, force was the instrument to achieve the Palestinian aim of national self-determination. For Israel, force was the instrument to suppress the Palestinian aim of national self-determination.

Meanwhile, negotiations have been a minor footnote. Israel and Hamas have negotiated indirectly through Egypt and other mediators and, for example, those links produced a ceasefire for part of 2008 and the release of a long-time Israeli prisoner in Gaza, Gilad Shalit, in 2011. But they have not negotiated directly or at high levels. Both parties contend that they are open to talks as long as those talks conform to their stipulations. For Hamas officials, that means not prostrating themselves to Israel as the PLO did in the past and instead aiming to negotiate a long-term ceasefire, not a final peace treaty. For Israel, it means Hamas accepting the pre-conditions noted above: the renunciation of violence, acceptance of negotiated Israeli–Palestinian agreements from the past, and the recognition of Israel.

A major Israeli goal in attacking Gaza in 2008 was to use military force to weaken Hamas and lessen the threat Hamas posed to Israel. The first day of the war included massive aerial strikes on Gaza: 'On Saturday, that was the IDF's goal: to shock and awe Hamas with a blow the likes of which has not been seen in Gaza since the territory was conquered by Israel in 1967'.[54] In early January 2009, Israel launched a ground invasion of Gaza. Both sides declared unilateral ceasefires that began on 18 January.

Israel's three top leaders spoke about this use of force in similar fashion. The prime minister, Ehud Olmert, was perhaps the most restrained in his explanations, but even he wanted

Force as the dominant policy

to change reality and the impact on Israeli cities like Ashdod, Ashkelon, and Sderot:

> The ground operation, that we started last night, is meant to set the foundations for our desire to change the security reality in the south. IDF forces set out to damage the military infrastructure set up by Hamas, and to take over launch areas from which many rockets were fired that hit Sderot in recent months and weeks, and Ashkelon and even Ashdod in recent days.[55]

He was focused on deterrence:

> We didn't start this operation just to end it with rocket fire continuing as it did before it began. Imagine if we declare a unilateral ceasefire and a few days later rockets fall on Ashkelon. What will that do to Israel's deterrence?[56]

The foreign minister, Tizpi Livni, also sought to change reality: 'Military actions are not easy to support. But this is the only way we can change realities on the ground.'[57] 'We have made a change in the equation, gone are the days in which Hamas fired at us and we kept quiet', Livni said. 'They erred in thinking that when Israel restrained itself, it would not respond'.[58] Note that she saw Israel as correcting a misimpression on the part of Hamas.

The word 'blow' captured the strong nature of Israel's move. Ehud Barak, the defence minister, said the goal was to deal Hamas a 'severe blow'.[59] The chief of military intelligence, Major-General Amos Yadlin, concurred:

> Hamas understands that violating the lull was a strategic mistake. It suffered a great blow. Dozens of headquarters have been damaged, the ammunition warehouses and production infrastructure were destroyed. The ability to smuggle through the tunnels was damaged.[60]

A few days into the war, on 4 January 2009, Barak said that Hamas had suffered a very heavy blow, 'but we have yet to reach a situation of changing the reality in the southern part of the country'.[61] As similarly expressed by Olmert and Livni, the point of the blow was to change reality. The status quo was unacceptable.

The idea of Israel deterring Hamas was a central and recurring theme, as already noted in Olmert's statement. A senior Israeli commander echoed the prime minister's viewpoint: 'If they want to go for another round, they have to take into consideration the consequences'.[62] Israel needed to teach Hamas a lesson, to cause Hamas to recalibrate its formula for calculating whether and how to confront Israel. According to the Israel Defense Forces, the ground operation's goal was 'to seriously damage the Hamas layout by taking over launch areas and strengthening deterrence, in order to create a better security reality for a longer time'.[63] For David Makovsky, an analyst at a Washington think tank, 'Israel believes its deterrence was lost in that war [against Lebanon in 2006] and Israel's current campaign against Hamas should be seen as an effort to regain that deterrence'.[64]

Many Arabs noted Israel's reliance on force. At an Arab summit in Qatar in mid-January 2009, Bashar Assad, the president of Syria, angrily declared that Israel's bombing of Gaza and the resulting civilian deaths showed that the Israelis spoke only 'the language of blood'.[65] This is, retrospectively, an especially notable statement given Assad's vastly bloodier approach during the Syrian civil war that started in 2011. But Hezbollah's general secretary expected Israel to break first: 'Should Gaza stand firm for days or weeks, the aggression will stop'. He explained further that Israel 'cannot go on for long. Eventually it will be forced to end its aggression.'[66]

Israel also pursued a second, indirect form of deterrence, hoping that physical damage and casualties would compel the people of Gaza to abandon Hamas politically. The idea was that force would compel political isolation or, to put it more broadly, the Israeli use of force would lead to Palestinian concessions in the political arena. The *New York Times* explained: 'The larger [Israeli] hope was that subduing Hamas would delegitimize the group's leadership in the eyes of the Palestinian people and eliminate its power to prevent a two-state solution'.[67] Jeremy Bowen, the BBC's Middle East editor (writing in the *Guardian*), offered the same understanding: 'The [Israeli] government hopes the people of Gaza will stop blaming Israel for what is happening to their families and start blaming Hamas'.[68] Tom Segev, an Israeli historian and columnist, agreed: 'The latest operation was aimed at demoralizing Gaza's residents and inciting them against Hamas'.[69] Thomas Friedman, a columnist at the *New York Times*, said Israel had used the same approach in 2006, with Israel hoping that Lebanese civilians would eventually turn against Hezbollah: 'What were you thinking? Look what destruction you have visited on your own community!'[70] Israel hoped force would generate 'a popular revolt against Gaza's present rulers'. Gazans themselves believed that this is what Israel was trying to do in the war.[71] The extreme version of this idea is known as the Dahiya doctrine, after a Shiite neighbourhood in Lebanon that Israel heavily attacked in 2006.[72] While the Dahiya doctrine can be understood in different ways, it is the Israeli use of disproportionate force on Arab civilian areas that may house supporters of the enemy. Israel's goal has variously been: to deter the enemy from attacking; to turn the enemy's civilians against the enemy military force as a result of the Israeli use of disproportionate force; to defeat enemy military forces operating in Arab civilian areas; to punish the enemy by harming Arab civilians; and perhaps to make clear that 'civilians' are as responsible as 'military' personnel for attacks.

The Israeli attacks on Gaza caused major damage, with 'heavy civilian suffering', a pattern of damage that is consistent with an effort to affect popular Gazan views of Hamas. Palestinian casualties totalled as many as 1,430 killed and 5,300 wounded.[73] Israel hit Palestinian police stations and government ministries, including 'interior, foreign affairs, finance, public works, justice, education, labour, and culture'.[74] About 14 per cent of the structures in Gaza were destroyed or damaged, including 4,100 homes. Eight schools were destroyed and 179 'incurred significant damage'. Ninety-two mosques were 'fully or partially destroyed'.[75] Many factories also were damaged or destroyed, including all seven textile factories and twenty-two of twenty-nine concrete factories. Hamas facilitated this strategy by operating in populated and residential areas. As one Fatah leader in Gaza, Ibrahim Abu al-Najjah, ironically noted, 'another victory or two like this, and we'll be finished'.[76]

Critics of this Israeli idea argued that Israeli force would strengthen, not weaken, Palestinian support for Hamas in Gaza. One interviewee summarized the problem:

> Abdel Hafez, a 55-year-old history teacher, waited outside a Gaza City bakery to buy bread, one of the few people visible outdoors. He said he was not a Hamas supporter, but believed the strikes would only increase support for the group. 'Each strike, each drop of blood are giving Hamas more fuel to continue'.[77]

Some Israeli analysts were equally sceptical: 'Gazans aren't the prisoners of Hamas tyranny – this is the government they chose, and pressure and suffering simply reinforces their solidarity and their loyalty to their leadership'.[78]

Some Israelis put their scepticism in broader, historical terms. Yossi Alpher, an Israeli analyst, commented on Israel's economic blockade:

> Over the past 42 years, Israel has periodically invoked collective economic punishment and incentives toward Palestinians on the theory that empty or full stomachs – impoverishment or development – would effectively alter Palestinian political behavior. There is not a shred of evidence that this has worked.[79]

Force as the dominant policy

Ha'aretz, a left-wing Israeli newspaper, editorialized in a similar vein:

> The lessons of previous wars, during which the IDF destroyed infrastructure targets and the homes of civilians but did not gain the quiet it had sought, have not been internalized.[80]

Analysts Amjad Atallah and Daniel Levy echoed these concerns:

> For anyone to believe that this time everything will be different, they would have to be incredibly optimistic or foolish. The most likely script will be a variation on previous wars. Israel will 'punish' the Arabs in Gaza as they have never been hurt before. Hamas will find ways to attack Israelis, either through rockets or through attacks inside Israel.[81]

Meanwhile, Britain's *Economist* magazine editorialized on the limits of force:

> Since Hamas is not going to disappear, some way must be found to change its mind. Bombs alone will never do that.[82]

Still, diplomacy was not absent from Israeli thinking, though it would not be equal parties negotiating. Two Israeli analysts saw a Hamas defeat as opening the door to a viable Israeli–Palestinian peace process:

> It may also be the last chance to reassure Israelis of the viability of a two-state solution. Given the unfortunate historical resonance, Israel should refrain from calling its current operation, 'Peace for Southern Israel'. But without Hamas's defeat, there can be no serious progress toward a treaty that both satisfies Palestinian aspirations and allays Israel's fears. At stake in Gaza is nothing less than the future of the peace process.[83]

In short, according to an Israeli official, 'The diplomatic window is open, but in the meantime the IDF will carry out the cabinet's orders to continue operating on the ground'.[84] Israeli Foreign Ministry spokesman Yigal Palmor was clear: 'If a real proposal with credibility and guarantees is submitted to us, we will give it a very serious examination'.[85]

Of course, critics charged that Israel needed to be more proactive on the diplomatic front. After just a few days, Israeli author David Grossman called for Israel to hold its fire to allow for the possibility of a negotiated political opening.[86] Israeli Muhammad Barakei (of the left-wing Hadash party and Member of the Knesset) said: 'It's clear that these attacks will not bring quiet or calm, only negotiations will'.[87] A *Ha'aretz* editorial agreed: 'This war needs to move immediately to the diplomatic track and agreements that will end the fantasies and delusions of both sides'.[88]

Moreover, some argued that the ferocity of the attack would make such a diplomatic pathway disappear and instead increase hostility. Neve Gordon, an Israeli academic, feared the approach would backfire: 'Ironically, Israel's attempt to destroy Hamas using military force has always ended up strengthening the organisation, thus corroborating the notion that power produces its own vulnerability'.[89] Haim Watzman questioned the deterrence dynamic:

> Israelis should be wary by now of national leaders who promise that this war, finally, will end Palestinian (or Hezbollah, or whatever) attacks on Israel.... The current operation is the bloodiest one Israel has ever launched against its Palestinian neighbors. Inevitably, in a place as densely populated as the Gaza Strip is, the civilian death toll is high. That will increase Palestinian and Arab resentment against Israel.[90]

Gideon Levy, a columnist and one of the most outspoken critics of the war, asked about Israeli pilots who dropped bombs on Gaza: 'Do they think about the burning hatred they are planting not only in Gaza but in other corners of the world amid the horrific images on television?'[91] Gordon described a pattern:

> Rather than continuing the truce, the Israeli government has once again chosen to adopt strategies of violence that are tragically akin to the ones deployed by Hamas, only the Israeli ones are much more lethal. If the Israeli government really cared about its citizens and the country's long term ability to sustain itself in the Middle East, it would abandon the use of violence and talk with its enemies.[92]

One Israeli soldier fighting the war agreed: 'We did not go there to sign a peace agreement', he said. 'It was a very aggressive operation....'[93]

In sum, Israeli political and military decisionmakers believed in the idea that force was the best means to achieve the basic goal of security, including by limiting or preventing the success of Hamas in moving Palestinians closer toward their goal of national independence. As is often the case, Israeli officials and analysts were not united behind a single idea, the primacy of force. That idea was dominant and shaped Israel's actions but a number of observers questioned the utility of that idea, arguing it would leave Israel in a worse place in terms of national security and the Palestinian question.

What about on the other side, Hamas? Hamas has long argued that military force is the only way to gain Palestinian independence. Force has overshadowed the negotiations option, as a senior Hamas leader explained in February 2009: 'Resistance has had successes, but Fatah's attempts to negotiate a political settlement have achieved nothing at all'.[94] Israeli sources understood Hamas this way as well. Barry Rubin, an academic, wrote in the *Jerusalem Post*: 'Hamas crows: You are weak, you are confused, you are helpless. Come, people, arise and destroy the paper tiger! ... Israel is helpless against the rockets.'[95] After the initial aerial bombing, one official claimed in early January that Hamas's position had 'hardened'.[96] When Israel launched the ground invasion, Hamas warned Israeli forces that 'Gaza will not be paved with flowers for you, it will be paved with fire and hell'.[97]

In public, Hamas leaders highlighted the centrality of force. Ismail Haniya, the (former) Palestinian prime minister, said in a televised speech: 'We say in all confidence that even if we are hung on the gallows or they make our blood flow in the streets or they tear our bodies apart, we will bow only before God and we will not abandon Palestine'.[98] He added: 'We will not leave our land, we will not raise white flags and we will not kneel except before God'.[99] Khalid Mishal, a top Hamas leader then based in Damascus, offered similar thoughts: 'This [third] Intifada will be peaceful for the Palestinians but lethal for the Zionist enemy'.[100] This third intifada or uprising would 'rescue Gaza and protect the West Bank'.[101] On Al-Jazeera television, Mishal said: 'We called for a military intifada against the enemy. Resistance will continue through suicide missions.'[102] Another Hamas leader, Mahmoud Zahar, spoke on Hamas TV: 'The Zionists have legitimized the killing of their children by killing our children. They have legitimized the killing of their people all over the world by killing our people.'[103] Hamas representative Osama Hamdan spoke to a gathering outside the United Nations offices in Beirut: 'We in the Hamas group and other resistance factions in Gaza know we don't have many alternatives. We have one alternative which is to be steadfast and resist and we will be victorious.'[104] Nizar Rayyan of Hamas, later assassinated by Israel, promised to send suicide bombers to kill Israelis in attacks that would 'humiliate the enemy to ashes'.[105]

Gaza under Hamas is not a democratic territory. Not surprisingly, there was not a public split among elites over whether the best idea for advancing the Palestinian cause was that of relying on military force or the belief that negotiations could better achieve Palestinian ends. Had Fatah under Mahmoud Abbas, Palestinian president, still been a strong player in Gaza, we might have had evidence of contestation between these two ideas. But since the Hamas takeover of Gaza in 2007, local Fatah loyalists were in a very weak position.

Israel, meanwhile, wanted explicitly and publicly to demonstrate that Hamas could not gain concessions, such as the opening of the Gaza border crossings, through rocket attacks or other uses of force. Hamas thought the rockets could do that but, as a former senior IDF officer noted, 'they were wrong'.[106] Israel wanted to prove it would not appease Hamas militancy.

Before and during the Gaza conflict, both Israel and Hamas spoke in terms of force and violence. They each believed in the idea that military force and coercion were the best means to achieve their objectives vis-à-vis the other. As noted in the first section of this chapter, the dominance of this idea is consistent with the view that many Arab and Israeli actors have held over the course of the Arab–Israeli conflict: the only way to get the other side to concede or capitulate is to use military force. The only way to advance core objectives is to use military force.

If the first two sections of the chapter have illustrated that conflict participants believe in the effectiveness of military force, is such a belief grounded in Arab–Israeli history? In short, the initial sections outlined the idea without demonstrating whether it has ever actually worked or not. In the next section, I suggest several historical examples that bolster the view that force is an excellent means of achieving political, military, and territorial objectives. In these examples, force was not the only factor, but it helped an Israeli or Arab actor achieve its military or political objective. People believe that only force works or that force works best in part because they can point to past episodes where that proved to be the case.

The historical record: cases where force leads to concessions

The history of the conflict provides some support for this idea that force and strength are the best means at the disposal of the rival parties. This section provides brief, illustrative cases of where force led the other side to change its policy by backing down or moving toward concessions. These are not meant to be exhaustive examples but rather illustrations using some of the common and not-so-common examples. In the 1967 war, Israel won an overwhelming military victory, marking the beginning of the end of Egypt's confrontational approach with Israel. In a second example from the late 1960s and early 1970s, the Palestinian national movement, led by the PLO, tentatively moved away from maximalist goals. This shift was not wholly due to Israel's strong military position but Israeli reliance on force did demonstrate the limitations of the forceful Palestinian approach, opening the door to more compromising positions. In the late 1980s and early 1990s, the first intifada pushed some Israelis toward negotiating a resolution with the Palestinians, support that contributed to the diplomatic agreement negotiated at Oslo, Norway, in 1993. While the legacy of the Palestinian use of force in the second intifada was mostly negative for the Palestinian cause, it did lead to one short-lived gain, the withdrawal of Israeli settlers from Gaza. That example is often mentioned in tandem with Hezbollah forcing Israel out of southern Lebanon in 2000, also through an Israeli unilateral withdrawal.

The 1967 war and beyond

Israel won a dramatic victory in the 1967 war. Israel launched its attack on 5 June 1967 and won the war in just six days. Egypt initially tried to claim it was winning but from the first Israeli attack, the Arab militaries were overwhelmed. Cairo misled

Jordanian leaders, claiming Egypt had defeated 75 per cent of the Israeli force, in order to get the West Bank front into the war.[107] But soon these misperceptions were swept aside by the rapidity and enormity of the Israeli victory.

Although one could date the start of the war to a number of events, Egyptian policy in May 1967 played a central role in escalating the situation toward war. In relatively rapid succession, Egypt: sent additional military forces to the Sinai Peninsula, the part of Egypt that borders Israel; asked for the United Nations to remove its peacekeeping force from Sinai; closed the nearby Straits of Tiran to Israeli shipping; and signed a military pact with Jordan. Israel was deeply alarmed.

The Israeli military crushed the Arab armed forces in what Israel saw as a pre-emptive attack. On the morning of 5 June 1967, two waves of Israeli bomber attacks destroyed 304 of Egypt's 419 aircraft. Syria lost half its air force and moved the other half out of Israeli range.[108] Egypt lost 10,000–15,000 soldiers; Syria had 500 dead and 2,500 wounded. Close to 800 Israeli soldiers died.[109] Jordan's air force and 80 per cent of its armoured forces were destroyed, 700 soldiers were killed, and 6,000 were injured or missing. It lost the West Bank, which accounted for over one-third of its gross national product, and 300,000 Palestinian refugees fled to Jordan's East Bank.[110]

Israel captured vast chunks of territory, including the Sinai Peninsula and Gaza Strip from Egypt, the West Bank from Jordan, and the Golan Heights from Syria. The territory under Israel's control tripled in size, and Israel took control of additional sources of the Jordan River. In the Gaza Strip, at least 360,000 Palestinians came under Israeli rule; another 900,000 lived in the West Bank, including East Jerusalem.[111] As of 1965, Israel itself already had about 300,000 Palestinian citizens.[112]

The Arab side was totally defeated and utterly humiliated, underlined by the rapidity of the war. The result of defeat, then, included the loss of land and life, the destruction of a large amount of military material, a large number of Palestinians coming under Israeli rule, and hundreds of thousands of Palestinians displaced from their homes. Nasser tried to resign on 9 June, but the Egyptian public, spurred on by Egyptian elites, rallied to oppose his resignation. Though he stayed on until his death in 1970, Nasser was 'forever tarnished and discredited'.[113]

The 1967 war and its aftermath contributed to Egypt and Syria both moving away from the policy of confronting Israel: 'A slow and gradual process towards the recognition of Israel was set in motion after 1967'.[114] What many Arab actors did hope was to put up an honourable fight and thereby achieve a political or symbolic, but not military, victory. What is the evidence for the claim that the outcome of the 1967 war, on top of Arab military defeats in 1948 and 1956 and episodic Israeli military strikes, started to transform the Arab approach to Israel?[115]

First, the destruction of Israel was never the aim of a post-1967 war in which Egypt and Syria were involved. In wars in 1969–1970 and 1973, the Arab aim was not the destruction of Israel as it arguably had been in 1948 and 1967. Instead, the aim was to get back land Israel captured in 1967. In the Khartoum summit statement of 1 September 1967, many observers have highlighted the Arab side's three 'no's and used the statement as the archetype of Arab rejectionism.[116] But commenting on the same statement, the late Fred J. Khouri, a political scientist at Villanova University, instead noted the explicit mention of political action and the absence of any explicit call for Israel's destruction.[117] Overall, the 1967 war shifted the terms of the Arab–Israeli territorial conflict from pre-1967 Israel to the territories occupied in 1967.

Second, Egypt and later Syria both accepted UN Security Council Resolution 242. The resolution, passed on 22 November 1967, 'affirms further the necessity … for guaranteeing the territorial inviolability and political independence of every State in the area'. While that clause did not explicitly mention Israel, the effect of Arab acceptance of the general statement included guaranteeing Israel's territorial inviolability and political independence. In 1975, Anwar Sadat, president of Egypt, explained: 'When we accepted UN Security Council Resolution 242 in 1967, Israel became an existing fact'.[118] In February 1971, Sadat launched an initiative that sought a peace agreement with Israel; he later wrote that if Israel and the United States had been more responsive to his initiative, the 1973 war 'would not have taken place'.[119] According to Sadat, 'Every door I have opened has been slammed in my face – with American blessings'.[120] Overall, then, 'Between 1967 and 1973, the attitude of the confrontation states toward Israel had undergone an essential change, from a conflict over existence before 1967 to tacit acceptance of Israel within its 1967 borders on the basis of Resolution 242'.[121]

Third, Egypt and Syria shifted their policies from total war to less direct military tactics and then to diplomacy. Egypt fought two limited wars (1969–1970, 1973), signed interim agreements (1974, 1975), and then negotiated a peace treaty (1977–1979). Egypt did not want a peace treaty with Israel in the summer of 1967 just after the war, but it did start to shift away from the idea that total war was the best means to confront Israel. Force became a tool not to destroy Israel but rather a means to try to get the political negotiations underway:

> These [post-1967] years also witnessed an unprecedented intensity, scope, and diversity of hostilities in between the all-out wars in the Arab–Israeli conflict. Yet this military escalation, combined with diplomacy, indicated a new Egyptian approach to the conflict with Israel. In hindsight, this intensified violence proved to be a crucial element in the process of adjustment to the limits of capabilities and departure from the lure of romantic visions.[122]

The romantic vision of endless confrontation with and possible destruction of Israel lost its allure in the wake of Israel's vastly superior military performance in 1967. The limited use of force in 1969–1970 and 1973, perhaps possible only because the Soviet Union was there to prevent Israeli routs, also was costly and ended up solidifying the ascendance of the belief in negotiations and decline of the idea of military force and war.[123] In the decade after 1967, Egypt's diplomacy became diplomacy to get back Egyptian territory *and* to accept Israel.

The reality was that war is costly economically. The war with Israel hampered Egypt's economic development efforts. Egypt, Sadat wrote, allocated twice as much to defence as to development. The wars with Israel were 'tremendous obstacles' on Egypt's 'road to progress'.[124] That meant, though, in relation to chapter 3, that Egypt could probably have ended the wars but not signed a peace treaty and still focused more on the economy. In short, non-belligerency would have been sufficient for economic development.[125] Prior to Sadat's Jerusalem trip, according to former Egyptian foreign minister Ismail Fahmy, Suez Canal revenue, oil sales, and worker remittances from abroad were growing and boosting Egypt's economy. In 1976, the United States provided almost $1 billion in aid to Egypt.[126]

Heading into the 1973 war, Egyptian leaders acknowledged that their options were limited due to Israeli military superiority, but they believed that even a limited war could help move the Arab–Israeli political process. Lieutenant-General Saad el-Shazly, the Egyptian military chief of staff, argued:

> it was impossible for us to launch a large-scale offensive to destroy the enemy's concentrations in Sinai or to force enemy withdrawal from Sinai and the Gaza Strip. All that our capabilities would permit was a limited attack. We could aim to cross the canal, destroy [Israel's] Bar-Lev line and then take up a defensive posture.[127]

Force as the dominant policy

Shazly recalls Sadat remarking:

> when we plan the offensive, I want us to plan within our own capabilities, nothing more. Cross the canal and hold even ten centimeters of Sinai, I'm exaggerating, of course, and that will help me greatly, and alter completely the political situation both internationally and within the Arab ranks.[128]

In short, Sadat 'seemed to have realized that even with Syria's aid he could not impose a military defeat on Israel'.[129] When another Arab head of state proposed a more aggressive plan that aimed to impose the 1947 UN partition plan, Egypt rejected it:

> Finally, if the plan's political goal was to impose the Partition Resolution of 1947, did a comparison of Arab and Israeli forces suggest that Israel could be destroyed militarily? And where had Arab military superiority come from at a time when we were suffering from Israel's military superiority?[130]

The reality, in Egyptian eyes, was that Arab military inferiority was not a fleeting phenomenon, and thus demanded a new Arab policy idea for relating to Israel and, ultimately, the Palestinian question.

Syria fought Israel in 1973 but signed an interim diplomatic agreement with Israel in 1974. Even in the 1973 war, Syria had limited aims. After all, Syrian forces stopped at the Jordan River when they had the opportunity to push deeper into Israel.[131] Although the 1974 agreement did not lead to a peace treaty, Professor Yaacov Bar-Siman-Tov noted that it was a 'major breakthrough'. He added: 'Syria, which was known as the most radical Arab state in the conflict, not only drafted a formal agreement with Israel but implicitly recognized Israel and accepted to cooperate with it'.[132] After the 1973 war, Syria pursued its opposition to Israel through proxies in Lebanon and via arms sales from the Soviet Union that Syria hoped would lead to strategic parity with Israel. It did not directly attack

Israel. But with the end of Soviet arms subsidies in 1987 and then the end of the Soviet Union itself in 1991, this approach was also abandoned. In the 1990s, peace became Syria's strategic choice.[133]

Thus, Egypt and others took steps post-1967 that they did not take pre-1967, including limiting the scope of the 1973 attack, speaking in non-confrontational language, negotiating and often signing contractual peace agreements, and embracing a two-state solution (thereby accepting the results of the 1948 war). Meanwhile, other Arab voices for war clung to the pre-1967 policy of confronting Israel. In summary, then, the 1967 war provided evidence that the Arab idea of confrontation with Israel, of using military force to advance national security and territorial aims, was a failure. After nearly twenty years of challenging Israel in military terms, Egypt and Syria were soundly and rapidly defeated in June 1967. Both lost soldiers, material, and sovereign territory that brought Israeli forces uncomfortably close to their capitals. Egypt consolidated its policy shift with a 1979 peace agreement, but Israeli–Syrian talks failed to achieve the same aim.

The Palestinian national movement

In the case of the Palestinian cause, force contributed to the loss of support for armed struggle, though it was not the sole or necessarily the most important cause of the transition to an acceptance of independence on part of Mandatory Palestine instead of fighting for the total removal of Israel. Arab defeat in the 1967 war, the failure of post-1967 popular uprisings in the West Bank, the civil war in Jordan, and the 1973 war were all direct or indirect setbacks for the Palestinian national movement. These setbacks, all stemming from the idea that reliance on and application of military force would lead to the achievement of major goals, did not automatically lead to more modest Palestinian goals, starting with the ten-point programme of 1974; it may be that competition for Palestinian allegiance with Jordan and Palestinians inside the occupied territories mattered more. But by discrediting the armed route to total victory, they opened the door to some change in the movement's objectives.

After the 1967 war and the humiliating defeat of the Arab states, the PLO took the lead in trying to advance the Palestinian cause, but the idea of liberating all of Palestine quickly ran into the reality of Israeli power. The Palestinians were initially seen post-1967 as 'standard-bearers of Arab nationalism and a source of pride'.[134] The 1968 PLO charter was a maximalist, rejectionist document. But from 1967 to 1970, the Palestinians first failed to 'dislodge' Israel from any occupied territory and then the PLO was defeated in the Jordanian civil war.[135] In 1974, the PLO adopted the plan of stages: while still pledging fidelity to the armed struggle, the PLO said it would establish Palestine on any section of liberated Palestine. Two smaller factions of the PLO, the Popular Front for the Liberation of Palestine (PFLP) and the Democratic Front for the Liberation of Palestine (DFLP), saw any liberated territory as a staging ground for future conquest but Fatah, the largest PLO faction, increasingly saw it as a state that would sit alongside Israel.[136] One sympathetic observer later called this an 'implicit acceptance to the two-state solution'.[137]

The League of Arab States moved closer to a two-state resolution by adopting a modification of the Fahd plan at a summit in Fez, Morocco, on 9 September 1982. The plan called for Israeli withdrawal from all the territories occupied in 1967 – not 1947–1948 – including 'Arab Jerusalem'. Arab Jerusalem could mean Israeli withdrawal from only part of Jerusalem, meaning the other part of Jerusalem would remain in Israeli hands. It asked the United Nations Security Council to guarantee the 'peace between all States of the region'. Implicitly, that latter phrasing included Israel.¹³⁸ The plan also was ratified by the sixteenth meeting of the Palestinian National Council.¹³⁹ In 1988, the PLO – on its own – formally accepted Resolutions 242 and 338 of the United Nations Security Council, and a two-state solution.¹⁴⁰ This PLO policy shift was confirmed by the PLO's participation in the Oslo peace process in the 1990s.¹⁴¹ The results of the 1967 war, aided by other factors, started a process that led to a diplomatic opening. Bassam Abu Sharif, a PLO official, later explained: 'Why pretend we could defeat Israel by force of arms? If that wasn't possible, why not face reality and deal?'¹⁴²

Helga Baumgarten, in her historical study of three organizational manifestations of Palestinian nationalism – the Movement of Arab Nationalism, Fatah, and then Hamas – concluded that all three,

> up against the stark reality of Israel's overwhelming power, were led – by stages and with varying degrees of explicitness – to scale back their objective from a Palestinian state in all of historical Palestine to a Palestinian state alongside Israel in the West Bank (including East Jerusalem) and Gaza. In other words, all three moved (in fact if not in ideology) from the goal of ending 'the occupation of 1948' with the creation of the State of Israel on 78 percent of historical Palestine to ending the occupation of 1967.¹⁴³

The first intifada, or Palestinian uprising, reinforced this shift. True, the Palestinians had surprised Israelis with the uprising in late 1987 and staked a claim to being a legitimate nationalist movement that Israel could not ignore. As noted below, the intifada changed Israeli perspectives. But it was clear the Palestinians would not be able to liberate any territory through the uprising.¹⁴⁴ Israelis questioned prevailing assumptions, but they did not capitulate there and then or halt the Israeli settlement project. Israel defended its position through force, with the minister of defence, then Yitzhak Rabin, calling for a policy of 'force, might, and beatings'.[145] One later commentator succinctly summarized Israel's and Rabin's aim as restoring the 'psychological status quo ante: Israeli strength, Palestinian submission'.[146]

Thus far, the examples have all been of Israeli power and use of force deterring Arabs and advancing Israeli objectives. Israeli force narrowed Arab aims, lending some historical credence to the Israeli belief that military force is the optimal means for achieving national ends. However, Israeli policy has also been affected by Arab uses of force, though the primary examples all came later in the conflict. The Palestinian intifadas and attacks by Hamas and Hezbollah on Israel have all been understood to have led to Israeli political and territorial concessions, both in conceptual terms and on the ground.[147]

Israeli policy and the first intifada

The actual Palestinian use of force undermined Israeli maximal policy ideas in the occupied territories and rejection of Palestinian nationalism. The Palestinian uprisings, and especially the first one, not only led to greater Israeli recognition of the Palestinian question but also harmed the dreams of the Israeli expansionist movement spawned by Israel's territorial conquests of 1967. The first intifada was direct evidence that the Palestinians would not quietly accept Israeli control or moves toward annexation.

For twenty years, Israelis could act as if the cost of controlling the West Bank and Gaza were minimal. From 1967 to 1987, Palestinians sometimes protested and sometimes used force or violence against Israelis. Yet Israel faced no continuous, systematic opposition movement or violent campaign at the grassroots level inside the occupied territories, and Israelis came to expect low-cost occupation. That changed dramatically with the first intifada, which lasted from 1987 to 1993. The status quo had a heavy cost; even if Palestinians could not displace Israel, they could make Israel's continued stay in the territories into a question rather than an answer. Israel had pushed Arab states toward accommodation with its powerful military, and now the Palestinians moved the Israeli mainstream through their own use of force.

For Israelis across the political spectrum, the start of the intifada in December 1987 was a shock. Palestinian protests and violence meant the occupation was not cost free; the intifada communicated that 'Palestinians will never submit to Israeli rule'.[148] Ze'ev Schiff and Ehud Ya'ari, Israeli journalists, summed up the impact:

> What Israel had so long refused to see was splashed across the horizon. All that had been suppressed, quashed, shelved, ignored, papered over, pushed aside, and swept under the carpet for two decades now forced its way out into the open, tearing through the veil of hypocrisy and self-deceit that what Israel had practiced for over twenty-one years was a 'benevolent occupation'.[149]

Don Peretz, a political science professor, agreed: 'Most Israeli factions have recognized that continued occupation will require harsh, even brutal measures, and that if there ever was an enlightened occupation, its time has passed'.[150] The Palestinians were 'a nation with a legitimate claim to statehood'.[151] Ultimately, peace was contingent on dealing with them and not the Arab states. The Green Line, the dividing line between Israel and the West Bank from 1949 to 1967, reasserted itself as Israeli–Palestinian contacts ebbed.[152] Even Jerusalem felt more like a divided city again. The status quo was not viable. In a June 1989 poll, only 13 per cent of Israelis 'consider[ed] the status quo a solution'.[153]

The fiscal costs of the first intifada mounted. In February 1988, the Israeli military was spending $5 million per day to combat the Palestinian uprising and soldiers were diverted from training for other military tasks. Israeli businesses lost $19 million per day, and Israel experienced a 50 per cent drop in tourism in the summer of 1988. Some sectors, such as construction and agriculture, especially citrus growers, suffered significant downturns. By the end of 1988, Israel had lost $650 million in exports due to the Palestinian boycott.[154]

The shock of the intifada, however, did not cause Israelis to embrace a single resolution but rather intensified feelings on the left and the right, and forced important tactical changes. The Israeli political spectrum became more polarized.[155] On the right, support for annexation and opposition to Palestinian statehood was mostly steady. Palestinian attacks were taken as proof that the Palestinians would never want to live side by side with Israel or Jews. But now more right-wing Israelis understood that Palestinians would not easily accept such Israeli positions and therefore the idea of expelling or transferring Palestinians gained traction. Though it had some limitations, one poll found support for transfer at 49 per cent in August 1988, including a number of Labor Party supporters.[156] Transfer, or ethnic cleansing, might be seen as a necessary step to maintain a Jewish demographic majority if Israel annexed the West Bank.

Yet a slight but meaningful number of Israelis shifted left, a shift that ultimately contributed to the diplomatic openings of the 1990s. More Israelis gradually accepted that Israel would have to talk with the PLO and possibly accept two states if Israel hoped to resolve the conflict.[157] From April 1987 – before the intifada – until March 1989, Israeli support for giving up 'at least some territory in return for suitable guarantees' rose from 41 per cent to 54 per cent; support for conducting negotiations with the PLO rose from 42 per cent to 58 per cent.[158] In 1989, a study group of the influential Jaffee Center for Strategic Studies concluded that the 'eventual establishment of a modified

Palestinian state and qualified negotiations with the PLO were measures least likely to harm Israel's interests over the long run'.[159] Holding onto the occupied territories came at a steep moral and financial price.

This slight leftward shift was enough, by the 1992 Israeli parliamentary elections, to tip the scales toward the left for its first outright victory since the 1974 elections. The shift brought the Rabin government to power and opened the door to several policy changes. First, in a letter from Rabin to Arafat, Israel formally recognized the PLO 'as the representative of the Palestinian people'. Second, Israel privately negotiated a two-state solution at Camp David (2000) and Taba (2001). Had a deal been struck, Israel would have relinquished the vast majority of the land of the West Bank and thereby forsaken Israel's annexationist dreamers.[160] Third, if Oslo had succeeded, one could have talked about not only a policy change on Israel's part in terms of the end of expansion through settlements but also the consolidation of the change. But since Oslo failed to lead to a two-state solution, not only was a new Israeli policy not consolidated but Israeli settlements continued to grow, thus leading some to doubt that a policy change had even taken place.

This explanation for the ascendance of one idea (negotiate) and the temporary decline of a different idea (rely upon military force) highlights several factors when thinking about how the dominant idea might change. Military force, including harsh treatment of Palestinians, had failed to quell the first intifada, potentially undermining the dominant belief. The Rabin government, as a *newly elected* government with different leaders, decided to push the idea of talks forward, along with a willing PLO leader, Yasser Arafat. The Israelis and Palestinians were aided by another factor in moments when ideas are in flux, a third-party mediator, Norway, that also provided support for the idea that negotiations and concessions could lead

Force as the dominant policy

to the achievement of basic national aims like security and independence.

One alternative hypothesis for changes in Israeli policy is that geo-strategic factors such as the end of the Cold War, defeat of Iraq in the first Gulf War (1991), and collapse of the Soviet Union (1991) better explain Israel's tentative policy shift away from expansion. The global and regional threat environment changed. While they were relevant factors, they alone are unlikely to be the explanation for the Israeli changes. First, the impact of such changes on the penchant for conflict resolution is indeterminate. Geo-strategic ascendance might lead states to negotiate from a position of strength, but they might also conclude they have no need to negotiate or, even if they sit down to talk with their adversary, no need to offer meaningful concessions because they are in such a powerful position. Second, the timing of the Israeli policy shift preceded these geo-strategic changes. In 1988–1989, the first intifada was already having an impact on Israeli thinking even before the end of the Cold War or the US victory in Iraq. In that sense, such larger factors probably reinforced Israeli changes already begun.

Unilateral withdrawal

In the 2000s, Israel unilaterally withdrew its military forces from southern Lebanon (May 2000) and then its settlers and military personnel from the Gaza Strip (August–September 2005). Both developments followed the collapse of negotiations on the Israeli–Syrian and Israeli–Palestinians tracks, respectively. The fact that the withdrawals closely followed negotiating failures cemented the belief that force, not talks, was the route to Arab achievements vis-à-vis Israel.

Hezbollah, a political and military organization in Lebanon, argued that Israel's unilateral withdrawal from Lebanon was a direct result of its military campaign against Israel's presence. After years of Israeli soldiers dying as a result of Hezbollah attacks, Israelis tired of the IDF's presence in Lebanon. Sayyid Hassan Nasrallah, Hezbollah's leader, offered the dominant metaphor:

> The road to Palestine and your road to freedom follows the path of resistance and intifada.... You do not need tanks, strategic balance, rockets or cannons to liberate your land; all you need are the martyrs who shook and struck fear into this angry Zionist entity.... I tell you: the Israel that owns nuclear weapons and has the strongest air force in the region is weaker than a spider's web.[161]

The spider image was meant to evoke the fragility of Israel and its military forces. Even without conventional warfare – tanks and the like – Hezbollah's use of force had brought about Israeli withdrawal. After eighteen years in Lebanon, the mighty Israeli military had been defeated. To Mohammed Dahlan, the head of the Palestinian Preventive Security Service, it demonstrated that 'violence wins'.[162]

Five years after its withdrawal from Lebanon, in 2005 Israel again unilaterally withdrew from an occupied territory, the Gaza Strip, in a process known as disengagement. This time, the lion of Israeli expansion, Ariel Sharon, as the then prime minister, led Israel out of Gaza. Israel closed twenty-one settlements in Gaza plus another four settlements in the northern West Bank. Israeli disengagement from Gaza was born out of frustration with negotiations with the Palestinians, coupled with Palestinian rocket attacks. The second intifada had taken its toll on Israel, and the Israeli public was firmly in support of separation from the Palestinians. If the split could not be a negotiated separation, Israel would take matters into its own hands and unilaterally determine Gaza's future.

Force as the dominant policy

In the context of the second intifada and the failed Oslo negotiations of the 1990s and 2000, the Israeli move looked like the Palestinian use of force had led to Israeli capitulation. Hamas, similar to other proponents of Palestinian military resistance, claimed victory:

> It is not a coincidence that Zionists' willingness to negotiate was evident when the first Intifada started taking a heavy toll on the occupation, and when Al-Aqsa [second] Intifada placed unprecedented pressure on the Zionist military, economy, and society as a whole.[163]

Asked about the disengagement plan, 72 per cent of Palestinians saw it as a victory for armed resistance and 66 per cent believed that 'armed confrontations have helped Palestinians achieve national rights'.[164] (Despite the high level of agreement with the argument that violence had forced Israel out of Gaza, Khalil Shikaki, a prominent Palestinian pollster, said other polling data showed Palestinians did not want to use more violence to achieve further aims.[165]) That meant that even many Palestinians who did not support Hamas saw the Israeli withdrawal as a victory for militant policies. Ghaith al-Omari, a former top aide to Mahmoud Abbas, the Palestinian president, 'remembers bitterly that Hamas strung up a huge banner after Israeli troops departed: "Three Years of Intifada Beat Ten Years of Negotiations"'.[166] Some Israelis agreed that the withdrawal bolstered the Hamas argument for armed struggle.[167]

The positive impact of the second intifada for Palestinians was important but short-lived, as I explain in greater detail in chapter 4. Life in Gaza took a decided turn for the worse, and Palestinians ended up further from their goal of independence. Although Israel withdrew it settlers, it maintained a tight hold on Gaza's borders. Israel, often with Egypt's support, shaped what went in and what went out of Gaza by air, land, and sea.

Under Hamas rule, which started in 2007, the Gaza economy declined, and Israel and Hamas had major military confrontations in 2008–2009, 2012, and 2014. Thousands of Palestinians died or were injured, and most survivors lived with PTSD (post-traumatic stress disorder). Vast amounts of housing and infrastructure were destroyed. Meanwhile, the second intifada (2000–2005) had convinced many Israelis they had no partner for peace.

Overall, the evidence that Israeli policy shifted as a result of the Palestinian use of force came on a number of levels. In addition to its recognition of the PLO (1993), Israel withdrew from Gaza and closed down its settlements there in 2005. Israel was involved in four private, high-level talks (Camp David in 2000, Taba in 2001, Annapolis in 2007–2008, and the Kerry talks in 2013–2014) to achieve a two-state solution based on Israeli territorial withdrawal. Two Israeli prime ministers, both with Likud roots, publicly endorsed a two-state solution, Ehud Olmert and Benjamin Netanyahu, though the latter's statement was quite limited, as I discussed earlier.[168] However, the main contrasting point was Israeli settlements. Although many Israelis talked about the end of Greater Israel, Israeli settlements continued to expand in the West Bank.

This section has demonstrated historical cases where the use of force caused the adversary to back down, narrow aims, or seek conciliatory policies. The dynamic has worked in both directions, with Israeli power and use of force leading to changes on the Arab side, and Arab pressure and militancy leading to Israeli concessions. The point is that the belief that force is the best means for achieving important national goals has some basis in historical interactions between the warring parties.

Conclusion

Arab, Israeli, and Palestinian actors have often articulated the idea that a reliance on military force is the dominant approach for attaining one's military and political goals. One can see this in foundational documents as well as in the rhetoric of political leaders and analysts.

One reason why one often hears the idea that 'the other side understands force' is that there is some historical basis for the claim – there are indeed moments in the conflict, such as the 1967 war, and the first intifada, that provide empirical support for it. The threat (and use) of force was not the only relevant factor, but it was an important one.

Interestingly, events can have multiple effects in different directions at the same time. The 1967 war is probably the best example of this dynamic, with the second intifada being another example. The same event, the 1967 war, started Egypt and Syria down the path toward acceptance of Israel, rejuvenated the push for armed struggle in the PLO, contributed to Islamism (and thus Hamas), and opened the door to Israel's massive expansion into the occupied territories, the settlement project. The use of force, the 1967 war, led to de-escalation and concessions as well as escalation and expanding aims.

This chapter has set the baseline of the commitment to military force as an effective tactic. In the next three chapters, I turn the tables and discuss the limitations and shortcomings of military force in terms of: attaining peace; avoiding counter-productive security outcomes; reaching fundamental political objectives; and taking diplomatic opportunities.

Chapter 3

PEACE CANNOT BE FORCED

On a sunny but cold day in Washington in 1979, the Egyptian president, Anwar Sadat, and the Israeli prime minister, Menachem Begin, signed a treaty of peace with the US president, Jimmy Carter, as their witness. After fighting five wars in less than thirty years, Egypt and Israel committed to a new, peaceful relationship. At the instigation of Carter – 'Let's have a handshake' – the three leaders stood and shook hands as a symbol of the new era of relations.[1]

The 1967 and 1973 Arab–Israeli wars played an important role in starting this transformation from war toward peace by demonstrating for both sides that the state of war was costly and, arguably, unsustainable. Egypt lost sovereign territory, the Sinai Peninsula, and the Suez Canal, an important Egyptian revenue source and the post-1967 de facto border between Egyptian and Israeli soldiers, was closed. But in 1973 Egypt's military regained some pride based on its military performance. In both wars, Israel demonstrated its military superiority, whether it attacked first (1967) or last (1973). But unlike in 1967, Israel suffered heavy casualties in 1973 and needed a massive US airlift of military supplies in the midst of the war. Its intelligence apparatus had failed, and the Israeli economy was hard-hit.

Though military force and the resultant human losses and economic costs played an important role in changing Egyptian and Israeli calculations, that alone was not enough to produce a peace treaty six years after the 1973 war. The wars led to a phase of non-belligerency – the absence of war – not a state of cold or warm peace. The move from no war to actual peace required a path-breaking move by Sadat and external mediation, as embodied by the US secretary of state, Henry Kissinger, and later Carter as well. After 1973, peace was possible not guaranteed, and the process almost stalled at several points.[2] In short, military force and the resultant wars cannot compel one or both parties to sign a final peace agreement.[3] Contingent factors like leadership and third-party mediation still matter for closing the diplomatic deal.

That has not stopped people from alleging otherwise, that peace can be forced. At a commemoration of the fortieth anniversary of the 1973 war, Benjamin Netanyahu, the Israeli prime minister, told the Knesset that 'Peace is achieved through strength'. His narrative jumped right from the 1973 war ('our neighbors learned that they could not defeat us by force') to peace with Egypt ('Five years later, Egyptian President Anwar Sadat and the Prime Minister of Israel, Menachem Begin, signed a peace treaty'). He did not mention any of the other factors that were key to that transition.[4]

By juxtaposing the Egypt–Israel example with a later case, Israel and Syria in the 1990s and 2000, the argument becomes even clearer. Through a combination of wars and Israeli superiority in arms racing, the Syrian government came to accept the need for a peace treaty with Israel. The two sides rarely clashed directly after 1973, a dramatic contrast with the 1948–1973 period, when wars, border clashes, and infiltrations were common. But leadership failings, domestic political factors, and problematic US mediation meant the two sides did not cement an agreement.

While Egypt and Israel moved from non-belligerency to peaceful relations after the 1979 treaty, they did not proceed from the peace agreement to a warm peace involving extensive cultural and economic exchange. At the popular level, many Egyptians opposed the treaty and, not surprisingly then, remained reticent about a deeper engagement with Israel as long as the Palestinian question remained unresolved. Israel was militarily stronger, which had set the stage for the treaty and, simultaneously, gave Israel tools to maintain its occupation of the West Bank and Gaza Strip. But that did not mean the average Egyptian had to like that reality or accept Israel and welcome Israelis as a consequence. In short, the reliance on force cannot compel a shift to a warm peace.

Thus, the point of this chapter is that the use of military force and the reliance on economic and military strength may create the opening for a peace treaty. National strength and force can help one or both parties realize that the military option is bankrupt and they must turn to negotiations and compromise. But it can neither guarantee a peace treaty will be signed nor ensure an emotional and symbolic shift from fear and opposition to warmth and acceptance. Absence of war, yes. Cold or warm peace, no. With Egypt and Israel, other factors (mediation, leadership) better explain the move from non-war to a peace treaty. Israel and Syria never reached a treaty, and their failure to do so reinforces the idea that force alone is not enough to reach a treaty, let alone warm relations.

Force has limits. Force is not a tool that brings about contractual peace agreements; only a turn toward negotiations, and the underlying idea that talking is a useful tool for achieving important ends, can secure peace.

The arguments presented here resonate with other academic works. For example, Peter Jakobsen's observation about the state of the field in coercion studies dovetails with this chapter:

Finally, several coercion theorists have pointed out that threats and limited use of force can only buy time for diplomacy and achieve short-term results that are likely to erode if they are not supported by diplomacy and positive inducements. This suggests that [for] coercion to be successful [it] should be accompanied by of [sic] an overall plan aimed at resolving the underlying source of conflict.[5]

I agree with Jakobsen's point that coercion has a hard time getting at the deeper factors that must change for peace, and especially a warm one, to break out. One also sees this in Charles Kupchan's *How Enemies Become Friends*: the strategic shift toward peace precedes the ideational one. The use of force cannot make the other like you or accept your narrative and national identity. Amos Oz, the late Israeli author, agreed: 'Enemies with their hearts full of bitterness and hatred sign a peace contract with clenched teeth and revengeful feelings. Then, in the course of time, eventually there may come a gradual emotional de-escalation.'[6]

I have seen a similar notion in a different topic, competing schools of thought on *non*-violence. As the sociologist Sharon E. Nepstad nicely frames the issue, the difference between Gandhi's principled non-violence and Gene Sharp's strategic non-violent approach is about what one needs to change in order to move toward achievement of the movement's objective. Is it changing hearts and 'conversion' – following Gandhi – or is it changing behaviour even if hearts stay far apart, as Sharp and others suggest?[7]

Getting to the 1979 Egypt–Israel peace treaty

The 1967 and 1973 wars created the conditions under which both Egypt and Israel were ready to negotiate, something they had not done seriously since the 1949 armistice agreement.[8] But there were two vital components that helped them move from not fighting wars toward signing a peace treaty, a move that was not guaranteed. One was the combination of Sadat's dramatic announcement in November 1977 that he was willing to travel to Jerusalem to speak directly to the Israeli Knesset (discussed below), and Begin's willingness to accept this dramatic gesture. Given the right-wing background of his party, Likud, and having finally, after almost thirty years of Israeli statehood, taken control of the Israeli government in 1977, Begin's welcoming of Sadat's move was not a preordained event. In combination, this created a powerful symbolic breakthrough that helped win widespread Israeli support for the central concession, withdrawal from the entire Sinai Peninsula and the closing of several Israeli settlements there.

The other vital component was US mediation, as embodied by Kissinger and Carter. Kissinger was vital to the process, and it is a fair argument to suggest that the negotiations might not have led to two agreements under the Nixon/Ford administrations had Kissinger not been as adept at bridging the gaps through step-by-step diplomacy. Carter was even more central. The Egypt–Israel treaty talks almost broke down on multiple occasions, including in the summer of 1978 and in March 1979. On both those occasions, Carter rescued the talks, first with the summit at Camp David and then, against the advice of many of his advisers, with a trip to the Middle East to bridge the last gaps in the treaty. In this section, I address these points in chronological order: Kissinger's role in 1973–1975, Sadat's trip in 1977, and Carter's diplomatic interventions in 1978–1979.

With the end of the 1973 war, a number of issues needed to be addressed. The Suez Canal, a vital source of revenue for Egypt, was closed. Although Egypt's armed forces had performed better than in 1967, its Third Army was trapped by Israeli forces in a small territorial pocket on the east bank of the Canal. Egypt,

Israel, and Syria all held prisoners of war. The military forces were entangled, the ceasefire was fragile, the economic damage was extensive, and many soldiers had been killed or wounded. Unlike before the war, however, Egypt, Israel, and the United States all felt some urgency to move toward negotiations to address some of these issues and, possibly, the larger territorial questions that had resulted from the 1967 war. The status quo of late October 1973 was problematic.

During Richard M. Nixon's abbreviated second term and then the Gerald R. Ford administration, Henry Kissinger, as secretary of state, shuttled between the Mideast leaders and negotiated an expansive ceasefire and three Egyptian–Israeli interim agreements. Egypt and Israel signed the six-point agreement (November 1973), the Separation of Forces Agreement (Sinai I, on 18 January 1974), and the Sinai Interim Agreement (Sinai II, on 4 September 1975). The result was Israeli withdrawal from a chunk of the Sinai Peninsula, the return of Egyptian forces to positions east of the Suez Canal, and commitments both to allow non-Israeli ships to pass through the Canal and not to settle matters through the use of force.[9] That means they agreed to repudiate a central idea that both governments had held, the primacy of military force, at least for the purposes of the Egyptian–Israeli relationship. The agreements laid the groundwork for the Camp David Accords (1978) and Egyptian–Israeli peace treaty (1979) and for massive additional US aid and arms for both Egypt and Israel. Nixon, accompanied by Kissinger, travelled to the region in June 1974 in order to revel in the diplomatic triumphs.[10]

The US effort under Nixon/Ford was a central element of reaching the agreements. In Nixon/Ford, the conflict 'became America's top foreign policy priority'.[11] Kissinger 'had successfully exploited the opportunity provided by the October [1973] War to initiate shuttle diplomacy'.[12] During the war, he had 'snatched control of events'. Kissinger's control was especially important because Nixon was politically weak (due to the Watergate scandal and Nixon's criminal cover-up), and thus Kissinger 'was in real measure running the world'.[13] Aaron D. Miller, later a US negotiator himself, noted Kissinger's personal impact, writing that Kissinger 'positioned the United States as the key mediator in the Arab–Israeli conflict'.[14] Kissinger's 'tactical skills as a negotiator and mediator were unsurpassed'.[15] Kissinger was not without fault. William B. Quandt, an important US official (in the 1970s) and scholar-author, criticized Kissinger on the Palestine question: he had a 'blind spot'.[16] Others complained about the limits of shuttle diplomacy. The step-by-step approach was too narrow to yield a comprehensive peace. But, at the end of the day, Kissinger shepherded the first major Arab–Israeli agreements since the 1949 armistice deals and started to transform the strategic fallout from the 1973 war into meaningful diplomatic agreements. Kissinger 'persuaded the parties to see the benefits of ... reciprocity as a basis for exchange'.[17]

In terms of Sinai II, Gerald Ford himself also played an important role. When he and Kissinger felt Israel was being obstinate in the spring of 1975, he 'lent his weight' to a reassessment of Israeli–US ties. Although that reassessment did not lead to a new US approach toward negotiations, it made Yitzhak Rabin, Israel's prime minister, 'anxious to end the painful and costly confrontation with the United States'. Ford later wrote that when he did not bow to 'home-front political pressure' then Israeli leaders 'were ready to resume serious bargaining'. Ford met with both Sadat and Rabin to spur the process forward, becoming 'very much involved'.[18]

Sinai I, the Separation of Forces Agreement, included a small Israeli military pullback from the Suez Canal and the introduction of UN peacekeepers. The Sinai Interim Agreement

(Sinai II) was much more extensive and moved the two parties in the direction of territorial withdrawal and non-belligerency. Israel pulled its forces back from key oilfields and to the eastern end of the Mitla and Giddi passes, strategic points on the Peninsula. Egypt re-opened the Canal to some ships bound for Israel. The two sides agreed not to use force against each other. In Article I of Sinai II, Egypt and Israel noted that the 'conflict between them and in the Middle East shall not be resolved by military force but by peaceful means'. They pledged to 'reach a final and just peace settlement ... this Agreement being a significant step towards that end'. They put an end to reliance on force in Article II: 'The parties hereby undertake not to resort to the threat or use of force or military blockade against each other'. The same ideas were repeated in Article VIII:

> This Agreement is regarded by the parties as a significant step toward a just and lasting peace. It is not a final peace agreement. The parties shall continue their efforts to negotiate a final peace agreement within the framework of the Geneva peace conference in accordance with Security Council Resolution 338.[19]

The latter phrasing also reinforced the idea that concessions and agreements are building blocks, noting the UN Security Council's role with Resolution 338 (22 October 1973) and the legacy of the Geneva peace conference, a multilateral gathering that did not directly lead to successful talks. In the Agreement, we see the shift from the idea of advancing foreign policy aims by force to the belief in doing so through negotiations and concessions.

The political process then stalled for almost two years. Kissinger's step-by-step diplomacy seems to have run out of steam and 1976, a US presidential election year, did not produce any further diplomatic breakthroughs. When Carter became president in January 1977, his administration actively pursued the Arab–Israeli diplomatic track, but his initial methods did not generate progress. For much of 1977, the Carter administration tried to build on the Geneva model, seeking to use a multilateral, Arab–Israeli conference to launch peace talks. This approach failed; Carter officials were, a later observer wrote, 'way offtrack'.[20] As part of the efforts to convene a conference, the United States provoked an outcry, first with a US–Soviet communiqué on 1 October 1977 that was taken as too supportive of the Arab position and then with an Israeli–US working paper on 5 October 1977 that was seen as too close to the Israeli viewpoint.[21]

In summary, just before Sadat's announcement in November 1977 that he was prepared to travel to Jerusalem, Egypt and Israel had solidified the state of non-war, but they had been unable to move further toward peace. The Carter administration had not found the right formula for moving to the next stage, and there was no guarantee that it would succeed.

Furthermore, Begin and Likud's commitment to the concept of the Land of Israel cast doubt on the idea that Israel would withdraw from territory as the price for securing a treaty with Egypt. While a withdrawal from Sinai might be possible, Likud adamantly opposed withdrawal from the West Bank and the establishment of a Palestinian state; an agreement with Egypt, especially if part of a comprehensive settlement, might very well require Sinai *and* West Bank withdrawals and thus, in theory, might not be possible under a Likud-led government.[22] The Likud position prior to November 1977, when Sadat did actually visit Jerusalem, comes through in party platforms, Knesset speeches, and a scholarly study of the members of Begin's governing coalition.

In 1969, 1973, and 1977, Likud platforms excluded a withdrawal from the West Bank but were less clear about Sinai. In 1969, they clearly rejected any 'renewed partition of the Land of Israel'.²³ The West Bank could not change hands. Although the party platforms did not explicitly call for holding onto Sinai, they did call for 'the maintenance of Israeli rule over the areas which serve the Arabs as bases of aggression'. Sinai was presumably an area that had served as just such a base since Israelis saw Egypt's Nasser as having initiated the 1967 crisis that led to war. In addition, Begin endorsed 'large-scale' settlement in every area captured in 1967, including, explicitly, Sinai. Again in 1973, Likud stated that 'Wide-scale, Jewish settlement in the regions of Judea, Samaria, Gaza, the Golan Heights, and Sinai is of supreme importance'.²⁴ In 1977, Likud clearly opposed withdrawal from the West Bank though it made no explicit mention of Sinai.²⁵

Begin's speeches from before he was prime minister provide a second source of evidence demonstrating that Israeli territorial concessions were not a certainty. In 1968, Begin 'flatly rejected the return of any territories to the Arab states "under any circumstances"'. Moreover, the 'attainment of a peace treaty does not necessitate any concessions'.²⁶ These comments are directly counter to what was then the recently passed UN Resolution 242, which called for Israeli withdrawal from land in exchange for Arab–Israeli peace treaties. The comments also are a direct refutation of the kind of process that actually led to peace with Egypt under Begin as prime minister. Begin also had a strong, negative reaction to Israeli concessions to Egypt that led to the Sinai II agreement in 1975. On 30 July 1975, Begin told the Knesset that Israel would be weak as a result of 'the policy of continual withdrawal from political and defense positions after every Egyptian utterance'. With Israel planning to move back in parts of Sinai, he asked, rhetorically, 'Does it not constitute unprecedented foolhardiness?'²⁷ When, in early September, the Knesset debated the just-signed Egypt–Israel Interim Agreement (Sinai II), he was even more caustic:

> You surrendered, gentlemen, you gave in to pressures, you withdrew from your positions, one by one, one line after another.... Now you are trying to create rejoicing in Israel by artificial means. There is no rejoicing in Israel. This is no disengagement. It is withdrawal. It is throwing away the fruits of victory of the Six Day War. And you are already being assured that when there has been further withdrawal no deadlock will be tolerated and further withdrawals will be demanded. This is not a step towards peace, it is a step towards additional pressure and concessions.[28]

It was a stark image: territorial concession in Sinai was 'throwing away the fruits of victory' of 1967. In addition to comments like these about Egypt and Sinai, over and over again Begin expressed his unshakeable commitment to the West Bank, in terms of both Jewish history and Israeli security needs.[29] It was quite reasonable to assume that Begin, should he ever become Israeli prime minister, would be both sceptical about a full withdrawal from Sinai and totally unwilling to withdraw from the West Bank, even if that was the only way Israel could make peace with Egypt. The retention of the West Bank was not up for negotiation; retention was Begin's 'closing position'.[30]

Lastly, one estimate made in May 1977 was that 34 per cent of Likud members of Knesset (MKs) would not agree to withdrawal from any territory and another 64 per cent would agree to return 'a substantial part' but not all of the Sinai Peninsula. The preferences were similar among the MKs of the religious parties that also joined Likud's governing coalition, the National Religious Party and Agudat Yisrael: 35 per cent no withdrawal, 65 per cent substantial but not total withdrawal.[31] While those numbers did not mean an Egyptian–Israeli deal would be impossible, they surely cast some doubt on the Begin government's ability to meet the Egyptian demand of total Israeli withdrawal from Sinai. And that assumes Egypt would not hold out for an Israeli commitment to withdraw from the West Bank, something that was, for certain, not going to come from a Begin government. No Israeli territorial withdrawal from Sinai, no peace treaty with Egypt. In short, the move to a treaty and, someday, warm relations remained plausible but far from certain.

When, on 27 September 1978, the Israeli parliament ratified the Camp David Accords, the Knesset vote looked similar to the above figures. The Accords, which promised a full Israeli withdrawal from Sinai but no territorial change on the West Bank, were supported by about two-thirds of the MKs from the governing coalition.[32] Presumably those who had been open to a withdrawal from a substantial part of the Sinai accepted a total withdrawal.

Before turning to Sadat's moves, I want to highlight the importance of this Begin and right-wing opposition to territorial withdrawal in terms of the beliefs about military force. Indirectly, this rejection of territorial withdrawal is also evidence of a belief in the idea that military force will predominate and is the best way to advance Israel's national interests. How so? Israeli leaders surely knew that, in the absence of any diplomatic effort that might lead to Israeli territorial withdrawal, Arab parties eventually would be tempted to use force to challenge Israel's occupation and its continuing hold on sovereign Arab land in the case of Egypt and Syria. Thus, an unqualified opposition to territorial change post-1967 was also a commitment to military force and coercion to maintain the Israeli position. Even a benign occupation, if Israel wanted to see its rule that way, is a military occupation.

Against what looked like a Begin government uninterested in territorial withdrawal, Sadat's decisions shook up the situation, generated momentum toward talks, and created an opening that led, for a brief window, to the primacy of the idea of negotiations and concessions in Egypt and Israel. On 9 November 1977, Sadat announced that he was willing to travel to Jerusalem to address the Israeli parliament, the Knesset. Within days, he did just that and transformed how Israelis saw Egypt. Sadat arrived on 19 November and spoke to the Knesset the next day. Yet the process did not truly start with Sadat's announcement in November 1977.

Prior to Sadat's bold move, Egypt and Israel explored each other's positions through secret contacts in Morocco that proved informative. Hassan Tuhami and Moshe Dayan met secretly in Morocco in September 1977 and agreed that the United States, not the Soviet Union, would mediate the talks. By the end of September, the two sides 'had measured each other sufficiently to realize that a deal might be struck between them'. Egypt had secretly checked with Israel that Israel was interested in a land-for-peace exchange with Egypt.[33] But the United States was largely ignorant of the content of the secret talks.[34]

On 28 October, just weeks days before his monumental speech, Sadat had told Ismail Fahmy, Egypt's foreign minister, that he was thinking about travelling to Jerusalem. Fahmy was sceptical of Sadat's move; he feared a Sadat visit to Israel would waste Egypt's bargaining leverage and undermine the Palestinian cause. Had Sadat come around to his views, Sadat's trip to Jerusalem might not have taken place.[35] When Sadat committed to the trip, Fahmy resigned. In many steps along the way, Sadat overrode the prevailing position of the Egyptian political-military establishment. The symbolic gesture to Israel, and subsequent concessions, were not foreordained but rather contingent on Sadat's decisions.

Sadat's decision to travel to Jerusalem was partly influenced by the Carter administration's struggles to set up a multilateral gathering. Sadat was unwilling to wait indefinitely for the Arab parties to agree to negotiate, and he told Carter so in a letter in late September. Carter publicly said that 'Sadat decided on his own to go to Jerusalem'. That said, Carter had sent Sadat a letter, dated 29 October 1977, calling for Sadat to take a 'dramatic' step to break the diplomatic deadlock.[36] The trip to Jerusalem signalled a break with the comprehensive approach, a loss of patience in other Arab actors like Jordan, Syria, and the PLO.

Sadat later explained that the 1973 war 'taught us that we could gain less by war than by our peace initiative'. The war helped transform Sadat's ideas about how effective force and negotiations could be for helping Egypt achieve its central goals, like the return of sovereign territory. Many wars had made him wary of war: 'Egypt became a backward country because of the slogan "war is supreme"'. He had come to the conclusion that peace 'can be achieved only through direct meetings between the parties to the conflict'. Sadat took credit for shifting the Israeli public to be in favour of peace negotiations with Egypt; his willingness to come to Jerusalem in 1977 led the Israeli people to become 'a pressure group in favor of peace'.[37]

Initially, some Israelis expressed scepticism about Sadat's gambit and saw Sadat's first remarks as mere 'rhetorical flourish'.[38] Many people 'saw it as a publicity stunt or even as a trick'.[39] After all, 'Israel was prisoner to a concept that Arab leaders could not and would not make a true and real peace with Israel'.[40] Privately, former prime minister Golda Meir told her close confidante, Israel Galili, that 'Grass will grow in my hand if he [Sadat] comes to Jerusalem'.[41] Israel's military chief of staff, Mordechai Gur, told an Israeli newspaper that Egypt might be setting up a deception reminiscent of the surprise Arab attack on Israel in 1973. Egypt was still preparing for war against Israel in the following year, 1978, he added. Gur cautioned: 'The Israeli and international public should be careful not to get carried away with too much enthusiasm'. Ezer Weizman, then the defence minister, said Gur was not authorized to make such remarks.[42] Meanwhile, Shlomo Gazit led a 'skeptical' and pessimistic meeting of Israeli military intelligence.[43]

Sadat's speech to the People's Assembly in Cairo on 9 November staunchly defended the centrality of Palestinian rights, potentially giving Israeli leaders a reason to worry. Had Israeli observers sought material to demonstrate that Sadat was intransigent and the Knesset reference was an aberration in a speech otherwise dedicated to goals diametrically opposed by the Likud-led government, they certainly could have done so. In the speech, Sadat made at least seven references to the centrality of Palestinian rights, homeland, and self-determination. He praised the Geneva option – the idea of a multilateral and comprehensive Arab and Israeli meeting – because it would be 'an historic opportunity to compel Israel to relinquish the occupied Arab territories, give up its expansionist dreams and stop preventing the Palestinian people from enjoying their right to a free prosperous life in their homeland'.[44]

In reacting to Sadat's speech, a sceptical Israeli MK in the government could have made the following claim: Yes, Sadat wants to come visit us here in Israel, but why should we bother, given his statements on the Palestinian issue? We will not make progress on Egypt and Sinai because Sadat will demand simultaneous movement vis-à-vis the Palestinians, and we refuse to part with Judea and Samaria (the West Bank). Again, this point about Sadat's references to the Palestinian question reinforces my larger argument that peace was not a certain option after the wars of 1967 and 1973; the road to contractual peace was shaped by Egyptian and, in this case, Israeli policy decisions.

Nonetheless, the Knesset overwhelmingly supported issuing an invitation to Sadat. US diplomats conveyed the invitation letter from Begin to Sadat.[45] Initial uncertainty changed to growing expectations of a Sadat visit. At Ben-Gurion Airport in Israel, a red carpet was removed from storage and 'aired and dusted'. The *New York Times* described the mood in Israel as 'buoyant'. An Israeli official said Sadat's offer to visit was 'an extraordinary step that creates a precedent'.[46] The day before Sadat's arrival, a major Israeli daily newspaper, *Maariv*, carried a banner headline in Arabic and Hebrew: 'Welcome President Sadat'.[47]

The impact of Sadat's trip on Israel was tremendous, both at that time and in subsequent years. In terms of the reaction at the time, the visit, 'and his speech in the Knesset, raised much hope in Israel that a new era in bilateral relations had begun'.[48] As Golda Meir, initially a sceptic, later recounted, Sadat's visit was 'as if the Messiah had almost arrived'. Many Israelis thought peace and normalization with the entire Arab world would quickly follow. To Abba Eban, a former foreign minister, Sadat 'changed the entire psychological and emotional context in which our relationship has been conducted'.[49]

For decades, Sadat's trip has remained the metric by which Israelis judge other would-be Arab peacemakers. In Israeli eyes, no other Arab leader has met the Sadat standards. Arafat, the Palestinian leader, certainly did not do so during the Oslo years, 1993–2001. Rather than boldly accepting Israel, Arafat was seen as equivocating, with Israelis increasingly questioning his commitment to a negotiated resolution of the conflict. Neither Arafat nor Syrian president Hafez Asad embraced the grand gesture in the way that Israelis came to expect after Sadat. When US president Bill Clinton and Israeli prime minister Yitzhak Rabin privately discussed the idea of an Israeli withdrawal from the Golan Heights in March 1993, Rabin said 'he needed Asad to do something akin to what Sadat did in journeying to Jerusalem to demonstrate his commitment to peace'. Of course, Asad and Arafat used Sadat as a metric too, in terms of territory. For example, since Sadat received 100 per cent of the Sinai Peninsula, Asad did not want to settle for any less than 100 per cent of the Golan Heights in an Israeli–Syrian agreement.[50]

While the importance of Sadat's move is clear, Begin's role in reaching a peace agreement should not be underestimated.

As noted already, he and Likud could have highlighted certain long-standing right-wing beliefs and selectively listened to Sadat and Egypt in a way that would have framed Sadat's offer as trickery and made peace impossible. Instead, they welcomed Sadat to Jerusalem, fully withdrew from the Sinai Peninsula, closed several Israeli settlements there, and agreed to the Framework for Peace in the Middle East, one of the two parts of the Camp David Accords (1978), which was more accepting of the Palestinians than one might have expected from Likud. Begin did not surrender and may very well have got the best of the overall deal. But he did make concessions and move in unexpected directions.[51]

Despite the fanfare of Sadat's visit to Israel, Egyptian–Israeli talks were unable to make sufficient progress in later 1977 into 1978. Another key ingredient was necessary for a successful peace agreement: the mediation of US president Jimmy Carter and his administration. By the time of Camp David, the 'atmosphere surrounding Egyptian–Israeli negotiations was anything but clear'.[52] Israel and Egypt made progress on some issues, such as the military and security aspects of Sinai withdrawal. But to reach an agreement they would still need the 'direct, continuous, and active support' of the Carter administration.[53]

With the process in trouble, Carter turned to a summit at the presidential retreat at Camp David to try to break the logjam in September 1978. It worked, as Egypt and Israel signed the Camp David Accords. The Accords included two frameworks, one on Egyptian–Israeli issues, including normalization and Israeli withdrawal from the Sinai Peninsula, and one on establishing a process for addressing the Palestinian question. The governments of Egypt and Israel signed a final peace treaty in March 1979, and Israel completed its withdrawal from Sinai in April 1982.

The 1979 peace treaty used similar language as the interim agreements, finalizing the shift from war to peace. In the preamble, Egypt and Israel expressed their joint desire 'to bring to an end the state of war between them and to establish a peace' and 'to develop friendly relations and cooperation between themselves'. In Article I, they terminated the state of war and established peace. In Article III, they agreed to 'refrain from the threat or use of force, directly or indirectly, against each other and [to] settle all disputes between them by peaceful means'. But what would happen if they could not agree on vital matters? Article VII was clear: 'Disputes arising out of the application or interpretation of this Treaty shall be resolved by negotiations'. If talks failed, the last resort was 'conciliation' or 'arbitration'.[54] The treaty embodied the idea that negotiations, not forceful interactions, are the best way to achieve one's foreign policy aims.

When the Egyptian–Israeli treaty negotiations were foundering in early 1979, Carter again successfully inserted himself, travelling to Egypt and Israel in March 1979 against the advice of many of his advisers, who feared a political failure. The March trip was, Carter later said, 'an act of desperation'. It worked though, and a few days later Egypt and Israel signed a peace treaty. Herb Kelman, a long-time academic analyst of the conflict, highlighted the 'vital' US role: 'In the end, the Egyptian–Israeli peace treaty would not have materialized without active engagement of the Carter administration before, during, and after the Camp David summit'. The United States was 'indispensable'.[55]

Especially given that Begin and Sadat had rocky relations, Carter himself was crucial: 'the only way to really get things done [on the peace process] is the way Carter did it. He and his Secretary of State doing it personally. He and Cyrus Vance.'[56] According to Israel's Moshe Dayan, Egypt and Israel 'would not have arrived at a final agreement' without Carter.[57] Most of the people to whom Aaron David Miller, author and former US negotiator, talked said 'no Carter, no peace treaty'. Carter's 'persistence proved invaluable', and Carter was the key at the

Begin–Sadat Camp David summit. In short, 'Carter's centrality to the success of the summit cannot be overemphasized'.[58] William Quandt, a US official at Camp David, was more restrained: 'American leadership' was a necessary but not sufficient condition for successful talks ('The parties to the conflict had to be ready for agreement').[59]

In addition to the multiple conciliatory steps, the Egyptian–Israeli process took on symbolic importance because of the way in which it stood the test of time. Egypt and Israel fought wars in 1948, 1956, 1967, 1969–1970, and 1973, but after the reconciliation process began, the two sides never fought a war. The treaty held for decades, as both sides received tens of billions of dollars in US aid. Cooperation begat cooperation, at least up to a point.

For the Israelis, the peace treaty ended frequent wars with Egypt and the human casualties that resulted. The State of Israel finally had diplomatic relations with an Arab country and not just any Arab country but Egypt, the self-proclaimed leader of the Arab world. Israel's strategic situation had changed much for the better. Even with the Egyptian armed forces, the Arab side had never bested Israel in war. Without the Egyptian military, the whole idea of a state-to-state Arab war against Israel was almost impossible using conventional weapons.

This treaty was one of the three monumental strategic events that greatly enhanced Israel's security from the late 1960s until the late 1970s: building nuclear weapons with France's assistance, cementing the US–Israeli alliance, and signing a peace treaty with Egypt. These remain the three most important elements of Israeli security today. And the treaty with Egypt was brought about by a cooperative spiral. One irony is that Israelis often complain about the cold peace with Egypt, meaning the absence of deep normalization, and France's tilt toward the Palestinian position. Yet Egypt and France have done as much as anyone to ensure Israel's long-term survival. Did they do it out of the goodness of their heart? No, they did it due to strategic realities and financial interests. But they did it nonetheless.

The Egypt–Israel peace, despite its flaws, stands as a testament to the power of the land-for-peace principle, a principle that exemplifies the idea of negotiations and concessions as a beneficial means to advance state interests. The two parties that formed the core of the early Arab–Israeli wars became locked in a peace agreement. Reconciliation could produce peace and security. It was a 'process of incremental peace-building whereby satisfaction with the successful implementation of an initial agreement generated sufficient momentum and incentive to manage greater risks of accommodation with third party assistance'.[60]

Why does it matter that Egypt and Israel signed a peace treaty anyway? Isn't a situation of 'no war' enough? In other words, why make a big deal over the idea that force cannot compel the signing of a treaty? Isn't it enough that force can compel two sides to stop fighting? While the end of war is beneficial, there are added benefits from a treaty. First, it may lock in the change, creating the perception that it is harder to disregard the end of reliance on military force even if domestic politics or strategic interests shift. Even when Mohamed Morsi of the Muslim Brotherhood served as Egypt's president for a year, in 2012–2013, the Egyptian government made no move to reverse or weaken the treaty. The implication is that the absence of war might last longer with a signed piece of paper, a treaty. Second, a treaty often includes, as does the Egypt–Israel treaty, mechanisms for monitoring and verification, for instance limited force zones, peacekeepers such as the Multinational Force and Observers in Sinai, and formal channels for consultation and dialogue for use in times of crisis. These elements help reinforce the treaty and contribute to the institutional staying power of peace. For example, when Egypt needed to increase its military forces in the Sinai Peninsula as a result of domestic unrest, it sought and received Israeli approval.⁶¹ That it took place inside the framework of the treaty meant there was time for consultation and acceptance. Third, a treaty may lay out terms for or be perceived as opening the door to further warming of ties, whether or not such terms are met. Though they were largely not met in the Egypt–Israel case, the treaty included precisely such terms.⁶²

Military force and war – as well as arms and superpower alliances – brought clarity to the assessment of the Arab–Israeli balance of forces. Although, this clarity pushed Egypt and Israel toward non-belligerency, it did not guarantee peace. The successful peace treaty was contingent on two additional factors: visionary leadership by Sadat and Begin, and third-party mediation by the Carter administration. Force alone cannot compel two sides to sign a peace agreement. By turning to the Israeli–Syrian case next, it will become clear that translating the absence of war into a peace treaty is not automatic. In contrast with Israel and Egypt and their 1979 treaty of peace, Israel and Syria failed at just such an endeavour.

The Israeli–Syrian case

Israel and Syria have never signed a peace treaty. They have fought far less since 1973 than they did from 1948 to 1973, but they do not have normal, peaceful relations. Through a combination of Israel's military strength and battlefield success, Syria came to recognize that it could not best Israel. Without Soviet support, Damascus could not even keep up with Israeli weaponry. In the 1990s, Syria's president, Hafez Assad, opted to pursue a peace of the brave, but the negotiations failed. So, Israel and Syria are stuck at a different stage than Egypt and Israel. A direct conventional war has not happened in almost half a century. At the same time, neither have the two countries progressed to normal relations. Since 2011, Israel's military intervention in Syria's civil war also demonstrates that periods of non-belligerency are fragile.

While Israel and Syria fought conventional military wars in 1948, 1967, and 1973, for most, but not all, of the period from 1973 to 2011 the Israeli–Syrian border was quiet. There are exceptions, including tensions along the border in 2011 as a result of the Arab uprisings and during the subsequent Syrian civil war. Israel also attacked Syria directly on a few occasions, such as the 2003 bombing of an Islamic Jihad camp in Syria, the 2007 counter-proliferation strike on a Syrian nuclear facility, and multiple strikes on Syrian weapons since 2011. But since 1973, the two sides have never engaged in a full-fledged conventional war. Part of this relative quiet might be explained by the fact that they have another arena in which to battle: Lebanon. For example, Israel and Lebanon's Hezbollah, a stalwart Syrian ally, have frequently clashed, including in the war of 2006. In Israel's invasion of Lebanon in 1982, the Israeli and Syrian air forces briefly fought each other.

But the shift is also about Israel's demonstrated military superiority. First, Israel won all three conventional wars, 1948, 1967, and 1973. It captured the Golan Heights in 1967 and, despite an initial setback, captured slightly more Syrian territory in 1973. Moreover, it became clear that Israel's air superiority meant that Damascus, Syria's capital, was vulnerable as well, given its proximity to the Golan.

Second, Israel won the combined arms race and superpower alliance contest. Granted, Israel's much stronger, high-tech economy gives it a stronger resource foundation than Syria for arms-making and war-fighting. But Israel's turn into a capitalist, globalized powerhouse did not really get started until the mid-1980s. Rather, Israel's alliance with the United States and the US commitment to maintain Israel's qualitative edge in weaponry and military technology left Syria without a military option against Israel. Even when the Soviet Union stood with Syria, the Syrians were not as well armed as the Israeli military. When Mikhail Gorbachev, the Soviet premier, ended Soviet military subsidies for Syria arms purchases in the late 1980s, the idea of even trying to contest Israeli superiority evaporated in an instant.

Syria opted for negotiations. To put it another way, the idea that Syria could best advance its interests by means of negotiations and possibly concessions took hold. In 1991, Assad agreed to attend the multilateral Madrid peace conference. For the next decade, Israel and Syria, usually with US mediation, tried to work out a final peace agreement. During Bill Clinton's first term, the United States was involved but never tried anything comparable to Kissinger's shuttle diplomacy or Carter's summit. The US mediation was limited, not intensive.[63] In Clinton's second term, the United States tried a summit. However, at talks in Shepherdstown, West Virginia, in January 2000, Israeli prime minister Ehud Barak got cold feet and, despite Clinton's presence, then proved unwilling to meet Syrian demands for the exact delineation of the Israeli withdrawal from the Golan Heights. Polling data told him he would not get enough support from the Israeli public for the withdrawal line that Syria wanted. Clinton tried again in March 2000, by meeting an ill Hafez Assad in Geneva, but that meeting immediately collapsed when Assad rejected Clinton's phrasing of the border delineation.[64] Both the United States and Israel mistakenly thought they could finesse Assad's position; they misread Syria's bottom line – literally a line in the sense of where the post-withdrawal Golan border would be drawn – for a mere bargaining position.

A few years later, Ehud Olmert, Israel's then prime minister, conceded at the end of his tenure that at least on the Syrian front, Israel could achieve its security aims more effectively through diplomacy than another war. Olmert had held talks with Syria through Turkish mediators but the talks fell apart in late 2008, when Israel attacked the Gaza Strip. Negotiations, not war, would advance Israeli interests, he explained:

> Were a regional war to break out in the next year or two and were we to enter into a military confrontation with Syria, I have no doubt that we'd defeat them soundly. We are stronger than they. Israel is the strongest country in the Middle East. We could contend with any of our enemies or against all of our enemies combined and win. The question that I ask myself is, what happens when we win? First of all, we'd have to pay a painful price. And after we paid the price, what would we say to them? 'Let's talk.' And what would the Syrians say to us? 'Let's talk about the Golan Heights.' So, I ask: Why enter a war with the Syrians, full of losses and destruction, in order to achieve what might be achieved without paying such a heavy price?[65]

Force would not advance Israel's cause but rather return the parties to the same point as before any conflict. Thus far, no evidence has emerged that Syria had turned away from the idea of a final agreement with Israel. But with the outbreak of civil war in 2011–2012, Syria became consumed with internal matters and uncertainty, leaving little time or focus for a deal with Israel. US recognition in 2019 of the occupied Golan Heights as part of the State of Israel seems to make any Israeli–Syrian agreement even less likely.

What was lost with Israel and Syria stuck in a state of non-belligerency rather than reaching a treaty of peace? There was a greater risk of backsliding; any of the periodic confrontations could have spun out of control. This became especially apparent as Israel attacked targets in Syria in order to weaken Iranian and Hezbollah forces in Syria during the civil war. The growing Iranian presence inside Syria signalled a changed threat environment for Israel that contributed to the resurgence of the idea that only the threat and use of force could protect Israeli interests vis-à-vis Syria. In addition, the fighting continued in Lebanon, whereas an actual peace agreement might have forced Israel and Syria to come to terms over their differences in Lebanon as well. Whatever gains there might have been from peace, such as reduced military expenditures, or, for the optimist, economic and cultural cooperation, were lost.

The contrast of this Syrian–Israeli example with the Egyptian–Israeli one is meant to demonstrate that force alone does not lead to peace agreements. In both cases, force demonstrated to the Arab side that the military option was not going to lead to the defeat of Israel or the return of territory lost in 1967. The military pathway was a failure. The idea of negotiations as the better means to attain foreign-policy goals gained hold. But the cases differed on what came next. On the Egyptian track, successful leadership and mediation led to an agreement. With Syria, the two sides failed to sign a deal. The contrast makes clear that force, arms, and military factors alone are not enough to push states from ending war to peace.

Yet there is a third step as well – after the transition from war to non-war *and* after the move from ending war to peace – where countries move from a formal peace to a warm peace, with trade relations, cultural exchange, and a deeper acceptance of the other. This, too, does not result from winning wars and having more weaponry and superior alliances. The next section turns back to the Egypt–Israel case and the cold peace.

The cold peace

The change in relations between Egypt and Israel not only illustrates the role of factors other than force in moving from the absence of war to a cold peace, but it also helps us understand that warm relations are also predicated on factors other than military force. Egypt and Israel's cold peace, or 'cool normalization', is thus doubly instructive.[66]

The Egyptian–Israeli peace contains several positive, peace-like elements consistent with the definition of a cold peace. The two sides agreed not to settle matters by military force, and they stuck by that provision. Israel fully withdrew from the Sinai Peninsula on schedule, in 1982. When the two sides disagreed about who was entitled to an area in Sinai known as Taba, they settled it by arbitration, not military force (Egypt won). They exchanged ambassadors, maintained an open border, and, when Hosni Mubarak was Egypt's president, cooperated to contain Hamas in Gaza. When Israel fought Hamas and others in Gaza in 2012, the post-Mubarak government's policy did not look much different than that during the Mubarak era. The treaty has stood for over forty years, and the long duration of the peace is noteworthy. In 2012, the Israeli president, then Shimon Peres, commented, 'the fact that there was peace between us and Egypt saved the lives of hundreds of thousands of young people in Egypt and in Israel'.[67] On the financial side, Giora Eiland, a retired Israeli major-general and former national security adviser, noted that Israel had since 1975 been able to reduce military spending from 33 per cent of its gross domestic product to 6 per cent, 'and this is largely because the peace agreement with Egypt has allowed us to restructure the resources devoted to the military'.[68] Israel's peace dividend was mammoth.

At the same time, the sense of peace is far from complete. In the deepest peace, the use of military force to settle differences becomes sub-rationally unthinkable; it does not even cross one's mind as an option to be weighed. Yet Egypt and Israel still seem to suspect each other, at both the governmental and the popular levels, even if they have not attacked each other in many decades. There is no harmony of interests, and no evidence of change in popular attitudes. 'In the words of the retired Egyptian general

Adel Sulaiman [in 2012], "the Egyptian people want peace. They don't want normalisation"'.[69] In 2008, Israel's ambassador to Egypt proposed adding Hebrew to a list of foreign languages that could be taught at the university level in Egypt. The result was negative: 'Several opposition and independent lawmakers sent urgent requests to the government asking them to officially reject [the] proposal, on the grounds that it was improper and "damaged the country's sovereignty"'.[70] In short, neither side has stopped thinking about the possibility of a prolonged violent clash or even war.[71]

Moreover, though the treaty called for extensive cultural and economic relations, the reality has been more limited. As part of the initial diplomatic process, the Egyptian and Israeli Ministries of Agriculture signed a memorandum of understanding on 24 March 1980; the US Agency for International Development (USAID) also worked to facilitate joint research projects. Egypt and Israel signed a cultural agreement on 8 May 1980 that 'spoke in sweeping terms of promoting understanding and friendship'. They signed related documents in late 1981 and into early 1982.[72] But then the relationship got stuck and little was actually implemented. In the 1980s, Egyptian tourism to Israel – by Egyptians, not foreigners visiting Egypt who also wanted to visit Israel – was 'virtually nonexistent'. Egypt's professional trade unions boycotted Israel and cultural contact at the intellectual and popular level was limited. The Egyptian press was harshly anti-Begin.[73] In December 1994, fifteen years after the treaty, a clear majority of Egyptians opposed buying Israeli goods (71 per cent opposed), visiting Israel (63 per cent), and industrial cooperation (75 per cent).[74]

With the fall of Mubarak in 2011, Egypt's sale of natural gas to Israel, a significant part of what economic trade did exist and an important source of fuel for Israeli electricity generation, was undermined and then halted. In April 2012, Egypt's state-owned gas company cancelled the agreement signed in 2005. Egypt had started selling oil to Israel as far back as late November 1979.[75] Egypt's post-Mubarak leaders were unable or unwilling to stop anti-Israel attacks emanating from Sinai and targeting both the natural gas pipeline and Israel itself.[76] In August–September 2011, the situation escalated; Israel killed several Egyptian border guards as Israeli forces fought with militants based in Sinai. Egyptians protested and rioted outside the Israeli embassy in Cairo, forcing Israel to evacuate its diplomatic personnel from Egypt.

One could argue that Egypt and Israel are not natural trading partners and that may be correct.[77] But that does not preclude all theoretical economic possibilities. For example, Egypt could sell Israel oil and gas (as it did in the past), send workers to Israel from its labour surplus, or boost Egyptian tourist visits to Israel as well as to Jerusalem and its Muslim holy sites. In 2018, Israeli and Egyptian companies considered a deal for natural gas to go in the other direction, with Israel exporting to Egypt.[78]

To re-state the general point, Israel's military superiority could not make Egypt trade with Israel. It could not make Egyptians visit Israel. It could not compel a change in attitudes or automatically generate a hunger for cultural or economic exchange.

The fact that Israel and Egypt were not alone in a bilateral world greatly undermined the prospects of further normalization. Actions Israel took with regard to other Arab actors – attacks on the PLO, Iraqi nuclear facilities, and Lebanon – created a negative environment. Egypt could not or would not simply overlook such interactions between Israel and other Arab players. For example, Kenneth Stein claims that already by mid-1981, a year before the Israeli invasion of Lebanon, 'cultural, trade, tourist, and commercial relations were put into a deep freeze'.[79]

The Israeli invasion of Lebanon came six weeks after the conclusion of Israel's full withdrawal from the Sinai Peninsula in 1982 and worsened the already troubled ties. According to Ann Mosely Lesch, 'Egyptians universally perceived the invasion as a slap in their face'. With the invasion, 'all pretense of cultural cooperation ended'.[80] Egypt withdrew its ambassador from Israel after the September 1982 massacre at Sabra and Shatila, Palestinian refugee camps in Lebanon. Lebanese Phalangists carried out the massacre with the knowledge and support of Israel.[81]

Egyptian–Israeli talks over Palestinian autonomy also fell apart, leaving Egyptians feeling as if an important part of the Accords had been ignored. According to the Framework for Peace in the Middle East, one of the two frameworks of the 1978 Camp David Accords, Egypt and Israel were to agree within one year on elections for a Palestinian 'self-governing authority'. The autonomy talks, as they were known, faltered in 1980, with Egypt suspending them on at least two occasions. In 1982, a US effort to restart the talks failed.

In 1984, Ezer Weizman, an Israeli air force commander and politician, pointed the finger at Israel for the less than warm relations with Egypt: 'We didn't take the autonomy issue seriously; we said "no more war" and went ahead and made war; we went into Lebanon ... and we killed and bombed – and then we have the effrontery to complain that Egypt is returning to the Arab world!'[82] In 1997, Kenneth Stein wrote about the Egyptian–Israeli relationship and the word choice in just his first paragraph aptly conveyed the nature of relations: 'tension, mistrust, and strain'; 'norms of disenchantment'; 'coldness and uneasiness'; they 'irk, confound, and disappoint each other'; and 'frosty relationship'.[83] In 2013, Akiva Eldar, a long-time Israeli journalist, observed that Israel's 'peace with Egypt is, at best, a formal agreement between two countries, or what we like to call a "cold peace"'.[84]

In some ways, the likelihood of a cold peace was indicated in the very process that led to a peace treaty. Many of Sadat's advisers did not want a treaty with Israel unless Egypt wrested strong concessions on the Palestinian front, the kind of linkage and concessions that Israel declined to include. Ismail Fahmy, minister of foreign affairs, and Mohamed Riad, minister of state for foreign affairs, both resigned when Sadat went to Jerusalem in November 1977. By the Camp David summit in 1978, Mohamed Ibrahim Kamel, who had replaced Fahmy, thought that were Sadat the head of a small family, 'the family would have taken prompt action to revoke his legal competence'. On 16 September 1978, Kamel made a final, private plea to Sadat, succinctly explaining the failings of the likely agreement and urging Sadat to reject it. His transcription of his plea in his memoir remains a lucid telling of the position of those Arabs who saw the agreement as deeply flawed. When Sadat dismissed Kamel's objections, the foreign minister offered his resignation and Sadat accepted it.[85] Those sentiments, reflected on a much wider scale, did not simply disappear after the 1979 peace treaty but rather manifested themselves in Egyptian behaviour at both the popular and the elite levels.

I can only imagine that the assassination of Anwar Sadat in October 1981 at the hands of Egyptian Islamists also soured Egyptian leaders on closer ties with Israel. The peace with Israel was not the only reason for the assassination, but Sadat's murder did suggest moving against societal currents could come with the ultimate price for an Egyptian politician.

Conclusion

By comparing the cases of Israel–Egypt and Israel–Syria, we see that the use of force cannot compel the other side to sign an agreement. The same wars, 1967 and 1973, helped lead both Israel and Egypt and Israel and Syria to a state of non-belligerency. But Israel and Egypt moved on to signing a peace treaty while Israel and Syria, despite attempts to do so, did not. The difference was the leadership and mediation that came later. As Albert Einstein once said: 'Peace cannot be kept by force, it can be achieved only by understanding'.[86]

Or, in the midst of yet another Israeli–Hamas battle in 2014, former Israeli defence minister Amir Peretz noted that Iron Dome, Israel's anti-rocket defence system, was no more than a stopgap measure. 'In the end, the only thing that will bring true quiet is a diplomatic solution', Peretz said'.[87]

But the Egyptian–Israeli relationship reveals a second limitation on force: it cannot compel states to have warm relations. Even though Egypt recognized it was militarily weaker than Israel, it did not seek a warm cultural and economic relationship. The Palestine issue festered, the Israeli occupation and settlement project continued, and that fed Egyptians' unwillingness to deepen ties with Israel.

We also see that the idea that military force is the best way for Arab and Israeli actors to achieve their aims has not always been the dominant idea. Egypt, Israel, and Syria all had moments when they changed their beliefs about the best means available to improve their political and security positions and turned to negotiations in which they offered significant concessions. That they came to believe such an idea did not guarantee a successful negotiating outcome, as Israel and Syria learned, but it did provide a break from the dominance of a different idea, that military force is the primary means available.

Chapter 4

FORCE, INSECURITY, AND FAILURE

An overemphasis on the belief that military force is the best means to advance political and national security goals can have severe negative repercussions. That relying on force cannot bring about peace agreements illustrates the limits of forceful means. But turning to shortcomings means acknowledging that this idea, the primacy of military force as an instrument of statecraft, can often create greater insecurity, failed political objectives, and new problems.[1] In short, the reliance on force not only cannot seal a peace, but it also may cause the possibility of peace to grow more distant as the threat or use of force spurs violence, unintended escalation, war, and greater insecurity.[2]

The point is not that either these negative consequences or the claim that only force achieves objectives is accurate to the absolute exclusion of the other. Many historical examples provide evidence of *both* tendencies that follow from the threat or use of force. Sometimes the same historical example provides conflicting evidence. I agree with David Baldwin: 'In some situations, force works very well, but in others it is actually counterproductive'.[3]

For example, Israel's 1982 invasion forced the Palestine Liberation Organization (PLO) out of Lebanon. Israel destroyed the PLO mini-state in Lebanon. The PLO ended up in distant

Tunisia and that, along with other important factors such as the first intifada, contributed to the PLO's 1988 declaration accepting Israel, the PLO dialogue with the United States, the Madrid peace conference (1991) and the Oslo peace process (1993–2001). From this vantage point, one could say that the use of force helped Israel weaken its adversary and push the PLO toward offering concessions, both achievements that would help Israel achieve greater security. Furthermore, because the PLO exit came before the assassination of Lebanon's president-elect Bashir Gemayel, before Hezbollah became a powerful military and political force, and before Syria reasserted control over Lebanon, the upside for Israel initially looked compelling. The expulsion of the PLO from Lebanon, coupled with the bombing of Iraqi nuclear facilities in 1981 and the continued growth of Israeli settlements in the West Bank, looked like a notable achievement.

But Israel's invasion of Lebanon had other effects that deepened conflict, not diplomacy, and contributed to Israeli insecurity in the ensuing years, as some had warned inside the Israeli military establishment. The invasion set the stage for the 1982 Phalangist massacre of Palestinians at Sabra and Shatila, Palestinian refugee camps in Lebanon, an event that has long featured in anti-Israeli perspectives – cited as proof of Israel's total disregard for Arab human life – and motivated some of Israel's adversaries. More importantly, the invasion led to the rise of Hezbollah in Lebanon, a more potent fighting force than the PLO and one that continues to oppose Israel to this day. It contributed to Egyptian alienation with Israel and thus the cold peace that has long typified the Egyptian–Israeli. It set the stage for Israel's eventual withdrawal from Lebanon in 2000, one of two unilateral Israeli withdrawals that signalled Israeli weakness and invited attacks such as the rocket attacks against Israel from Gaza and Lebanon. And, in turn, these attacks led to a further war and military operations against Hezbollah in 2006 and against Hamas, the major Palestinian Islamist organization, in Gaza in 2008–2009, 2012, and 2014. I come back to this case in greater depth later in the chapter.

When states seek to increase their security, what do they hope for? They want to avoid losing territory, avoid occupation of their territory, and avoid total defeat or destruction. To put it another way, they want to maintain their territorial integrity and independence. They may want to weaken, degrade, displace, or topple rivals. They want to deny their rivals weaponry, training facilities, allies, funding, and propaganda victories. They do not want their actions to create new rivals or increase sympathy for the other side. They want to avoid war, if possible, but, if they must fight or if they choose to fight, they want to win at a reasonable economic and human cost. They want to minimize their own casualties. They want to avoid losing control of the military situation or facing unintended negative consequences such as escalation.[4] If matters turn to politics, they want to force a political dialogue or possible resolution on their own terms. They want to generate diplomatic defeat and capitulation or the closest to it that they can arrange. These hopes are often dashed when military force is the main instrument to achieve them.

Despite these hopes, what we may actually see when states use or threaten force is the negative repercussions for their own national security and/or fundamental political aims. On the basis of four short case studies in this chapter, I identify nine negative potential impacts in terms of national security:

(1) human casualties and suffering
(2) counter-attacks
(3) an arms race
(4) an improvement in a rival's international political standing
(5) a decrease in support at home for negotiations
(6) a strengthening of a rival's view that one is hostile or hawkish

(7) expenditure of resources (e.g. financial, territorial)
(8) creation of a new enemy or rival
(9) generation or fuelling of other detrimental policies (e.g. expansionism).

While I think it is important to consider what goals each state or organization had in mind when it turned to military force, this chapter is ultimately built on my judgement as to whether it managed to improve or worsen its military-political situation.

For example, Hamas was opposed to the Oslo peace process and wanted to end it. So, in that sense, was the second intifada a success, given that it marked a decisive end to Oslo and created significant Israeli opposition to a negotiated resolution? I would say no, because: it worsened the daily lives in social and economic terms of the average Palestinian; it made Palestinian self-determination seem less likely; and Israel did not capitulate, though Israel's disengagement from Gaza is noteworthy. In short, the overall impact should be seen as a setback for the Palestinian cause. The metric here is 'did security improve?' or, especially with regard to the Palestinian national movement, 'was progress made toward achieving fundamental political goals?' rather than 'were those goals achieved?'

Questioning the reliance on force

Through much of the Arab–Israeli conflict, the idea that the escalation, insecurity, and failed objectives resulting from a reliance on force were common and dangerous was a distinctly minority view, but some prominent leaders articulated it. Not all participants have embraced a reliance on force as the best approach. Moshe Sharett, in the 1950s, as Israel's second prime minister, and Mahmoud Abbas, in the 2000s, including as Palestinian president, both pushed for recognition of the dangers of always turning to a forceful resolution. The argument came in two variants. A weaker version simply rejected the idea that force would help actors win concessions. A stronger rejection suggested not only that force would not lead to concessions, but that its use was actually counter-productive and would worsen the political and security situation.[5] In doing so, these leaders put forth the historical limitation of a reliance on force: it can lead to problems, including dangerous escalatory spirals that worsen one's security situation.

In a speech in 2002, Mahmoud Abbas, who later became the Palestinian president, criticized the Palestinian reliance on military means during the second intifada (uprising): 'We cannot achieve our aims by the use of force'. Israeli settlements in the occupied territories expanded despite the second intifada and territories that had been liberated through the Oslo process in the 1990s were retaken by Israel during the second intifada. While Oslo had failed in its ultimate goal, a two-state solution, he said that:

> at least the phenomenon of homelessness came to an end with the [Oslo] negotiations and with peace, when it could not have been ended through war. We have gone to war many times, and you all know what the results were. Were Arab tanks surrounding Tel Aviv when we reached agreement at Oslo?

His answer to this rhetorical question was that tanks had not produced Oslo. He called on ridding the intifada of its 'negative aspects, especially its militarization'.[6] The then Palestinian interior minister, Abdel Razak Yehiyeh, echoed Abbas's argument, telling Palestinian factions, 'Stop the suicide bombings, stop the murders for no reason. Return to the legitimate struggle against the occupation, without violence and following international norms and legitimacy.'[7] He was unable to achieve consensus on that point with all the Palestinian organizations.

On other occasions since that time, Abbas has reiterated his distaste for reliance on forceful action to achieve Palestinian goals, including, most importantly, Palestinian independence.[8] In 2008, he took a similar position but was not categorical about the future: 'I do not support a return to armed struggle at this point in time. But, at a later date, this could be an option for the Palestinian people.'[9] At least at that time, he was opposed. The latter caveat may have been to provide some political protection or it could have been recognition that other Palestinian groups, such as Hamas, did not share his rejection of armed struggle and might push for its return in the future if he did not lead a successful effort to reach a two-state solution. In a 2012 example, however, Abbas returned to a much more definitive phrasing during an interview broadcast on Israeli television:

> As far as I am here, in this office [of the Palestinian president], there will be no armed, third, armed, Intifada. Never. We don't want to use terror. We don't want to use force. We don't want to use weapons. We want to use diplomacy. We want to use politics. We want to use negotiations. We want to use peaceful resistance. That's it.[10]

So not only did he reject violence and force as a means for achieving Palestinian ends, but he also affirmatively endorsed diplomacy and political tactics. In 2014, in the midst of the Hamas–Israel war, Abbas, in an interview on Al-Mayadeen News (Lebanon), 'declared that the armed struggle is over and he is opposed to rockets, armed resistance and any kind of fighting against Israel'.[11]

Decades earlier, Moshe Sharett had gone further and decried the connection between the use of force and escalation. So, Sharett explained, not only did force *not* make the situation better, it actually made it worse. At the time, Sharett was locked in a leadership struggle with David Ben-Gurion, the serving Israeli prime minister. When Ben-Gurion retired in 1953,

Sharett became prime minister and lasted into 1955. Ben-Gurion returned, first as defence minister and then, after pushing Sharett aside, as prime minister again. Ben-Gurion favoured an activist, force-reliant foreign policy as the preferred Israeli approach for stopping Arab opposition and aggression.

In contrast, Sharett was very aware of the way in which the use of force became a self-fulfilling prophecy. Israel's threats and use of force sparked Arab threats and use of force. Israel should stay its hand sometimes in order to escape this endless, escalatory spiral:

> In principle, Sharett was not opposed to retaliation, but he was concerned that it might precipitate escalation of the conflict and exacerbate Arab hostility towards Israel. Moreover, there was no evidence that such a policy indeed resulted in amelioration of Israel's security stance; in the absence of such proof it should refrain from reprisal unless absolutely necessary.[12]

He understood the dynamic:

> Sharett was fearful that reprisals would degenerate into an unthinking military routine which would only fuel the cycle of violence and escalate the conflict to higher levels.[13]

More broadly, he raised the point rhetorically:

> Do people consider that, when military reactions outstrip in their severity the events that caused them, grave processes are set in motion that widen the gulf and thrust our neighbors into the extremist camp?[14]

It is these grave processes that form the core of the insecurity argument.

The ideas about military force embedded in the debate between Sharett and Ben-Gurion continue to inform debates about Israeli practices to this day. Some commentators present the weaker version, arguing that force does not lead to concessions and the advancement of security goals: 'The notion that the country's security problems can be resolved by the unilateral use of extreme force is a persistent delusion among Israeli politicians'.[15] It is a delusion. Yuval Diskin, former chief of Israel's Shin Bet, a security agency, criticized the Netanyahu government in 2014 for its delusions, including 'the illusion that everything can be solved with a little more force'.[16]

Others endorse the stronger version whereby force is dangerous and promotes insecurity. Looking at Israeli–Hamas interactions, as well as France and its Algerian opponents and Turkey and the PKK, Steven Cook of the Council on Foreign Relations noted: 'The problem in each of these cases is that force was (or is) being employed to suppress nationalism or a nationalist issue. Under these circumstances, the consequence is not the pacification of the target population but an intensification of violence.'[17] The suppression of nationalism can backfire. In another example, Tom Segev, an Israeli journalist and historian, wrote that Israeli military operations led to escalation and deepened Israeli–Palestinian hatred but did not lead to an improvement in Israel's security or standing.[18] Israel Radio reported the following from a Palestinian official in Nablus during Israeli military operations in June 2014: 'But does all this [Israeli military] activity affect Hamas? I don't think so. If you respond with violence, you won't weaken Hamas. Just the opposite.'[19] In outlining the anti-war position in July 2014, Dahlia Scheindlin, an Israeli pollster and analyst, put it succinctly: 'escalation breeds escalation'.[20] Sobhi Salim, a Palestinian in Gaza, was sceptical as well: 'The violence will never bring a solution if there is not a political agreement. They all say, "We'll bring freedom with the rifle," but it's all empty talk.'[21]

On both the Palestinian and the Israeli side, there is some recognition of the shortcomings of threatening and using force, even if it remains the minority position. Turning to historical cases, we see evidence supportive of this minority viewpoint.

The historical record: force leads to greater insecurity and failed objectives

While force sometimes lessens confrontations, other times it arouses a powerful and violent counter-reaction: 'just as force can have a sobering effect, it also arouses other passions'.[22] We see this counter-reaction in the Gaza Raid and Suez war (1955–1956), the 1967 Arab–Israeli war, the 1982 Israeli invasion of Lebanon, and the second intifada, which began in late 2000. Again, the point is not that the threat or use of military force leads only to insecurity and possibly escalation but rather that greater insecurity is a common outcome of the use of force.

Gaza Raid and Suez war

In 1955–1956, Israeli military efforts to better its security standing did not do so. Neither the Gaza Raid nor the Suez war had the desired effect of uniformly improving Israeli security. The raid in February 1955 increased Egyptian support for cross-border infiltration and contributed to the Egyptian pursuit of Eastern bloc arms. The Suez war in the autumn of 1956 was a prelude to a decade of relative quiet with Egypt, but Gamal Abdel Nasser, Egypt's president, was not removed or weakened. In fact, the war came at a huge cost for Israel: it catapulted Nasser to a position of great leadership and power in the Arab world and the global non-aligned movement. It was that very position that helped shape Nasser's fateful decisions in May 1967.

What were Israel's security concerns in relation to Egypt in 1955–1956? Israel wanted Egypt to stop the cross-border attacks, many of which originated in Gaza, by the Palestinian Fedayeen (guerillas). From 1948 to 1967, Egypt controlled but did not annex Gaza. Israel worried about a conventional military attack by Egypt and other Arab states. As Nasser tightened his grip on power, Israel worried about a resurgent and radical Egypt leading an anti-Israel movement across the Arab world. For David Ben-Gurion and Israel, an Arab leader who could unify the Arab states against Israel was 'the great danger'.[23] That meant that weakening or toppling Nasser was important not only vis-à-vis Egypt but also with regard to Israel's regional security concerns.

On 28 February 1955, Israeli forces attacked Gaza, resulting in what many accounts consider to be an important moment of escalation. The raid was intended to pressure the government of Egypt to stop Palestinian infiltration and attacks on civilian and military targets inside Israel.[24] The raid was quite large compared with previous Israeli attacks; the Israel Defense Forces (IDF) caused 100 Egyptian casualties.[25] It 'represented another leap in escalation'.[26] The raid was 'unprecedented in scale'.[27] It was the 'bloodiest' since the 1948 war and 'severely shook Egypt and, ultimately, the entire Middle East'.[28] The raid 'put Israel and Egypt on a collision course'.[29]

Despite Israeli hopes, the Gaza Raid was unsuccessful in stopping cross-border attacks and illustrates the ways in which the use of force can be counter-productive. First, as a result of the Raid, Egypt shifted from trying to curb Palestinian Fedayeen attacks from Gaza against Israel toward using the Fedayeen attacks as 'an official instrument of warfare against Israel'.[30] The situation on the border worsened, including additional casualties and direct involvement of Egyptian troops. So, the central Israeli goal in launching the Raid was a failure; instead, the Raid was 'a great catalyst of Israeli–Egyptian violence'.[31]

Second, some authors claim that as a result of the Raid, Nasser decided Israel was not serious about negotiations.[32] The evidence is limited but, if accurate, the example reinforces the notion that the use of force can obscure or undermine diplomatic openings.

Third, according to Nasser, the Raid was a major impetus that led to the Czech arms deal, Egypt's major purchase of weapons from the Soviet bloc.[33] Critics largely attack the idea that the Raid was the sole factor to explain Egypt's arms build-up. I agree: it was not the sole factor. But even the critical views are consistent with the idea that the Raid was one of the important elements explaining Egypt's arms deal. As Michael Oren, an Israeli historian and politician, argued, the Raid 'served to accelerate Egypt's and Israel's efforts to acquire modern weaponry'.[34]

Critics have contended that the Gaza Raid had little to do with the Czech arms sales, but I think the evidence suggests it was a major factor. In terms of military hardware like tanks and planes, Egypt's preference had been US and Western arms, but that deal never materialized. According to Guy Laron's research with declassified documents, Nasser restarted arms talks with the Soviet side in 1955 in order to gain leverage vis-à-vis the Americans; to prepare to counter Egypt's exclusion from the Baghdad Pact, a pro-Western alliance; and in response to the Gaza Raid. While it is correct that the Egyptian government had sought Soviet arms in the years prior to the Gaza Raid, Nasser saw the raid as part of a Western campaign of growing pressure on Egypt.[35] He felt he was left with little choice but Soviet arms and the Soviet leadership was, at last, willing to deal. One month after the Raid, the talks that directly led to the Czech deal began.[36] On 18 June 1955, Hassan Tuhami, then head of the Intelligence Branch at the president's office, wrote to Nasser that Egypt needed Russian arms 'to stand against Israel'.[37] The Gaza Raid and Baghdad Pact were, Laron argues, 'catalysts'.[38]

Even critics make arguments that concede the importance of the Raid in spurring the Egyptian arms deal with a Soviet client, Czechoslovakia. Uri Ra'anan's major point was that the arms deal, and Egypt's turn toward the Soviet Union, was a response to Western efforts to form a Mideast alliance without Egypt – what came to be known as the Baghdad Pact and started with Turkey and Iraq – not the Gaza Raid. Egypt wanted to get arms 'in diametric opposition to contemporary Western aims in the region'.[39] But since, as Laron noted, Nasser saw the Raid as part of a broader campaign of Western pressure against Egypt, that way of thinking would mean the Raid *did* contribute to the desire for a Soviet arms deal. The Western alliance and the Gaza Raid melded together in Egyptian eyes.

Another critic of the importance of the Gaza Raid to Egypt's calculations on arms procurement, David Tal, nonetheless wrote:

> Still, it cannot be ruled out that Operation Gaza led the Egyptian negotiators to seek – and receive – larger quantities and more powerful types of weapons that [sic] might otherwise have been the case. Similarly, the operation may have persuaded the Soviets that the Egyptian request was reasonable.[40]

While Tal does not concede that the Raid caused Egypt to seek the arms deal, he does suggest very important ways it may have influenced the shape of the Czech arms deal that actually emerged in 1955. In fact, if the Raid affected Soviet thinking in that way, it is possible that absent the Raid, the deal would not have taken place, not due to Egypt, a common argument rejected by Tal, but due to *Soviet* reluctance.[41]

In sum, the Raid did not accomplish Israel's major security objective, reducing infiltration, but probably made that situation worse. Moreover, it contributed to Egypt's acquisition of weapons, thus putting Egypt in a *better* position to consider a conventional attack on Israel and forcing Israel to think more directly about a preventive war. The arms deal meant Israel had to consider whether to act militarily before Egypt received and absorbed the Eastern bloc arms. For Thomas Rid, sometimes Israel's activist or aggressive approach worked (e.g. with Jordan) but with Gaza and Egypt, 'the raids seem to have had an escalatory effect that ultimately helped pave the way for a conventional confrontation with Egypt in 1956'.[42]

Even before Egypt's Czech arms deal became known in September 1955, Israel was considering launching a war against Egypt and Israel too was seeking arms from an external great power. By spring 1955, Moshe Dayan, Israel's military chief of staff, and David Ben-Gurion, who had just returned as Israel's defence minister in February, agreed that Israel should launch a war against Egypt. Israel, and especially Dayan, used military raids to try to provoke Nasser's Egypt. Dayan was 'deeply committed to the retaliation principle'.[43] On 29 March 1955, the Israeli prime minister, Sharett, and cabinet voted down a Ben-Gurion plan to conquer Gaza, then under Egypt's control.[44] In late October 1955, Ben-Gurion and Dayan created plans to strike Egypt in January 1956.[45]

What was the impact of the Czech arms deal on Israeli national security thinking? First, it intensified Israel's search for an external patron to provide arms – to counter the weaponry that would flow into Egypt – and to protect Israel from external British or Soviet meddling. The arrival of Soviet arms created time pressure on Israel as the weapons 'dramatically changed the strategic situation' in Egypt's favour.[46] It would be harder to pressure Egypt once it trained with and assimilated the weaponry. Israel had other motives as well, but the preventive one was central to its joining Britain and France in curtailing Egypt.[47] In 1956, Israel and France signed a new arms agreement. An arms race was in full swing.

Second, Israelis were alarmed. In early October 1955, Peretz Bernstein, a Member of the Knesset, argued, 'It is hard to imagine that [Nasser] would make this move if he didn't intend to use the arms.... We must consider the serious intention now issuing from Egypt ... to attempt to destroy Israel'. In the full Knesset debate, Mordechai Bar-On later summarized, the central point was clear: 'The Czech deal threatened Israel's existence and presented a most palpable danger'.[48]

However, in the short term, the arms deal led Ben-Gurion, now prime minister, to *delay* attacking Egypt, even though Dayan still favoured war. The cabinet was not in favour of war – which was made clear at a 4 December 1955 meeting – and Ben-Gurion came to believe that an Israeli attack on Egypt, or even smaller retaliatory raids by Israel, would undermine the search for an external patron such as France or the United States.[49] Instead, Ben-Gurion's idea was that once Israel had a patron solidly in place, he would again support launching a war against Egypt. His hesitation about war was only a 'temporary delay', as became clear the next year, in the autumn of 1956, when Israel, Britain, and France agreed to attack Egypt.[50] By early March 1956, historian Avi Shlaim argues, Ben-Gurion was back to a pro-war position; neither an arms procurement deal with the United States nor serious negotiations with Nasser seemed possible. The need for delay was over in his mind.[51]

Note that Ben-Gurion's reaction to the Czech arms deal shifted. His initial response, as indicated by his war planning with Dayan in late October 1955, was to go to war, presumably before Egypt could absorb its new weapons cache. But he shifted, during December 1955, to securing great-power patronage and arms *before* launching that war. Perhaps this shift was because of Israeli cabinet opposition or because US officials, as well as the secretary of state, John Foster Dulles, told Israel that preventive war would, in Levey's telling, 'compromise their relationship with the United States'.[52]

What did Ben-Gurion want to do once Israel had the arms? Tal contends he had not decided whether the arms were meant for offensive action or to deter Egypt and thereby avoid war. In Tal's view, Israel, or really Ben-Gurion, was 'dragged to war' by France.[53]

The Suez war was meant to weaken Nasser, but ended up greatly bolstering his standing. It was a major political triumph for Egypt's president, which thrust him onto the Arab and international stage in a manner deeply unhelpful to Israel. Pan-Arabism, the idea of unifying all Arabs in a single political entity, became synonymous with Nasserism. The war 'gave Nasser almost unlimited credit in his own country and throughout the Arab world'.[54] Israel failed to use war to achieve its major objective, and it actually worsened the situation. In a conversation with a US diplomat after the war, Nasser said the war had changed Egyptians' opinion about Israel: 'popular indifference has given way to hate', something Tal links to the rhetoric that paved the way to the 1967 war.[55] At the same time, the border grew quiet.[56] Boaz Atzili and Wendy Pearlman argue that the border grew quiet *because* Nasser was greatly empowered by the 1956 war; they argue stronger states are much better than weak ones at cracking down on non-state actors operating militarily from within their territory.[57]

The rise of Nasser, synonymous with the rise of pan-Arabism, could have been much worse for Israel had it not been for two major obstacles that limited its impact. First, the pan-Arabist idea directly contradicted national identity and politics, the idea that a person is, say, Syrian or Egyptian first. Arab nationalists pushed back, such as when Syria broke off its short-lived union with Egypt. Second, the 1967 military debacle reflected poorly on Nasser and pan-Arabism. Nasser even offered his resignation as a result of the war; it was rejected. The fact that other obstacles arose, however, should not obscure the fact that pan-Arabism, building on the results of the 1956 war, could have boded much worse for Israel, had much of the Arab world actually united and retained anti-Israelism as a major military-political tenet.

The danger of pan-Arabism for Israel was not all hypothetical. Aspects of the 1973 Arab–Israeli war and crisis that flowed from pan-Arabism did complicate Israel's situation. Arab solidarity, which can be thought of as a limited manifestation of pan-Arabism, was instrumental in facilitating the Arab oil embargo against the United States and the Netherlands and its consequent impact on the global economy in 1973–1974. A second example was the presence of Iraqi military forces during the 1973 war, forces that constrained Israeli action in southern Syria. Both the embargo and Iraq's meaningful military participation were consistent with pan-Arab politics and rhetoric. Neither example helped Israel or, in the oil case, its allies, like the United States.

Neither the Gaza Raid nor the Suez war, both forceful Israeli policies meant to advance Israel's security objectives vis-à-vis Egypt, succeeded and, in some ways, they made Israel's security situation even worse, by facilitating Nasser's regional rise. Israel had a decade of relative quiet, but the price was an intensification of border incidents in 1955–1956, fuelling the Arab perception of Israeli hostility and expansionism, elevating Nasser to a regional (if not global) perch, and, possibly, undermining any hope for a negotiated deal with Egypt in the 1950s.

Can one imagine a different pathway in 1955?[58] What if Sharett had prevailed, tamped down calls for military strikes, and kept Ben-Gurion and his activists outside the government for years? One question is whether there could have been any kind of diplomatic opening between Egypt and Israel, especially given that Israel and Egypt had signed an armistice agreement in 1949. If, starting with secret talks, Egypt and Israel could have reached some kind of accommodation in the 1950s and thereby avoided the 1967 war, history would have unfolded very differently. The key question is the extent to which Nasser (and his Free Officers Movement) would have considered such a policy. The more that was a real possibility, the more Israel lost in executing the Gaza Raid. A counterfactual scenario built on a non-forceful, non-military Israeli policy, is plausible.

Imagining a different path in 1956 is more difficult because so many of the key relationships did not involve Israel but rather Britain, Egypt, France, and the United States. Even if Israel had had a different policy and had sought a non-forceful option, the other states might still have become militarily entangled in a way that would have precluded bettering Israel's security situation.

1967 war

Multiple parties fought the 1967 Arab–Israeli war, or what Israelis call the Six-Day War. It contains multiple examples of the force–escalation–insecurity dynamic. The growth of insecurity – not security – can be told on the basis of Egyptian, Palestinian, Syrian, and Israeli policy decisions. I focus on Egypt's forceful actions that set the stage for the Israeli attack, Israel's capture of massive amounts of Arab territory, and the resultant Israeli expansionism, the Israeli settlement project.

On about 13 May 1967, Soviet officials warned Egypt that Israel was concentrating military forces on the Israeli–Syrian border in advance of a planned Israeli attack on Syria. The Soviets regularly issued such warnings.[59] In this case, the Soviets may have learned of a 7 May Israeli cabinet decision to 'launch a limited retaliatory strike if Syrian-sponsored border incursions continued'.[60] Israel was not, however, massing forces.

Egypt responded with several moves in rapid succession that set Israel on edge. On 14–15 May, Cairo began moving soldiers into the Sinai Peninsula, the part of Egypt that bordered Israel. Prior to the build-up, Egypt had one division in Sinai; by the end of the month it had seven divisions there, or about 100,000 soldiers.[61] Egypt next asked the United Nations Emergency Force, peacekeepers stationed on the Egyptian side of the Egyptian–Israeli border in the aftermath of the Suez war, to depart. On 18 May, the UN secretary general complied and the entire peacekeeping force began to leave; the next day Egypt recalled some of its soldiers who were busy fighting in Yemen. On 22–23 May, the Egyptian president, Gamal Abdel Nasser, announced that Egypt was closing the Strait of Tiran to non-Israeli ships bound for the southern Israeli port of Eilat. On 30 May, Jordan's King Hussein travelled to Cairo and signed an Egyptian–Jordanian military agreement, thereby solidifying the anti-Israel front.

Egypt's military moves, whether intended as a bluff to prompt Israeli concessions or as actual steps toward attacking Israel, prompted an Israeli attack on 5 June, a devastating defeat, and Egypt's loss of Gaza and the Sinai Peninsula, results Egypt surely did not desire. So not only did Egyptian policy lead to escalation, but it also dealt a blow to Egypt's territorial expanse and national interests.

One could tell other stories about the origins of the 1967 war, but they too speak to the way in which force and counter-moves created an escalatory spiral. In 1966–1967, Palestinian militants launched, and Syria encouraged, raids against Israel with the hope of sparking a war. In November 1966, Israel launched a large-scale attack against Samu, a village in the West Bank then under Jordanian control. In early April 1967, an Israeli–Syrian dogfight resulted in the downing of six Syrian aircraft. In early May, Egypt feared, encouraged by the Soviets, Israel was planning to strike Syria. To the extent that any of these factors explain Egypt's belligerent moves in May, they still point to an escalatory spiral sparked by duelling moves exhibiting toughness and strength.

Israel justified its attack on 5 June as a pre-emptive strike against Egypt and Syria, but it also fed a confrontational dynamic on the Palestinian front. First, the PLO concluded from the war and the weak performance of Arab state armed forces that Arab conventional armies would not advance the Palestinian cause, and thus Palestinians needed to take over the fight.[62] One result, in 1968, was the revision of the PLO charter, with more aggressive and belligerent language. The belief that the Palestinians' future was in their own hands led to Palestinian–Israeli fights on the ground – notably the battle at Karameh in 1968 – but also, especially in the 1970s, a Palestinian campaign of international terrorism designed to hurt Israel and to draw attention to the Palestinian nationalist cause. That campaign included the 1970 plane hijackings as well as the 1972 Munich Olympics attack.

Second, the war contributed to a longer-term trend, the rise of Islamism. Islamists argued the war had exposed the bankruptcy of Arab socialism, the then dominant and largely secular ideology of the Arab regimes. Secularism had failed the Arab peoples, but there was an alternative: Islam was the answer.[63] One should be careful not to overstate the role of the 1967 war, as the Arab governments had already stumbled, most importantly, in terms of economic growth and development. But the war reinforced the perception of government ineptitude, which helped Islamism develop a growing social and political role in Arab societies. Twenty years later, Islamism in the Palestinian context formally crystallized with the formation of Hamas, the central organization that took over the mantle of resistance to Israel when the PLO went the route of negotiations – the Oslo process – in 1993.

Israel's immediate strategic and political considerations drove its decision to attack on 5 June 1967. States regularly follow short-term needs over longer-term pressures. Even had Israel known the impact the war would have on Palestinians, Israel likely would not have acted differently. Nonetheless, the war contributed to an Israeli–Palestinian escalation in the short term (PLO) and the long term (Hamas), and thus, in this dimension, offers up an additional case of force causing (or contributing to) escalation and undermining one's security.

In May 1967, had Egypt not escalated the situation through military moves, its security situation would have turned out much better. Egypt would have remained territorially complete because Israel would not have had the opportunity provided by war to capture and hold sovereign Arab territory, including Egypt's Sinai Peninsula. Israel would not have been able to move settlers into Gaza, the Golan Heights, Sinai, and the West Bank, a move especially detrimental to Palestinians, because Israel would not have occupied those spaces. Nasser himself must have known that such a devastating outcome from pressuring Israeli militarily was possible; for several years prior to the war he had been saying that the Arab military forces were not ready to confront Israel. Lastly, many factors contributed to the Islamist rise but perhaps the absence of the humiliating defeat of the 1967 war might have affected Islamist organizations' nature and characteristics as they grew in the 1960s and 1970s.

Lebanon, 1982

In June 1982, Israel invaded Lebanon in order to secure a friendly Israeli–Lebanese agreement and to drive the PLO out of Lebanon, where it had been headquartered since the early 1970s. Though Israel's invasion did have some of the desired effects, it also had several unanticipated consequences and generated some long-lasting security problems. In the end, Eyal Zisser concluded, 'Once again it became clear to Israel that striking a military blow on its enemies was not enough to remove the threat they posed to it'.[64]

The PLO operated as a quasi-state within Lebanon, in competition with the national government. Israel invaded, citing as a reason the attempted assassination of the Israeli ambassador to Britain, Shlomo Argov, on 3 June 1982, even though the assassins were affiliated with a rival of the PLO, Abu Nidal's terrorist group. Within a few months, Israel forced the PLO to abandon its headquarters and evacuate thousands of its fighters. Furthermore, in 1983, Israel was on the cusp of securing a new ally after Israel and Lebanon negotiated a treaty. But the Lebanese government was condemned for making a deal with Israel and the government backtracked, abrogating the agreement in April 1984. Israel pulled back but kept military personnel in southern Lebanon until a unilateral Israeli withdrawal in May 2000.

Israel's invasion in 1982 sparked three problematic countermoves. The immediate one was the creation and rapid growth of a new Arab nemesis, Hezbollah, a political and military organization based among Lebanese Shiites. In Yitzhak Rabin's words, 'It was as if the Shiite genie was released from the bottle, in a way that no one had foreseen'.[65] Hezbollah skirmished with Israel and its allies until the Israeli withdrawal in 2000. It 'was seen as the first agent in history that succeeded in ousting Israel by force from occupied Arab land'.[66] Hezbollah continued to confront Israel after that, with the two sides fighting a war in 2006 after Hezbollah crossed into Israel to capture and kill Israeli soldiers. The Shiite organization also provided an anchor for its close allies in the governments of Iran and Syria. Looking back, Ehud Eiran summarizes the problem well:

> Hezbollah was created as a result of the war, rose to [a] national leadership position and created an ongoing security challenge for Israel. Looking back from 2012, the greatest challenge posed by Hezbollah – [and] indeed the most undesirable outcome of the 1982 war – is the fact that the organization plays an important part [in] Iranian deterrence against Israel. In other words, a 1980s operational problem had become a strategic issue by the first decade of the 2000s.[67]

But there was no going back. Overall, 'the ambitious [Israeli] operation did not succeed in ending terrorism, but actually made it worse'.[68] Hezbollah replaced the PLO and then some.

Furthermore, the Israeli invasion indirectly set the stage for the outbreak of the first Palestinian intifada in the West Bank and Gaza in December 1987. After Israel forced the PLO out of Lebanon, the new PLO headquarters was set up in distant Tunisia. For the first time, PLO leaders were not based in one of Israel's neighbours. The organization 'remained in the wilderness', wrote one of the foremost scholars of the Palestinian movement, Yezid Sayigh.[69] Palestinians in the occupied territories, many of them PLO supporters or lower-level officials, ended up taking matters into their own hands with the intifada. And I mean 'hands' literally. Palestinian youths threw rocks and Molotov cocktails at Israeli soldiers. Moreover, Hamas's Khalid Mishal contended that Palestinian Islamists, too, sought to exploit the opening created by the PLO's failings, geographical distance, and turn toward negotiations.[70] One could note that the first intifada led to Madrid and Oslo, but those negotiations were certainly not what right-wing Israeli prime minister Menachem Begin wanted when he launched the Lebanon war in 1982. Israel's effort to rid itself of its main enemy – the PLO in Lebanon – set in motion two pathways of Arab resistance, Hezbollah and the first Palestinian intifada. The Palestinian question emphatically did not go away.

Moreover, the Israeli invasion of Lebanon led Syria to strengthen its armed forces and improve its political standing within Lebanese politics. 'While the PLO was removed from the [sic] Lebanon, Syria got stronger.'[71] In 1982, the lessons Syria took from Israel's military dominance, especially in the air, as Syria had lost over 100 aircraft, influenced Syria's subsequent build-up, fuelled by Soviet arms and aid. In the mid-1980s, Syria sought strategic parity with Israel and was seen by Israel as 'a palpable threat to Israel's existence'. Syria sought military equality with Israel. In terms of Lebanese politics, Syria also emerged in a better position after the 1982 war, especially because the attempted Israeli–Lebanese agreement failed and Hezbollah, with close ties to Syria, grew in stature.[72]

As in 1967, Israel's immediate strategic and political considerations drove its decision to invade Lebanon. But again here, those immediate considerations coexisted with the reality that the use of force by Israel fed the escalation of the conflict. Though it was forced to move to Tunisia, the PLO remained an Israeli adversary and now Hezbollah was added to the anti-Israel mix as well.

What would have been different if Israel did not invade Lebanon in 1982? Had Israel wanted to pursue a diplomatic pathway for dealing with the Palestinian question instead of trying to smash Palestinian nationalism and force the PLO out of Lebanon, it had one. The 1978 Camp David Accords between Egypt and Israel had two frameworks, one of which dealt with Egyptian–Israeli peace and the other of which addressed the question of Palestinian autonomy. The latter document, the Framework for Peace in the Middle East, called for autonomy talks, the maximum Begin, the Israeli prime minister, would allow for the Palestinians when the agreement was negotiated; he was strongly opposed to an independent state of Palestine. Under Jimmy Carter, the US president, those autonomy talks did get started but Jordan and the PLO declined to participate and the Egyptian–Israeli meetings did not generate progress. Israel could have tried to give those talks real meaning rather than letting them peter out under the late Carter and early Reagan administrations. The same kind of Israeli government that would have avoided an invasion of Lebanon would also likely have been more open to substantive, not just procedural, negotiations over the Palestinian matter. Had Israel signalled that those negotiations could be a real opening, rather than a diversion and a necessity agreed to only in order to open the door to peace with Egypt, not only might Arabs and Israelis have genuinely addressed the Palestinian issue over a decade before Oslo but also the PLO or Jordan might have joined the talks. (Even in reality, for a few weeks right after the agreement was signed in 1978, both did consider joining.[73]) In the early 1980s, the PLO was in the midst of a transition from the 1974 ten-point plan, the first major inkling it would accept a two-state solution, to its 1988 public declaration accepting Israel. It might have been an opportune time for talks.

Counterfactually, one is hard pressed to imagine an Israeli *diplomatic* pathway toward installing a pro-Israeli regime in Lebanon. But the PLO was the main irritant to Israel that was based in Lebanon. If, via autonomy talks, Israel had taken that Palestinian question seriously, at least Israel might have hoped for a less hostile Lebanese government and the overall environment would not have been one in which Hezbollah came into being as a result of an Israeli military attack.

Second intifada

The last example is another escalatory spiral, the second intifada, which began in September 2000.[74] The intifada itself contained a series of force–escalation interactions. Israel had planned an immediate, heavy-handed response that it thought would quash Palestinian protest, but instead it inflamed Palestinians and protest mushroomed. Israel was said to have fired one million rounds in the first three weeks of the intifada.[75] One specific mechanism by which protest expanded was through Palestinian funerals. A funeral itself became a venue for further Palestinian–Israeli confrontations; the more Palestinian dead, the more funerals, and the more the intifada boiled.

As the intifada dragged on, Palestinian groups turned to suicide bombings, increasing Israeli casualties: 'As Israel used targeted assassinations and a regime of stifling curfews and lethal incursions in a bid to break Palestinian spirits, the combined Palestinian factions retaliated with wave after wave of suicide strikes'.[76] Hamas was the most prolific, but Fatah, the Popular Front for the Liberation of Palestine (PFLP), and Islamic Jihad also had bombers. The first Hamas suicide bombing of the second intifada was in March 2001.[77] My interest is less in the specific tactic chosen than in the general choice to use a forceful tactic.

What did Palestinians hope to accomplish by using force? Hamas sought to use armed resistance as an alternative to the failed Oslo paradigm of negotiations, which Hamas would characterize as Arafat's capitulation to American and Israeli pressure. If the negotiations were going well and had popular support, Hamas felt constrained and would shy away from suicide bombings.[78] But the Oslo process, based on a negotiated resolution and the rejection of force, did not bring the Israeli occupation to an end. Thus, noted Khaled Hroub, Hamas pursued an alternative, summed up in this line: 'Wherever a military occupation exists, a military resistance should be expected and exercised. Such a resistance, taking various forms, would only stop when the occupation ends.'[79] In 2003, Shaykh Ahmad Yasin, a Hamas founder, was succinct in saying 'Only armed resistance can achieve liberation'. Ismail Abu Shanab, a Hamas leader, made a similar point at that time, suggesting 'pressure' – meaning bombings and resistance and the resultant Israeli death and destruction – was the means to make Israel withdraw.[80] Interviewed in 2010, Khalid Mishal, a long-time Hamas leader, agreed: 'When there is occupation and people suffering under occupation, the strategic response must be resistance – a steady and unwavering line of resistance until the occupation is brought to an end. No occupier was ever removed without resistance.' Mishal went on to highlight Israel's withdrawal from Gaza as a sign of the success of Palestinian resistance.[81]

The various Palestinian movements disagreed about the extent of the Israeli occupation. Some argued it constituted the entire territorial area going back to 1948, while others focused on the West Bank and Gaza Strip, territories Israel occupied in the 1967 war. Most militant groups accepted such bombings but some wanted them focused on targets in the occupied territories and against the Israeli military, not civilians. In August 2002, many Palestinians organizations tried to negotiate a unified document on the aims of the second intifada and much of the discussion revolved around these issues.[82] There was also, as I have indicated in discussing the views of Mahmoud Abbas, some pushback against the use of suicide bombings anywhere.[83]

Scholarly sources highlight a range of factors in such bombings, some of which echo the views of Palestinian leaders. Two of these were revenge against Israel and internal political competition among Fatah, Hamas, and other Palestinian factions. Assaf Moghadam, in noting the many motives for the attacks, made a useful distinction between the individual and the organizational motives. In short, a specific suicide bomber had their own reasons for committing the act and an organization had motives for wanting such bombers to act in its name and thus for devoting resources to recruit, train, and execute the operation. Moghadam quotes Martha Crenshaw, a leading terrorism expert, who emphasizes the importance of a strategic perspective, meaning seeing a bombing as a course of action meant to achieve certain larger aims.[84] For an organization such as Hamas, the violent attacks supported official goals – destroy Israel – and operative ones like undermining the peace process or defying the Israel Defense Forces.[85] Mia Bloom, who highlights the internal political contestation between Palestinian groups, notes that these same groups used bombings in the hopes of hurting Israel, deterring Israel, and forcing Israel to withdraw and end the occupation.[86] By 'internal political contestation', I mean the way Hamas used bombings to try to elevate its political standing and weaken its domestic Palestinian rival, Fatah.

The bombings did not end the Israeli occupation. This use of force instead sparked more Israeli moves, including major military operations, such as Operation Defensive Shield in 2002, as well as the construction of the barrier or wall in the West Bank to block bombers and to informally incorporate some land into pre-1967 Israel. In the West Bank, Israel re-occupied land from which it had withdrawn in the Oslo years. True, Israel closed down its settlements in Gaza in 2005. But the external occupation of Gaza continued, including Israeli control of land and sea access, water, and airspace, and the Israeli hold on the West Bank did not change at all. Israel's West Bank settlements continued to grow in terms of population. In short, the Palestinian use of force (suicide bombings) led to more Israeli force and coercion, not an end to the occupation.

Moreover, in the years after the second intifada, the Palestinian national movement fragmented, growing politically and geographically weaker. With the Hamas victory in the 2006 Palestinian parliamentary elections and the Egyptian, Israeli, and US reaction, Gaza, where Hamas dominated, and the West Bank, where Fatah dominated, came to look like two different entities that to some extent were moving in different directions. Neither moved closer to independence.

By about 2005, the second intifada petered out, in part through Israeli military counter-measures. But one could also say it morphed into other combat, as Hamas launched rockets at Israel and Israel launched raids into Gaza, culminating in the 2008–2009, 2012, and 2014 Israeli–Hamas battles. Like the earlier cases in this section, the second intifada demonstrates the potential of the use of force to spark forceful reactions and moves *away from* the achievement of core national aims.

Interestingly, when the second intifada was occurring, Palestinians thought it was working. Had the second intifada achieved its goals? From 2001 to 2005, in the midst of it, polling showed an average of 66 per cent of Palestinians thought it had achieved its goals. By the end of 2006, however, the proportion had dropped under 50 per cent. On the question of who had 'won' the intifada, 49 per cent of Palestinians thought the Palestinians had won, with the rest divided between Israel, both, and neither. By the end of 2006, Palestinians were far more divided as to who had won: Palestinians, 24 per cent; Israel, 27 per cent; both, 18 per cent; neither, 29 per cent.[87]

In sum, for Palestinians, what resulted from the second intifada? From 2000 to 2008 – a period a little longer time than the intifada itself – Israeli security forces killed about 4,800 Palestinians; fellow Palestinians killed another 600 Palestinians.[88] Israel built a wall in the West Bank that enclosed some cities and villages and cut off many Palestinians from their land. To some observers, the route of the wall looked like an Israeli land grab of 8–10 per cent of the West Bank.[89] The wall and several major Israeli military operations negatively affected Palestinian property and livelihood. It was devastating for farmers separated from their lands. For example, agricultural output sank significantly in the village of Jayus as a result of the building of the wall between the village and the village's farmlands.[90] The wall cut off the village of Al Walaja on many sides.[91] The Israeli left collapsed, leaving far fewer voices in the Israeli body politic pushing for some kind of compromise solution and accepting of the idea of Palestinian self-determination. If the first intifada shifted the median Israeli voter slightly left, the second intifada moved that median voter dramatically to the right.[92] More Israelis said they had no partner for peace. The uprising, which ended in 2005, produced neither a Palestinian state nor any hint that the Palestinian people were any closer to achieving one. In the years just after the intifada, the Hamas–Fatah split became the dominant story, leaving the Palestinian national movement in a weak and fragmented position from which to push back against mighty Israel. 'Our worst mistake was the use of firearms and the violent attacks in the second intifada. This caused us tremendous damage', concluded Jibril Rajoub, a former Palestinian security chief.[93]

Another way to think about the results of the second intifada is in terms of Palestinian security. Occupied Palestinians live uncertain lives, often at the mercy of Israeli military personnel. They lack control of many physical, economic, and social aspects of their lives and, at best, have highly constrained political manoeuvrability.[94] Palestinians post-second intifada are not secure and, as I have emphasized, the second intifada did little to bring Palestinians closer to a day when they will be secure in their person, their livelihood, and their political future.

What if the Palestinian national movement had launched a protest movement not built on suicide bombings and the use of force? The first intifada was less violent than the second, and it did more to advance the Palestinian national cause. In 2000, what if instead of bombs and weaponry, as well as instead of stones, the intifada had solely consisted of protest marches, tax strikes, banging pots and pans, guerilla theatre, and the kind of actions that have brought attention to specific Palestinian locales in more recent times, such as Nabi Saleh, Budrus, or Sheikh Jarrah, a Jerusalem neighbourhood? These few protest movements have made only limited progress, but a stronger test of the tactics' success would be a national Palestinian movement simultaneously using many of those tactics but no violence, including stone throwing. Chenoweth and Stephan's work suggests such a movement would be consistent with the types of movement that have had greater success than violent ones.[95] The Israeli political spectrum would likely have looked very different, with greater support for non-military pathways, making the level of internal (Israeli) support for significant compromises higher.

The nature of the demand

One last point: when considering the success or failure of using military force, one needs to consider how much room the target state or non-state actor has to back down. The key point is whether, if a state backs down, it will still have anything left to lose. Forceful policies are probably going to be less effective when the potential losing side has nothing to begin with or will have nothing left if it capitulates. If the leaders will still be in charge and retain most or all of their sovereign territory, they may bend in the face of superior force, whether in the form of threats or actual military use. But if an actor has nothing, why back down? There is nothing to protect or preserve. For example, this may help explain limits on what Israeli force could do against Hamas in 2008–2009, 2012, and 2014. Hamas had nowhere to go; it was hunkered down in Gaza and its nationalist ethos dictated that Gaza was part of its homeland. There was no other place to go that would signal capitulation but that would still leave Gaza's Palestinians with something (with the obvious point that going to Israel or to the West Bank was not an option). Jibril Rajoub, a Palestinian politician not affiliated with Hamas, made the point: 'You can deport me. But you cannot deport Palestine from my heart.'[96] In 2014, Mohammed Deif, commander of the Izzedine al-Qassam Brigades, Hamas's military wing, said, 'The Zionist entity will not know security unless the Palestinian people live in peace'.[97] An Israeli analyst, commenting on the population in Gaza during the 2014 war, noted that 'nations fighting for their freedom will endure the worst sacrifices'.[98]

Ariel Ilan Roth, a scholar, took the opposite position about Hamas during the 2014 Israel–Hamas war. Since Hamas ultimately wants to destroy Israel, Roth wrote, battles between Israel and Hamas could not follow the pattern of the Egypt–Israel confrontations in the 1970s:

> Sadat had concrete objectives, namely the re-opening of the Suez Canal and the return of the Sinai Peninsula to Egypt – objectives that were reconcilable with Israel's own needs. Hamas, on the other hand, calls for Israel's elimination, an objective that leaves scant room for negotiation.[99]

Military force in such circumstances cannot set the stage for diplomacy because there is nothing to negotiate. Roth's view of Hamas is not universal. If one sees room for concessions, then the nature of the demand looks different, and force and diplomacy could be productively inter-related.

Contrast the example of Hamas in Gaza with Arab states like Egypt and Syria that lost territory in conventional wars with Israel in 1956, 1967, and 1973. The result of those conventional wars was negative and humiliating, but they still held the majority of their sovereign territory, including their capital cities. All was not lost when Israel captured the Sinai Peninsula and the Golan Heights. So, depending on the nature and needs of the target of a threat or use of military force, observers should expect different results. A non-state actor with unrealized nationalist aspirations makes different calculations in the face of force than a sovereign state does.

A similar example is when Israel unilaterally withdrew from southern Lebanon in 2000. Israel never had a sovereign claim on Lebanon. It could withdraw without compromising either its original (1948) territory or the expanded (1967) version, which included the Golan Heights, West Bank, Gaza Strip, and Sinai Peninsula. Even given all the ambiguity over Israel's borders, southern Lebanon fell outside those borders. Thus, military pressure, largely from Hezbollah, against Israel's presence in Lebanon worked. Israel could leave *and* still retain many assets.

These historical examples are consistent with work by scholars who have argued that the nature of the demand or concession matters. Using and threatening force does not guarantee the achievement of preferred outcomes. One can see this, for example, in an earlier debate about the effectiveness of coercive air power. Can a state achieve its objectives by bombing another state into submission?[100] This focus on aerial bombardment is a subset of a larger question: when does military coercion work? In Karl Mueller's extended critique of the seminal work that sparked much of the debate, Robert Pape's *Bombing to Win* (1996), Mueller noted that Pape assumed that if the dispute involves vital stakes for the target, coercive bombing for the sake of punishing the target – inflicting pain on the civilian population – will fail.[101] Yet, if vital stakes are not in play, Mueller noted, coercion can be a success or a failure.

In other words, one of Mueller's central critiques of Pape was about how Pape treated the level of interests in the target state. For Mueller, how vital the stakes are and whether the issue involves territory determine, in part, the success or failure of coercion: 'States and leaders are not inclined to concede important interests easily…'.[102] In a similar vein, one quantitative study found that the coercive use of air power is less likely to work when the attacker demands a change in leadership.[103] I take that as another example of how the nature of the demand matters, because demanding a change in leadership is big demand. Willem Dekker, also responding to Pape, explicitly built demands into a revised model of coercion.[104] Dekker's inclusion created space for varied levels of demands by the coercer and how they interact with the target's (vital) interests.

This brief foray into a debate on air power reinforces a broader notion highly relevant to this book: in conflict, the nature of the demand matters. What force can and cannot achieve in the Arab–Israeli arena is partly dependent on the objective. If the state or organization being pressured by the threat or use of military force believes a vital interest is at stake, it will be less likely to submit.[105] Even though force may be a useful tool in certain situations, it is not a panacea.

Conclusion

In studying the use of force in the Arab–Israeli conflict, history is not uni-directional. Those participants and observers who believe that force is always the answer, that force increases security, weakens the adversary, and leads to the advancement of national security interests are neither wholly correct nor incorrect. There are episodes that can be read to reinforce such beliefs. But events like the 1967 war or the 1982 Israeli invasion of Lebanon also demonstrate that the same event may have multiple implications, with conflicting lessons for policymakers. Sometimes, force leads to escalation and greater insecurity. At the start of this chapter, I listed a number of possible effects that hinder rather than help a state's national security.

States are not unaware of the possibilities outlined in this chapter. In 1973, Israel feared a mirror image of what happened in 1967, when Egyptian military moves, arguably intended to deter an Israeli attack on Syria, led to an Israeli pre-emptive attack. Israeli leaders feared that a military move to deter Egypt would be seen by Egypt as an offensive build-up, so Egypt would feel the need to launch a pre-emptive attack, just as Israel had done in 1967. Israel was hesitant to take steps toward full mobilization or other provocative steps, and under US pressure refrained from doing so.[106]

One detail from Israel–Hamas battles brought home for me the counter-productive possibilities that emanate from military force. When Israel bombs homes and other buildings in Gaza, the concrete is eventually recycled.[107] Given the limited quantity of concrete that is available in Gaza due to Israeli and Egyptian restrictions on importing building materials, it is very possible that recycled concrete from bombed-out structures was then used by Hamas to build underground tunnels for command and control, storing arms, surviving Israeli attacks, and attacking inside Israel.

Chapter 5
MISSED DIPLOMATIC OPPORTUNITIES

In the Arab–Israeli conflict, all the countries and organizations have proclaimed their desire for peace and simultaneously blamed the other side for lack of interest in peaceful relations. During the course of the conflict, multiple parties have called for more conciliatory relations. In addition to general calls for some version of peace, at times countries or organizations have pushed hard for concessions or even specific, concrete proposals. Yet such diplomatic or rhetorical overtures are often ignored, treated with suspicion, or actively undermined, seemingly at odds with the professed commitment to peace. These missed diplomatic opportunities are the third shortcoming or cost of the idea of relying on military force.

What is the connection between the dominant idea that military force is preferable and the outcome of missed diplomatic opportunities? I suggest two elements. The flip side of thinking that military force is the best policy tool available to achieve national aims has often been that negotiations and concessions are seen as an inferior means, one that signals weakness and that leads to one being taken advantage of by one's rival. The idea is that negotiations and concessions are a risky combination best avoided. In addition, structures of violence and coercion exert themselves, thereby undermining or leading to the premature closure of negotiating opportunities.

The institutions and mechanisms that embody the commitment to force do not simply stop working or go into hiatus because a negotiating opportunity might materialize. In short, ideas and institutions combine to undermine diplomatic pathways.[1]

I reject two alternative explanations for cases where talk of negotiations or concessions do not lead to structured diplomatic processes or to diplomatic breakthroughs. The first alternative to my argument is that these so-called opportunities are illusory rather than missed. The claim is that there are few if any genuine opportunities for de-escalation, conciliation, or resolution. One or both parties do not actually want a negotiated settlement. To put it another way, the initial question of this chapter is wrong. However, the history of the Arab–Israeli conflict *does not* support this objection. While there may be some illusory ones, there are also opportunities that could have changed the direction of relations and undermined the emphasis on force and war.[2]

The second alternative is that actors fail to pursue opportunities due to bureaucratic and domestic political constraints. A leader who wants to test the possibilities of a particular diplomatic opening may not be able to overcome public or elite opposition. Interest groups may fight the leadership. In some cases, civil and military leaders may have different perspectives. Rather than rejecting this argument, I sidestep it. These constraints do exist, but in choosing to pursue a diplomatic opportunity, a leader is choosing to push back against such constraints and to try to contain or redefine them.

This last point is connected to the underlying assumption of this chapter: if a government or organization had really wanted to try to change the direction of Arab–Israeli or Israeli–Palestinian relations by de-emphasizing the reliance on military force, violence, and coercion, there were numerous moments that could have been creatively built upon to effect change. Some have been concrete proposals inviting a different relationship, while others have been unilateral policy shifts or merely ideas floated in the public sphere. But what all of them have in common is that they could *potentially* have served as an opportunity to test an alternative to force and war, and to confront entrenched pro-force bureaucrats, politicians, and publics.[3] Yes, Anwar Sadat's visit to Israel in 1977 was a slap-you-in-the-face moment that was hard to ignore (though even there, some Israeli leaders started out sceptical when Sadat first proposed the idea). Dramatic changes are likely to have a greater effect on people's beliefs.[4]

But there have been moments when, had leaders been interested, they could have tried to find the 'properly executed concessions' that Robert Jervis, a leading scholar of international relations, wrote about as relevant even in a world dominated by deterrence thinking and the idea that shows of force are the key to survival and getting one's way.[5] The notion of properly executed concessions cuts directly against the notion that *any* concession is too risky to attempt because it will be taken for weakness and that states cannot afford to leave themselves vulnerable, even in the most minute way.

The next section illustrates the idea that negotiations are a poor instrument for advancing state objectives. This is followed by three cases that illustrate how reliance on force and security demands have undermined or muddied possible diplomatic opportunities, in 1974, 2002, and 2005. I then address two objections: that these alleged diplomatic openings are not genuine openings but are illusory; and that other domestic actors, not a commitment to military force as the best policy, may serve as the key obstacles to negotiations.

Beliefs about the inherent flaws of negotiating and conceding

Why do two countries that both profess to want peaceful relations miss opportunities to negotiate and resolve the conflict?

After all, opportunities to negotiate, whether as informal proposals or concrete plans, are not infrequent. Conflicting parties, as well as external patrons and mediators, offer up many ideas that could serve as a starting point for negotiations. Building upon Jeffrey Legro's emphasis on highlighting ideas about means or policy options, I argue that the deeply embedded idea of relying on military force obscures these opportunities for talks. Diplomatic overtures are considered an indication of weakness. The belief is that while force causes the other side to back down, attempts at conciliation are seen as appeasement and invite further depredations.

I define a diplomatic opportunity narrowly here, to mean concrete proposals and plans. I am interested in situations where an actual text, approved by a government, describes a process or desired outcomes in order to move away from war and conflict. One could argue that informal ideas floated by leaders or organizations are also diplomatic opportunities, but in this chapter I do not generally address those types of opportunities. A formal proposal is harder to ignore, whereas a sceptical government might more easily dismiss off-the-cuff or informal suggestions.

By *missed* opportunity, I am looking at moments when one side did not engage or did not try to use a text or event as a springboard for talks or to create other diplomatic interactions. I am not including failed negotiations where the two sides did engage, often at great length, but were unable to reach an agreement. With a missed opportunity, the talks never got started.

By using the word 'opportunity', I am not suggesting that the potential for opening diplomatic pathways is always obvious. Take the Oscar-winning short film *West Bank Story* (2005), in which an Israeli Jewish restaurant and a Palestinian restaurant compete for customers and national vindication. The confrontational approach of most of the Israeli and Palestinian characters leads to a sad outcome: both restaurants burn to the ground.

But the story does not end there. In the midst of the rubble, two oblivious customers ask for food from Ahmed (of the Palestinian Hummus Hut) and Ariel (of the Israeli Kosher King), respectively. Ahmed and Ariel each rebuff the requests but David and Fatima, an Israeli Romeo and Palestinian Juliet, say, yes, we can help you. Even as they pull together bits and pieces of both facilities that survived the fire and start to serve people food, Ahmed and Ariel begin to argue and shout about who owns the table from which David and Fatima are serving. Meanwhile, a line of customers forms, David and Fatima successfully appeal to Ariel and Ahmed, and soon more workers from both restaurants join together in order to feed the customers. Food trumps fighting.

In an environment in which conflict has burned the restaurants to the ground and most workers outwardly are unsympathetic to the other side, David and Fatima change the culinary trajectory. They see an opening, they exploit it to cooperate, and they draw others in. Before they start, one could have said that such a breakthrough was impossible because of the entrenched opposition. But they see an opportunity for change and pursue it, changing others as well along the way.

This short, simple, silly movie – a winner of the 2006 Academy Award for best live action short film – nicely illustrates my key underlying assumption. In an environment saturated with ideas preferring military force, diplomatic openings require creativity and leadership. A particular plan may have serious shortcomings, but it can be used as a springboard for talks and conflict resolution. Instead of categorical rejection, a proposal may spur a counter-proposal, back-channel talks, or renewed engagement. I assume a certain diplomatic malleability here. If leaders want to reduce the dominance of force, conflict, security rhetoric, violence, and the like, there are moments that lend themselves to such a turn. Success is not guaranteed, but it is plausible even in many hard situations because leaders can amend, reframe, and mould ideas.

What does it mean to say that the reliance on force obscures and undermines opportunities to pursue negotiations and concessions? A common belief associated with the reliance on force, nicely captured by the political scientist Robert Jervis in one of his two models of international affairs, the deterrence model, is that negotiations and concessions signal weakness and invite further attack. They undermine a country's drive to achieve its basic objectives.

The idea behind the preference for force actually has two elements. First, the threat and use of force prevails. Force is thought to be the best instrument with which to achieve one's objectives, including the most fundamental one, state survival. Second, conciliatory policies are a sign of weakness and invite further attacks. This very idea undermines potential diplomatic openings and the possibility of negotiations.

Negotiations require concessions, and they require countries to take risks. That is hard enough. But for some, the expectation is that not only will such moves not be reciprocated but that they will be interpreted as weakness and an invitation to demand more concessions. They fear looking weak to their immediate adversary and to other countries.[6] They may also fear the *domestic* political implications of being called weak in relation to foreign policy. Concession 'may be too costly in terms of the internal opposition it would arouse'.[7] That is not a recipe for enticing states to explore the possibility of negotiations or to pursue concrete talks about hard issues related to security, identity, and survival.

Until his death in 1994, Yehoshafat Harkabi was a prominent Israeli strategic thinker who served as a chief of Israeli military intelligence in the late 1950s and was later a professor at Hebrew University. Harkabi was not a policymaker, but he was a part of the mainstream Israeli national security establishment and, as such, his views are likely to reflect wider views within that establishment. Although Harkabi eventually became open to the positive aspects of compromise, his 1977 book, *Arab Strategies and Israel's Response*, predicted little in the way of genuine Arab compromise.[8] In the book, Harkabi asserted that post-1967 changes in the Arab world were merely tactical shifts to adopt incremental approaches toward achieving absolutist objectives. He concluded that 'Arab moderation is still very relative and remains within the framework of extremism'.[9] The Arabs had learned they could not achieve Israel's destruction through direct conventional attack, but they had not abandoned the core objective. They had simply shifted tactics to ones more palatable to the international community. It was a 'process of nibbling'.[10] They would destroy Israel slowly rather than all at once.

The logical conclusion was that any Israeli concessions simply played into an Arab trap. Concessions did not help end the conflict but rather confirmed for the Arab side that a gradualist strategy could work to end Israel as the Jewish state. If there were Israeli territorial withdrawals, for example, 'Egypt [would] then exploit the new situation to transform its open-ended position into binding national objectives.... The conciliatory stance is only a means of pursuing the struggle.'[11] More generally, Zeev Maoz later noted, many Israelis suspected that any Arab political settlement would be 'actually a ploy designed to deprive Israel of important strategic assets and to renew the military pressure on it when Israel became weaker'.[12]

Harkabi's thinking in 1977 is a particularly powerful argument because it is not falsifiable. No matter what Arab policy was pursued, it seemingly proved he was correct. If the Arab side expressed a desire to defeat and destroy Israel, then Harkabi's wariness about the possibility of compromise was justified. But even if the Arab side stated more conciliatory or moderate positions, such as accepting a Palestinian state in part of Palestine, Harkabi would still have described that as evidence for the deeper desire to defeat and destroy Israel. The Arabs were simply cloaking that deeper desire in a mantle of respectability because direct confrontation had not worked (1967) and seemingly nice or compromising words led to greater international support. Moreover, Harkabi could always point to previous statements, even if dated, as proof of the Arab side's real intentions. Again, the framing of the argument could explain why Arab officials switched from honest (run the Jews into the sea) to misleading (pseudo-compromising) statements without admitting a true shift in Arab goals.

Harkabi's 1977 argument is not an isolated one. Begin, at the time a member of the opposition in the Israeli parliament, decried the Sinai II agreement (1975) with Egypt, saying Israeli territorial withdrawal 'is not a step towards peace, it is a step towards additional pressure and concessions'. That perfectly embodies the concerns about diplomacy opening the door to further pressure and demands, not peace and cooperation. Harkabi-style claims that diplomacy and concessions only encourage Arab pressure on Israel continue to resonate, as Efraim Karsh demonstrated: 'For Arafat and the PLO leadership, the Oslo process has always been a strategic means not to a two-state solution ... but to the substitution of a Palestinian state for that of Israel'.[13] During the second intifada, the Israeli military chief of staff, Moshe Ya'alon, offered a tactical example: any unilateral withdrawal 'would give a push to the struggle against us.... That was my argument when the question arose of withdrawing from Joseph's Tomb [in Nablus in the West Bank]. It was clear to me that leaving the tomb would be an incentive for the Palestinians.'[14]

In opposing Israel's disengagement from Gaza in 2005, Benjamin Netanyahu, then a minister in Ariel Sharon's cabinet, highlighted his fear that this concession, Israeli withdrawal from its Gaza settlements, would worsen Israeli security: 'But I am convinced today that the disengagement will eventually aggravate terrorism instead of reducing it'. He situated his concerns in the larger context: 'Like in Oslo, the warning signs are being ignored. I understand the intentions here – who doesn't want peace? But here in the Middle East this is not the way to attain peace – it has failed before and it will fail again.'[15] Netanyahu, as he has done frequently, suggested that the rules 'here in the Middle East' are different from those that apply elsewhere.

On 1 April 2009, Avigdor Lieberman articulated similar sentiments at his inauguration as Israel's foreign minister. Most attention to the speech focused on his questioning of the two-state solution. But what was equally striking about Lieberman's talk was his succinct description of decades of the sceptical perspective within Israeli security policy:

> Does anyone think that concessions and constantly saying 'I am prepared to concede,' and using the word 'peace' will lead to anything? No, that will just invite pressure, and more and more wars. 'Si vis pacem, para bellum' – if you want peace, prepare for war; be strong.[16]

Again, the wording is clear: concessions invite further pressure.

Even Moshe Sharett, the exemplar in the 1950s of the position that concessions could be productive and retaliation could lead to spirals of violence, was wary of Israeli concessions that ran too deep. The one-time Israeli prime minister preferred '[m]utual advantages' to concessions. He used the term 'concession' to mean Israel forsaking its core aims, such as agreeing to curtail Jewish immigration to Israel. Concessions understood in Sharett's way would lead, he feared, the Arabs to the following conclusion: 'We were stubborn for 10 years – now they [the Israelis] are beginning to falter; let's be stubborn just a little longer and they will give away more and more'.[17]

Among Palestinians, displeasure with the Oslo framework often suggested Palestinian concessions had led only to further Israeli expansion or aggression. Israel took advantage of the Palestinians after the Palestinians had made significant concessions. Haidar Abdel Shafi, a Palestinian negotiator at the 1991 Madrid conference and talks, later expressed concern that the Oslo process had hidden an ever-deepening Israeli occupation:

> The negotiations for implementing the Oslo accords provided a good cover for Israeli violations on the ground in the shape of its notorious strategy of settlement and creation of facts, which is the basic strategy of the Zionist movement. Our remaining at the negotiating table gave the international community an excuse for ignoring its responsibility to confront Israel's blatant aggression against the Palestinian people and violations of international conventions.[18]

The general view is that 'negotiations have afforded Israel cover to consolidate its control over the West Bank and, until recently, Gaza. From average Palestinian to political cadre, the verdict is striking in its similarity: the U.S. process of bilateral negotiations at best has been a charade.'[19] One American analyst echoed these concerns:

> Israel's interest in a peace process – other than for the purpose of obtaining Palestinian and international acceptance of the status quo – has been a fiction that has served primarily to provide cover for its systematic confiscation of Palestinian land and an occupation whose goal, according to the former IDF chief of staff Moshe Ya'alon, is 'to sear deep into the consciousness of Palestinians that they are a defeated people'.[20]

In late October 2013, Israel announced plans to build more settlements in the midst of Israeli–Palestinian talks that had been facilitated by the United States. In reaction, Nabil Abu Rudeina, a spokesman for the Palestinian president, Mahmoud Abbas, said the move 'destroys the peace process'. Sami Abu

Zuhri, a Hamas spokesman, was more blunt: 'It is ... the PA's [Palestinian Authority's] negotiations with the occupation that are now providing (Israel) with a *cover* for these crimes'.[21]

What all these examples share is the idea that a concession does not help a state or organization achieve its goals of security and survival. Rather, concessions signal weakness and invite the other side to take advantage through pressure, expansion, coercion, and war. Concessions jeopardize survival and undermine security. That view leaves little if any room for a positive reception of plans, talks, or proposed accommodations.

One corollary is also noteworthy: since negotiating efforts also have a mixed historical record – some successes and some failures – the fear of diplomacy inviting further attack might not even need to be present to spur a lack of interest in political opportunities. Even if this book demonstrates flaws with an (over)reliance on military force, critics of diplomacy may point to diplomatic failings as evidence for questioning whether there is a genuine alternative pathway to relying upon force. In short, we would love to negotiate but (1) it signals weakness, (2) it may very well fail, and (3) its failure could make the confrontation even worse. Options 2 and 3 could be persuasive even without option 1.

Historical cases

The following three cases illustrate the difficulties of capitalizing on possible opportunities. In 1974, the PLO adopted the ten-point programme that officially introduced the idea of the partial rather than total liberation of Palestinian territory. Most Israelis saw it as just a more gradual approach to the destruction of Israel, a change in tactics, not ends. In 2002, the League of Arab States passed a resolution calling for a two-state solution, but most Israeli leaders were lukewarm to dismissive. In 2005, Israel unilaterally disengaged from Gaza. While in later years Israeli officials framed it as an olive branch, at the time Israel declined to negotiate its exit with the Palestinian Authority. Hamas – and most Palestinians – interpreted the move as a victory for military force, not diplomacy. Israeli withdrawal of its civilian settlers was a big deal, even if it included a lot of baggage. In each case, my aim is to show how commitments to force and security prevented an initiative from spurring further positive developments.[22]

I selected these three cases to illustrate the claim that real opportunities for talks that could have led to breakthroughs have existed. They are not cases of failed negotiations but rather moments prior to negotiations, when the *possibility* of negotiations or concessions became apparent but were not pursued. These are not the only cases that could be studied in this light, but each illustrates the scepticism about negotiations, the perception that talk and proposed concessions signal weakness, and/or the ability of policymakers to undermine the extension of olive branches when they are committed to the idea that military force is the best means to achieve their objectives.

What characteristics should we expect these and other cases to share? First, the reaction of the other side to such initiatives will be underwhelming or dismissive. Moreover, the proposal, whether concrete or amorphous, may be characterized as a trick or ruse: that is, the alleged concessions are really mechanisms designed to achieve the same ends as force. The fear is that the alleged concession or discussion that could lead to concessions will still help impose one's will on the enemy.[23] For example, Moshe Ya'alon, when Israeli military chief of staff, said that PLO leader Yasser Arafat 'saw Oslo as a Trojan horse that would enable the Palestinians to enter Israel'.[24]

Second, diplomatic creativity or a stated commitment highlighting the possibilities of a proposal, even if also noting its initial flaws, will be absent. The parties will not take the approach of 'let's sit down and figure out how to make this work'. The interaction will look more like rejection or standoffish-ness than mutual problem-solving. The same old security-based and forceful approaches will predominate. Caution will dominate creativity and courage.

The PLO's ten-point programme, 1974

Conflicting understandings of Palestinian territorial ambitions are clearly illustrated by starting with interpretations of a 1974 PLO policy statement and the impact those interpretations have had to this day on Israeli wariness of Palestinian compromise. Any time the Palestinian national movement, whether as the PLO or the Palestinian Authority (PA), has said it would accept some of the disputed land and thus a two-state solution, some on the Israeli side have seen that not as a genuine concession but as a tactical trick designed to facilitate Israel's elimination. This debate was prominent during the Oslo process in the 1990s. As charges of PLO 'salami' tactics have evolved, it becomes clear that *any* Palestinian policy may be interpreted as a means for destroying Israel whether that is the Palestinian intent or not: a call for all the land, a call for part of the land, acceptance of continued occupation, and a push for implementing the Palestinian right of return.

On 8 June 1974, at the twelfth session of the Palestine National Council in Cairo, the PLO adopted a ten-point programme framing Palestinian aims, the precise meaning of which continues to be in dispute. In the second point of the programme, the Council stated it 'will employ all means, and first and foremost armed struggle, to liberate Palestinian territory and to establish the independent combatant national authority for the people over every part of Palestinian territory that is liberated'. Over the years, policymakers and pundits debated how to interpret the meaning of this phrasing. If the PLO was willing to start by establishing the Palestinian homeland – with 'the independent combatant national authority' – on any 'liberated' territory, would the PLO be satisfied with only *some* of the land between the Jordan River and the Mediterranean Sea? Some people came to argue that this language hinted at a strategic shift within the Palestinian national movement toward territorial compromise. If they were right, a US-led peace process would have room for manoeuvre. Others saw it only as a tactical change meant to better achieve the same goal, Israel's total destruction. If they were right, a peace process would never lead to peace.

In his comprehensive history of the Palestinian national movement, Yezid Sayigh argued that the ten-point political programme was the result of a 'pragmatic trend' among Palestinian leaders, and he noted that the tone of the final statement was designed to 'placate rejectionist sentiment and prevent an open split' among the PLO factions. When, a few months later, on 21 September, Arafat signed a statement with Egypt and Syria that seemed to focus on territories occupied in 1967 only, the Palestinian 'rejectionists' opposing the programme were further concerned. But for Sayigh, the PLO's direction was ambiguous: 'What, precisely, the mainstream leadership really sought in the long term remains open to contention'. Most Palestinian leaders probably still dreamed of the total liberation of Palestine and the establishment of a secular, democratic state, he argued, 'but whether or not the mainstream leadership believed this to be a likely eventuality, it was perceptive enough to realize that attaining its statist ambitions could only come about through major compromises in historic claims and opportunistic enough to make that choice'.[25] If Sayigh's last assessment was correct, it would make the Palestinian move a concession – an unhappy concession that cut against Palestinian hopes and dreams – but a concession nonetheless.

Inside the PLO, those who came to be known as the rejectionists believed that the establishment of a national authority on any liberated land, notably the West Bank and Gaza, was a betrayal of the original PLO goals. So even though, as we will see, many Israelis saw no distinction between the PLO moderates and extremists, the rejectionist front withdrew from the PLO executive committee in September 1974 over this very issue.[26] They saw the ten-point programme from June as too accommodating.

Writing in the *Journal of Palestine Studies* in 1976, Hussein Agha exhaustively catalogued the Palestinian arguments for and against a 'WBS', a West Bank State, which might or might not include Gaza.[27] He looked at it in terms of a final resolution of the conflict and as merely a stage toward the establishment of a secular, democratic state in the West Bank, Gaza, and pre-1967 Israel. His careful examination of the many advantages and shortcomings from a variety of perspectives nicely reflected the lack of certainty within the Palestinian national movement about the role a WBS could or should play in Palestinian self-determination. Was it a prudent move, a betrayal of principles, or something else altogether? Looking back, his writing suggests that acceptance of a WBS, and thus the Palestinian move toward a two-state solution, did not happen overnight in 1974. At most, the ten-point programme was a step in that direction. That in 1977 the PLO reaffirmed the 1974 programme and, in 1988, both issued its declaration of statehood and met US conditions for the inauguration of a direct PLO–US dialogue is all evidence that the 1974 plan was an elevation of compromise politics over militant absolutism.

At the time, though, some opinion writers were uncertain as to whether the PLO was moving toward a two-state solution.[28] Initially, the *New York Times* interpreted the decision as a victory for Palestinian moderates.[29] But the same paper later described the Palestinian position as follows: the West Bank 'should revert to the Palestinians so they can establish an independent state there'.[30] That phrasing left unstated whether the establishment of a state in the West Bank was seen as an endpoint or a step toward total control of Mandatory Palestine. Another reporter defined Palestinian national rights in the Palestinian National Council's text as 'meaning minimally the right to establish a Palestinian state on the West Bank and in Gaza'. Note the use of the word 'minimally' so as to leave the door open to multiple interpretations of Palestinian intent.[31] 'Minimally' meant it might or might not be a final resolution.

Israel's defenders referred to this PLO policy as the plan of stages and tended to see it as a tactical shift only. The PLO, they argued, was open to the step-by-step dismantlement of Israel, akin to slicing a salami where the salami is Israeli territory and the occupied territories, including the West Bank and the Gaza Strip. In 1975, Shlomo Avineri, an Israeli political scientist, offered a textbook characterization of what Israelis saw as PLO salami tactics:

> The only difference between the 'extremists' and the 'moderates' within the PLO is that while the 'extremists' believe that Israel should be eliminated in one stroke, the 'moderates' believe in salami tactics – getting power in the West Bank first, and from there continuing to fight against what remains of Israel.[32]

The difference between hardliners and moderates was, according to Richard Cohen, an official with the American Jewish Congress, only whether they sought to destroy Israel 'all at once' or 'gradually'.[33] In short, all members of the PLO were deemed to have the same aim, the end of Israel, and to differ only over tactics. Thus, Israeli withdrawal from the West Bank would not be a final resolution but rather a Palestinian stepping stone toward Israel's destruction.

In a related light, Yehoshafat Harkabi, the prominent Israeli strategic analyst mentioned earlier, contended that a 'strategic school' in the Arab world saw United Nations Security Council Resolution 242, passed just after the June 1967 war, as an opportunity. Actors 'must sometimes acquiesce temporarily to undesired courses of action'.[34] Accepting 242 would force Israeli withdrawal to the 4 June 1967 lines, the pre-war lines, something the Arabs could not hope to achieve on their own, given Israel's military advantage. It would not mean an end to the larger conflict because true Arab–Israeli reconciliation was impossible; rather, it was a phase where a distasteful move (Arab acceptance of 242) could nonetheless bring great Arab gains (Israeli withdrawal from the territories occupied in 1967). The PLO could then continue to press Israel for further concessions.

Harkabi also argued that other Palestinians, within a school of thought that rejected any settlement with Israel, feared a phased approach precisely because they thought it might become the new status quo as temporary measures meant to serve as a springboard for total Palestinian victory actually turned into a permanent compromise. In short, an interim solution to the problem would become lasting and final.[35] So, even as some Israelis decried the phased approach as a trick, some Palestinians opposed it because they thought it was a genuine compromise or would slide into one over time. One heard echoes of this same Palestinian concern in the 1990s, when Palestinians worried the 'Gaza first' element of the Oslo Accords – Israeli pullbacks from much of the Gaza Strip but only the small city of Jericho in the West Bank – actually meant Gaza first and last.

The Palestinians' own ambiguity probably fed the sceptical Israeli reaction in the mid-1970s. As is often the case with policies that could be understood as concessions, the alleged concession was not presented as such in clear-cut fashion. Palestinian leaders were deeply divided about the policy, and the armed struggle continued simultaneously. Coming out of the meeting of the Palestinian National Council in June 1974, Nayef Hawatmeh, secretary general of the Popular Democratic Front for the Liberation of Palestine (later the organization dropped the word 'popular' from its title), presented a clear example of this tactical duality: 'The council has given a mandate to the leadership to use all military and political means available to obtain for the Palestinian people the right of self-determination within its territory'.[36] So it was easy for Israel to assume that the concession was anything but a true conciliatory move, given the context. It was a muddy message. The elements pushing the idea of the greater effectiveness of military force continued to exert influence.

The way in which Fatah shifted from liberation of all to some of historic Palestine and from armed struggle alone to accepting political action also undermined the impact of the shift itself. As Helga Baumgarten of Birzeit University succinctly explained, Fatah changed its 'actual strategy' but did not adjust its rhetoric accordingly. Because diplomacy often took place in secret, the armed struggle retained its 'sacred nature' in public. In part because of Arafat's style of leadership of both Fatah and the PLO, the Palestinian public was never educated and conditioned to accept these major policy modifications. Only the 'unarmed struggle of the [first] intifada' brought the Palestinian public into the equation, setting the stage for the ascent in 1988 and 1993 of a political compromise with Israel.[37]

In addition, the PLO and other Palestinian organizations remained involved in the armed struggle. Palestinian militants continued terrorist attacks on Israelis. Around the time of the PLO's 1974 programmatic changes, prominent Palestinian attacks included the killings at Ma'alot (May 1974), the Nahariya attack by sea (late June 1974), and the attack at the Savoy Hotel in Tel Aviv (March 1975). Furthermore, with the important exception of Egypt, the relationship between Israel and most Arab states remained hostile throughout the 1970s.

The combination of continued violence and rhetorical ambiguity fed Israeli suspicion. Palestinian leaders disagreed about both the goal (liberate all of Palestine or just the West Bank and Gaza) and the tactics (armed struggle and/or political means).

Arab Peace Initiative, 2002

After first emerging as a Saudi proposal, the League of Arab States endorsed the Arab Peace Initiative (API) on 28 March 2002.[38] In the plan, the Arab countries: mention Israel by name; support a two-state solution through Israeli withdrawal to the 4 June 1967 lines and the establishment of a Palestinian state in the West Bank, Gaza Strip, and East Jerusalem; and call for a 'just solution' to the Palestinian refugee problem. Although the text references UN General Assembly Resolution 194, the resolution Palestinians cite as the basis of the right of return for Palestinian refugees, the API does not use the phrase 'right of return' and the term 'just solution' leaves the door open to the Palestinians to make concessions to Israel on the refugee issue. In exchange for Israeli withdrawal, the Arab countries would 'consider the Arab–Israeli conflict ended, and enter into a peace agreement with Israel, and provide security for all the states of the region'. The Arab states would establish normal relations with Israel.[39] In 2013, they added the idea that Israeli–Palestinian land swaps would be acceptable as part of a two-state solution. A land swap would mean that for any land that Israel annexed in the West Bank, Palestinians would receive compensatory land from inside pre-1967 Israel. For example, Israel might want to annex large Jewish settlements in the West Bank like Modi'in Illit or in the Etzion bloc in exchange for relinquishing equivalent amounts of Israeli land along the West Bank, which would no longer be the West Bank but rather the largest part of the new State of Palestine. The members of the Organisation of Islamic Cooperation also supported the API.

The plan emerged at the height of the second Palestinian intifada. On 27 March 2002, a Palestinian suicide bomber killed thirty Israelis and over 100 were wounded. Israelis refer to the attack as the Passover massacre. Including those killed that day, approximately 200 Israeli civilians had been killed by that stage in the intifada.[40] Within days, Israel launched a large-scale military operation in the West Bank, Operation Defensive Shield. As attention turned to the bombing and Israel's military moves, reporters noted that the 'events on the ground overshadowed' the Arab League's statement.[41]

The initial response of the Israeli foreign minister, Shimon Peres, to the API revealed the challenges of seeing the API as a positive, peace-seeking message. Peres's 105-word statement of 28 March 2002 opened with one line of general praise for the API but then qualified it in two important ways.[42] He twice noted that continued terrorism undermined the possibility of pursuing the peace plan: 'the Saudi step is an important one, but it is liable to founder if terrorism is not stopped'. The Saudi reference was shorthand for the API because Saudi Arabia had first proposed the initiative. Furthermore, Peres criticized the comments of other speakers at the Beirut summit at which the API was approved. So even though he liked the text, he was distracted by the rhetoric of others speaking at the same venue, many of whom still subscribed to the idea that only military force would lead to the achievement of Arab aims. And this reaction is from a politician, Peres, who was regarded as the strongest major proponent of peace in Israeli politics.

Although Peres did not mention any Arab leaders by name, several of those who spoke at the Beirut summit endorsed the

Palestinian use of force during the second intifada. This may have been part of the mixed message that Peres heard. For example, Syria's president, Bashar Assad, said at the summit, 'This intifada has started to make the Israeli people understand. So, the more we want peace, the more we will support the intifada.' An Iraqi official, Izzat Ibrahim, vice chairman of the ruling Revolutionary Command Council, added 'That intifada has given positive results.... That is what is going to produce liberation over the enemy.'[43] Nonetheless, both Iraq and Syria supported the API declaration.

When the Israeli prime minister, Ariel Sharon, reacted to the API, his comments did not suggest he sought to engage with the plan as the foundation of Arab–Israeli peace. In a speech to the Knesset on 8 April 2002 that was largely about the second intifada, terrorism, and the Israeli military operation then underway, Sharon used the word 'positive' to refer to the proposal but, as Netanyahu later did as well, said talks 'cannot be dictated'. He then pushed back against the API's vision of Israeli borders and method for addressing the Palestinian refugees. He nevertheless offered to meet 'immediately' with Arab leaders, 'without any pre-conditions from any party, to discuss peace'.[44] For Sharon, the API fell into the category of pre-conditions and thus was not a legitimate or useful starting point. Israel's cabinet approved fourteen reservations to the Roadmap (2003), a diplomatic proposal issued by the US president, George W. Bush, including one reservation that rejected the API as a possible basis for negotiations.[45] No subsequent Israeli government decision formally changed that official position.[46]

Rather than seeing the word 'East' before Jerusalem instead of only 'Jerusalem' or 'just solution' instead of 'right of return' as linguistic progress or slight changes worth exploring, Israelis expressed concern. The phrase 'just solution' made the plan 'a non-starter in its current form', according to an Israeli

Foreign Ministry spokesperson, Emmanuel Nachshon.[47] Gilad Sharon, Ariel Sharon's son, later wrote that, 'On the surface, the proposal looked appealing.... But the details made the offer unacceptable.'[48]

In the decade or more after the API first appeared, it stayed a part of the discussion but was never embraced by either the Sharon (2001–2006) or Netanyahu (2009–present) governments. The Arab League reaffirmed it in 2007 and 2013. In 2007, Hamas indicated it would neither endorse nor oppose the proposal – a stance worth noting since Hamas is generally seen as hostile to a two-state solution.[49] In June 2013, Israel's minister of defence, Moshe Ya'alon, said Israel would sit with anyone without pre-conditions but that the API did not meet that standard; it was a 'dictation' that did not leave room for negotiations.[50] The plan, Ya'alon said, was 'spin'.[51] The deputy defence minister, Danny Danon, was even more sceptical, saying, 'You have to sacrifice a lot, and on the other hand you're not really going to get peace'. He did not think Israel should even consider the API. And yet another minister, Yuval Steinitz, was also critical: 'We need to worry about genuine peace with genuine security – these items are not included in the Arab Peace Initiative'.[52] The word 'genuine' is quite revealing, highlighting the frequent Israeli claim that alleged Arab peace efforts are not genuine. In sum, 'Ever since the initiative was first presented, most Israeli decision-makers, as well as the public, have regarded it with doubt and suspicion'.[53]

Only occasionally have Israeli officials taken a different stance. In 2007, in the most significant exception, Ehud Olmert, the Israeli prime minister, expressed his support for the API and some meetings took place between the Egyptian, Israeli, and Jordanian foreign ministers. Tzipi Livni, then Israel's foreign minister, endorsed the idea that differences over details should not drive Israelis to dismiss the document: 'I think that it would be a mistake today, at this juncture, for us to start waging some kind of debate about each clause'.⁵⁴ In 2013, forty MKs forced the prime minister, then Benjamin Netanyahu, to speak at a special parliamentary meeting on the API.⁵⁵ Israel's science and technology minister, Yaakov Peri, later called the API a 'good alternative' that needs to be 'examined'. Netanyahu's office denied that Peri's comment reflected the coalition government's policy and stuck to the idea that the API was a diktat, not an offer.⁵⁶ One Israeli reporter asked the core question about Israel's hostile response to the API: if some clauses are not to Israel's liking, 'why doesn't Jerusalem at least try to engage with the Arab world by professing interest in the initiative, if only to demonstrate the will for peace and avoid being labeled as the party that prevents an agreement?'⁵⁷

For Elie Podeh, an Israeli scholar and expert on missed opportunities, 'The story of the Arab Peace Initiative is the story of Israel repeatedly missing an opportunity'.⁵⁸ It first emerged at a time of intense Israeli and Palestinian confrontation, the height of the second intifada. In such an atmosphere, Israeli leaders were less likely to engage with the plan, especially given that, at the time, Hamas, Palestinian Islamic Jihad, and other Palestinian militants continued to confront Israel with force. That continued fighting concretely illustrates the way in which a commitment to the idea of force for achieving national ends undermines the possibility of moving forward with openings for negotiation.

Israeli disengagement from Gaza, 2005

Israel's disengagement could have served as a turning point for Israeli–Palestinian relations but the force- and security-dominated environment in which it emerged greatly undermined that possibility. A year earlier, in May 2004, the

Quartet – the European Union, Russia, United Nations, and United States – called the idea a 'rare opportunity in the search for peace in the Middle East'. It was, as many observers noted at the time, a monumental shift, as Israel, led by one of the foremost proponents of the establishment of Israeli settlements in the occupied territories, Ariel Sharon, closed down all twenty-one settlements in the Gaza Strip as well as another four in the northern part of the West Bank. But Israel did so in unilateral fashion, unconvinced that the Palestinian Authority (PA) was a partner for peace after years of attacks during the second intifada. Disengagement was neither embedded in a negotiated framework nor led to a restarting of Israeli–Palestinian talks after the pull-out. Furthermore, Hamas saw the Israeli withdrawal as vindication of the armed struggle. Perhaps most importantly, nothing changed for the better on the ground, especially in Gaza. Violent Israeli–Palestinian confrontations continued; Israel continued to build settlements in the West Bank; and the Gaza economy went from bad to worse, with the possibility of Israeli–Palestinian economic engagement and growth trumped by force and Israeli security arguments.[59] All of these obstacles were directly or indirectly tied to the emphasis on force and security.

In August–September 2005, Israel removed approximately 8,000 civilian settlers and its military forces from the Gaza Strip. Although there was some limited coordination to discuss future economic matters and between Israeli and Palestinian security services to help the withdrawal run smoothly, disengagement was designed and conducted as a unilateral Israeli move. The most compelling explanation for Sharon's unilateralism was his belief that bilateral diplomacy (e.g. the Camp David summit of 2000) and military options had failed, and he was facing a rising tide of plans and proposals, many of them put forward by Israelis, that involved Israeli concessions not only in Gaza but also in the West Bank. In order to seize the initiative, Sharon proposed a plan of his own that would work despite his opposition to bilateral talks with the PA: unilateral withdrawal from Gaza. By taking back the initiative, he could, as his close adviser Dov Weisglas later suggested, protect what he saw as the real prize, the Israeli occupation of the West Bank. He would buy time but not have to make the kind of concessions Palestinian negotiators would have demanded in a bilateral context.[60] By moving unilaterally, he also would not reward the PA with an achievement – in the absence of a bilateral agreement for Israeli withdrawal, the PA could not claim credit for Israel leaving. The government of Israel did not want to offer the PA such a political reward as the PA had not cracked down on Hamas in Gaza.[61] An alternative explanation is also consistent with Sharon's move: he would reduce Israeli Jewish concerns by removing 1.5 million Gaza Palestinians from the demographic equation.

The international community never pressed Israel to make the Palestinians 'stakeholders in the process'. It chose the certainty of unilateral withdrawal over the possibility of a negotiated agreement.[62]

Despite the unilateralism, the PA recognized the importance of Israel closing settlements and sought to build on disengagement. The president of the PA, Mahmoud Abbas, talked to Sharon, as well as Moshe Katsav, the Israeli president, and called the withdrawal 'a brave and historic decision'. Abbas hoped to work with Sharon to bring about peace.[63] Withdrawal was a step in 'the right direction', Abbas told *Al Quds*, a Palestinian daily.[64] Saeb Erekat, a top Palestinian negotiator, said 'We invite Sharon to resume negotiations'.[65] When Abbas visited the White House in October 2005, the US president, George W. Bush, said Israel's withdrawal was a 'magnificent opportunity'.[66] Silvan Shalom, the Israeli foreign minister, suggested disengagement 'could constitute an encouragement for returning to the peace process'.[67]

Sharon and Abbas did consider meeting but the meeting kept getting delayed and, with it, the chance of seizing the initiative. They had spoken about the idea in a telephone call in August 2005. It was reported that Sharon and Abbas were scheduled to meet in September, at the United Nations.[68] Then the date was changed to 2 October.[69] The next reports said it had been pushed back to late October or early November 2005.[70] In October, the United States sent David Welch of the US Department of State to try to arrange a Sharon–Abbas meeting. Erekat and Weisglas met in preparatory talks on 9 October 2005, but only for half an hour. Weisglas gave Erekat a written proposal on renewing a joint committee to deal with Palestinian prisoners, and on transferring West Bank cities to the PA.[71] The weeks slipped away and, meanwhile, other factors worsened in the Israeli–Palestinian arena.

The central negotiating obstacle to meeting and, more importantly, restarting bilateral talks was Israel's commitment to sequencing the next steps. Israel's argument was that the PA must first disarm and dismantle terrorist organizations, including Hamas, before Israel would sit down for renewed bilateral talks with the PA.[72] Shalom, Israel's foreign minister, stated that: 'So far there is disappointment in the world from the steps taken by Mahmoud Abbas to eradicate terrorism'.[73] Wary of Hamas violence in general, and having lived through five years of the second intifada, the Israelis were firm that their security needs demanded a crackdown first.

Abbas never was willing to take this step in the late summer and autumn of 2005. Instead, he favoured integrating Hamas rather than confronting it, an effort that culminated with Hamas's participation in the January 2006 Palestinian parliamentary elections. At one time, Abbas said he would not confront or disarm 'militant organizations' in Gaza.[74] Later, though, Abbas said he would, but the PA would determine 'when and how'.[75]

But this disagreement about sequencing remained unresolved and the call for renewing bilateral talks remained unfulfilled.

This was all taking place in the context of Hamas celebration of disengagement as proof of the supremacy of armed struggle against Israel and with continuing Hamas–Israel confrontations. In other words, even as Abbas and Sharon were thinking about their next diplomatic steps, violence was in the air in both theoretical and actual ways. Hamas argued that the Israelis understood only force and that armed struggle was the best means for advancing the Palestinian national cause. What better way to demonstrate that than with disengagement? For only the second time since 1967, Israel shut down civilian settlements in the occupied territories and Hamas could convincingly claim that it was the result of Hamas fighting against Israel in Gaza. When Palestinians first heard of Sharon's idea, two-thirds 'viewed it as a victory for armed resistance'.[76] Later, Hamas spokesman Sami Abu Zuhri noted 'Hamas's struggle and Hamas's role in liberating this precious part of the homeland'. He added that resistance 'made this victory possible, and this victory can be repeated'.[77] Hamas was happy to lead the destruction of synagogues Israel left behind in Gaza after withdrawal.[78] It was not a negotiated outcome so the PA could make no claim that the diplomatic path had been reinforced. In fact, Sharon may have intended to deny the PA its key argument, the use of negotiations to advance Palestinian nationalism.[79] The only interactions to plan the disengagement were low-level contacts, and the officials engaged in these talks 'lacked the political authority or the mandate to address the central security issues involved'.[80]

Israel, Hamas, and other Palestinian factions continued the tit-for-tat violence. Fighting inside Gaza, rockets launched at Israel, and Israeli air strikes were not conducive to further co-operation, economic or otherwise.[81] Hamas cells in the West Bank planned attacks.[82] Hamas fired forty rockets at Israel in late September 2005.[83] Over the four months following disengagement, 283 rockets were fired at Israel.[84] On 24 October 2005, Israel killed an Islamic Jihad commander in the West Bank. Later, Islamic Jihad in Gaza responded with rocket fire. On 25 October, Israel fired missiles at two Islamic Jihad sites in Gaza. Erekat was exasperated: 'We're back in the same cycle of violence'.[85] The result of disengagement, one astute observer noted, was that the 'violent confrontation escalated tremendously'.[86] Sara Roy, a long-time Gaza analyst, noted that it was not only violence against Israel but also internal Palestinian contests: 'The weeks since the last Israeli soldier pulled out of the Gaza Strip have been marred by violence. There are almost daily battles between the PA and Hamas, Fatah and Hamas, and Gaza's many clans, militias, and security forces.'[87]

Roy's analysis is a reminder that the situation in Gaza immediately after the pull-out was not conducive to the PA asserting control and presenting Gaza in way that would be positive for renewed talks with Israel. There was a power vacuum in Gaza with a weak PA, a rising Hamas, and the continued power of Gaza clans. James Wolfensohn, the Quartet's envoy on economic matters in Gaza, noted PA fragmentation in a letter to the UN secretary general, Kofi Annan.[88] Hamas was in a much stronger political position than Fatah, as it later proved in the Palestinian parliamentary elections.[89] In short, it was hard for the PA to govern and it would have been hard if not impossible for the PA to disarm Hamas had the PA even wanted to proceed.[90]

Another process that continued in the backdrop was the Israeli building of settlements in the West Bank. This cast a pall over disengagement, especially because it seemingly confirmed the way Weisglas, a close Sharon adviser, had linked the two: disengagement as the price for deepening Israel's hold on the West Bank. From June 2004 to June 2005, Israel's settler population in the West Bank grew by 12,800 (not including East

Jerusalem). For Ghassan al-Khatib, a Palestinian minister, this undermined the spirit of disengagement: 'The Gaza step will not be worthy unless the international community compels Israel to match it with a stop to settlement expansion in the West Bank'.[91] Israel was also building the separation barrier in the West Bank during this time.

The final important aspect of disengagement was the way in which it failed to lead to any improvement in the Gaza economy because of the force-laden environment. The PA acknowledged the importance of economic progress, as noted by Abbas's chief of staff, Rafiq Husseini: 'But mostly what we have to do is create jobs for people and this is what the government is bent on doing, giving people hope for the future'.[92] Even after the withdrawal of the Gaza settlers, Israel maintained a tight hold on the crossings in and out of Gaza, as well as Gaza airspace and the coast. It justified this hold as needed for security. Wolfensohn lamented Israel's tight control of the crossings: 'The Government of Israel, with its important security concerns, is loath to relinquish control, almost acting as though there has been no withdrawal'. Mark Regev, an Israeli foreign ministry spokesman, agreed with this logic: 'If Israel tomorrow allowed unimpeded passage at the crossings, I think everyone believes that would have negative consequences all around. There would likely be a series of suicide bombings and we would have to respond.'[93]

The result was further damage to the economy, not to mention the negative dynamic it contributed to between Israeli and Palestinian leaders. Even as the PA demanded control of the Rafah crossing into Egypt, Israel closed it in early September 2005.[94] The predictions were clear: without open passages to the West Bank, Gaza will see 'a rise in unemployment and poverty'.[95] In an opinion piece in the *Wall Street Journal*, Abbas complained about continued and detrimental Israeli air, sea, and border control.[96] In October, Wolfensohn wrote that the 'flow of workers and goods from Gaza to Israel has ground to a halt'.[97] Frustrated, he closed down his envoy mission in April 2006.[98] He said, 'Instead of hope, the Palestinians saw that they were put back in prison'.[99] In short, security arguments and years of a climate of violence and attacks overwhelmed the economic needs and thereby squandered the possibility that economic renewal could act as a positive, post-disengagement dynamic. Israelis and Palestinians 'seemed largely unable or unwilling to take full advantage of the momentum created by the pullout plan'.[100]

The United States tried and failed to improve the movement of people and goods to benefit Gaza's economy and raise quality of life. Then US secretary of state Condoleezza Rice helped negotiate an agreement in November 2005, the Agreement on Movement and Access, which addressed these very issues. But it was never fully implemented. The European Union briefly deployed a border assistance mission at the Rafah crossing, but the United States never got a Gaza–West Bank link off the ground.

The long-term economic consequences were even worse. The poor economy, both on its own and as proof that disengagement had done nothing to advance the Palestinian national cause, bolstered Hamas. The results of disengagement, both economic and in terms of the Hamas argument that it proved armed struggle was the best means to end the occupation, further strengthened Hamas in the January 2006 elections.[101] Hamas's electoral victory led to international economic sanctions and even tighter Israeli control of what came in and out of Gaza. In short, the Gaza economy, and the consequent human suffering, reached new lows in the years after disengagement.

In sum, the case of Gaza disengagement demonstrates that parties used to fighting have a tough time pivoting toward negotiations and creating a constructive environment. In a situation where violence, occupation, economic restrictions, and West Bank settlements remained a reality, the possibility of disengagement becoming the start of a new relationship did not come to pass.

Addressing the alternative explanations

As pointed out at the start of this chapter, there are two other explanations for why a potential opening for negotiations did not materialize. But I think both of these explanations or objections are flawed and do not really challenge the point I am making.

Objection 1

One alternative way of thinking about the failure in any of the cases just evaluated is that the particular formulation of the proposal, idea, or policy did not meet the other side's demands. In other words, the proposal itself was so far from what they were hoping for that it was not worth pursuing; it was not an opportunity for negotiations. The problem could have been with the wording. A leader might have hoped for meaningful compromise but the proposal did not move in that direction; it had too little compromise. Or, it could be that a leader did *not* want to make any meaningful compromises, and the proposal assumed otherwise. It would require too much compromise. In the latter case especially, the unwillingness to respond means continued reliance on force and coercion.

With the 1974 programme, the Arab Peace Initiative, and the disengagement, I demonstrated the real possibilities for diplomatic openings. Each case could have turned out differently, with progress in negotiating, rather than serving as a missed opportunity. All three proposals had the potential to meet the other side's demands.

But I also think it is important to consider three broader arguments that also suggest why these kinds of proposals are real political opportunities. There is evidence that Arab–Israeli compromise is not impossible. First, both sides have a rhetorical foundation calling for peace. Second, the Arab–Israeli conflict has witnessed many actual concessions, including territorial ones. The historical record does not support the idea that either side has been ideologically immune to actually implementing concessions. Third, many significant offers have been made, even if they have not been implemented.

On the Israeli side, the Declaration of Independence (1948) was quite clear on this matter:

> We extend our hand to all neighbouring states and their peoples in an offer of peace and good neighbourliness, and appeal to them to establish bonds of cooperation and mutual help with the sovereign Jewish people settled in its own land. The State of Israel is prepared to do its share in a common effort for the advancement of the entire Middle East.

This initial statement was aimed at the Arab states and the people therein. Thirty years later, in October 1978, Moshe Dayan echoed Israeli's founding document:

> Our dream has always been – not only since the founding of the State of Israel, but since the very beginning of the Zionist movement – of a Middle East in which Jew and Arab would live in harmony and cooperation for the mutual advantage of both peoples.[102]

Thus, just after the signing of the Egyptian–Israeli Camp David Accords in September 1978, Dayan emphasized that harmony was Israel's dream.

An in-depth study demonstrates that, in recent years, Israel's search for peace has been a consistent theme in speeches made by prominent Israeli politicians at the United Nations General

Missed diplomatic opportunities

Debate every autumn.[103] In 1998, Benjamin Netanyahu, then prime minister, said, 'no one wants peace more than we do'. The next year, David Levy, the foreign minister, said the same: 'Israel aspires to reach a comprehensive peace with its neighbours, a peace of harmony'. Shlomo Ben-Ami in 2000 said, 'Peace ... is the objective', while the next year Shimon Peres explained, 'Israel is committed to contribute whatever it can to renew a real peace process'. In 2002, Peres said, 'the real triumph is in the harvest of peace'. The following year, Silvan Shalom offered that 'we will go the extra mile, as we have proven before, to bring peace and security to both our peoples' and 'Whenever a true partner for peace has emerged, he has been met with Israel's extended hand'. He even noted that his family name means 'peace'. The next year Shalom mentioned peace more generally several times and mentioned his meeting with the United Nations secretary general 'to discuss peace in the Middle East'. In 2005, Ariel Sharon, the then prime minister, stated, 'Peace is a supreme value in the Jewish legacy and is the desired goal of our policy'. Peace, Tzipi Livni explained in 2006, is 'an integral part of our nation's sense of mission'. In 2008, the Israeli president, Peres noted, 'Israel, for its part, shall continue to seek peace sincerely and fully'. Netanyahu was adamant the next year: 'Make no mistake: all of Israel wants peace. Any time an Arab leader genuinely wanted peace with us, we made peace.' In 2010, Avigdor Lieberman told the United Nations that, in Israel, 'Everyone wants peace'.

Netanyahu's 2011 speech to the United Nations contained repeated mentions of Israel's pursuit of peace, more than any of the previous speeches studied. He said, for example, 'Israel has extended its hand in peace from the moment it was established sixty-three years ago. On behalf of Israel and the Jewish people, I extend that hand again today'; 'In Israel, our hope for peace never wanes'; and 'The truth is that Israel wants peace. The truth is that I want peace.'

In these speeches, Israeli leaders also marshalled a series of historical events to support their claim to be in pursuit of peace. The most common example was the peace treaties with Egypt (1979) and Jordan (1994). Other examples included negotiations with Syria and the Palestinians, and the withdrawal of Israeli settlers from Gaza in 2005 (disengagement).

On the Palestinian side, the Declaration of Independence (1988) also emphasized peace:

> The State of Palestine, in declaring that it is a peace-loving State committed to the principles of peaceful coexistence, shall strive, together with all other States and peoples, for the achievement of a lasting peace based on justice and respect for rights.[104]

As with Israel, Palestine's search for peace has been a consistent theme in speeches made by prominent Palestinian politicians at the United Nations General Debate since Palestine was given the right to participate in 1998. 'Our people chose the peace option', Yasser Arafat exclaimed in 1998. He added later in the same speech that 'There is no alternative to peace'. The Palestinians wanted, Arafat said the next year, to work hard at 'achieving real peace'. In 2001, Arafat used multiple phrasings: 'just and lasting peace', 'peace of the brave', and 'peace as an irreversible strategic choice of our people'. In 2004, Farouq Kaddoumi explained the Palestinian negotiators had accepted a number of different proposals 'so that we in the Middle East can all live in peace and security and stability'. The next year, Nasser al-Kidwa said, 'we are working to promote a culture of peace and to reject violence'. In 2006, Abbas, after quoting Arafat's 1974 speech to the United Nations, said himself Arafat's famous line two times, 'do not let the olive branch fall from my hand'. In 2009, Abbas said, 'Everyone agrees on the need to achieve peace in the Middle East'. The PLO was eager 'to achieve a just, lasting and comprehensive peace'. Mirroring Netanyahu, Abbas in 2011 extended 'our hand to the Israeli Government and the Israeli people for peacemaking'.[105]

Like the Israeli speeches, the Palestinians mentioned historical examples where they wanted peace (but were sometimes rebuffed by Israel). The list included Madrid, Oslo, Camp David (2000), and Annapolis, as well as the 1974 Arafat speech to the United Nations and the Arab Peace Initiative (2002).

Rhetoric is not a perfect yardstick. Critics may rightfully argue that rhetoric may be empty, misleading, or self-serving. So, to buttress the broader case that concessions and moves toward peace are genuinely possible, let me now turn to some examples of concessions, some of which have been implemented.

The history of the Arab–Israeli conflict is replete with *actual* concessions. In terms of territory, Israel withdrew from a sliver of Syrian territory after the 1973 war; from the Sinai Peninsula as part of the 1979 peace agreement with Egypt; from West Bank cities as part of the Oslo process in the 1990s; from its so-called security zone in southern Lebanon in 2000; and from settlements in the Gaza Strip and a little bit of the West Bank during Israeli disengagement in 2005. Meanwhile, Egypt recognized Israel and signed the 1979 peace treaty; the PLO recognized Israel (e.g. 1988, 1993); and Jordan recognized Israel and signed a peace treaty in 1994. The Arabs, one analyst noted, 'generally showed a remarkable tendency for compliance with their treaty obligations'.[106] So there is not a fundamental commitment permanently against concession and the pursuit of diplomatic openings.

In addition to the concessions that were actually achieved, Arab, Israeli, and Palestinian leaders have offered a number of other major concessions. Palestinian negotiators have accepted the idea that, in a two-state solution, Israel will annex some of the settlements (neighbourhoods) in East Jerusalem. They have also – now along with the Arab League – accepted the idea of land swaps whereby Israel would annex pieces of the West

Bank where settlements are located near the Green Line, the line that separated Israel and the West Bank before the 1967 war, in exchange for other bits of land along the Green Line being turned over to become part of Palestine. Meanwhile, some Israeli leaders have accepted the idea of Palestinian sovereignty in several core areas of East Jerusalem, as well as an Israeli territorial withdrawal from more than 90 per cent of the West Bank.[107] Israeli–Syrian negotiators came very close to a peace treaty in 1999–2000. Syria was willing to establish normal relations with Israel. Israel was willing to withdraw from about 99 per cent of the Golan Heights, though the exact border by the Sea of Galilee was a sticking point.[108] Lebanon and Israel negotiated a draft peace treaty in 1983, but Lebanon officially abrogated the draft agreement in 1984.[109]

The point is that there are such things as genuine offers and actual concessions. No party has proven fully immune to the appeal of negotiations and concessions. Many proposals and potential openings are real, and thus ignoring or bypassing them represents a missed opportunity.

Objection 2

Domestic politics and bureaucratic forces may impede the pursuit of diplomacy and peacemaking. One's own party or coalition, opposition groups or movements, or interest groups may stand in the way of change. Elected officials may be wary of shifting course and embracing negotiations because rivals could point to the shift as a sign of failure or weakness. State officials might try to thwart implementation or leak unhelpful information. That much is true.

But leaders are *not* stuck with a static domestic environment and a hostile bureaucracy that advocates military force. A capable and politically savvy executive or head of government can challenge the existing environment and push back against entrenched commitments to military force. In other words, suggesting that the domestic political climate is against a certain diplomatic plan or opening is legitimate and often accurate, but it fails to account for the role leaders play in shaping and reshaping that domestic political climate over time. The same goes for bureaucratic opposition to diplomacy (and bureaucratic support for a military and force-focused approach); it is real *and*, in my view, it is subject to manipulation and attempted redefinition by leaders seeking to pursue diplomatic tracks.

Ariel Sharon was a lifelong hawk and pro-settlements elected official. He was strongly associated with the use of force at both the tactical and strategic level, and the excess use of it on occasions (e.g. Qibya in 1953 or Lebanon in 1982). Yet as prime minister in 2005, Sharon closed down twenty-five Israeli settlements, including all twenty-one Israeli settlements in the Gaza Strip. Yes, Sharon may very well have done this to stave off several different peace plans floating around at the time and to divert attention from and/or buy time for deepening the Israeli occupation of the West Bank. But even so, it was a radical break with his past and with the idea that force is always the answer.[110] He did not let the fact that his closest Likud supporters were not advocates of shutting down settlements – far from it – stop him from moving toward withdrawal. With disengagement, Sharon changed the terms of debate until he suddenly entered a coma at the start of 2006.

Israeli settlements rely on Israeli military force to seize the land and then to protect the settlements once they are built. The land was initially occupied through war; the legal justification used for taking private Palestinian land is usually 'military need'; and the settlements survive based on governmental or settler threat of or the actual use of force. I agree with Haim Yacobi and Wendy Pullan: 'Israel has used its military might and economic power to relocate borders and boundaries, grant and deny rights and resources, shift populations, and reshape the occupied territories for the purpose of ensuring Jewish control'.[111]

Concessions like closing Gaza settlements are not easy to sell at home, even as they are crucial to win trust and counter-concessions from one's international adversary. That means that one way domestic politics could complicate the move toward diplomacy is by forcing leaders to speak in multiple, contradictory directions simultaneously, perhaps promising one thing in secret even as they take contradictory public steps or make use of aggressive statements to maintain their domestic support. The challenge of an environment with multiple actors is magnified by the problem of each single actor or leader needing to speak to multiple constituencies at the same time. A leader might send a strong or costly signal to their adversary by rejecting this dynamic and speaking the truth about a contested issue to the home front.

I recognize that it is possible that a leader will not be able to overcome domestic or bureaucratic opposition *in every case*. Sometimes the opponents may be too strong or the leader too weak. Israeli and Palestinian politics contain many obstacles. The timing may be off or the deal may be far from perfect and hard to sell. But I contend that there is a large middle area, where success is neither precluded nor assured. In this middle area, a leader's creativity, commitment, perseverance, and luck could open a diplomatic door that formerly appeared to be closed.

Leaders usually have political capital. They have to be willing to spend it to bring about change.

Conclusion

The idea that military force is the best way to advance policy and that negotiations and concessions are dangerous has a self-reinforcing quality. The diplomatic openings that might provide a route for moving away from conflict are, at best, greeted solely with suspicion and, at worst, undermined and dismissed without serious exploration. So, the 'military force' idea sticks. The cases in this chapter illustrate such missed opportunities.

At the same time, we know there have been some Arab–Israeli negotiations that have begun (e.g. the Oslo process) and even succeeded in reaching and implementing agreements (e.g. the Egypt–Israel treaty). How do such openings ever get traction in the face of the dominant idea? How does that idea shift? In the next chapter, I consider what makes it hard to move from the first idea (force is better than negotiations) to a different belief about state policy instruments. I also examine some reasons why the idea of negotiations as a beneficial means does sometimes become the dominant idea, if only for short periods.

Chapter 6
CHANGING THE DOMINANT IDEA

When do actors shift between ideas about the effectiveness of the different means or policies available to them? In the Arab–Israeli conflict, the dominant idea has been that force is the best way to achieve state aims, while negotiations and concessions are a poor choice. What makes that idea hard to change? At the same time, sometimes a secondary idea, that negotiations and concessions are the best available means and military force is counter-productive, has prevailed in this conflict. What leads to a change in the dominant idea?

A number of factors lock in an idea about how to best use policy instruments, while other elements can lead to change, where one idea about how to consider military force and negotiations is replaced by a different belief. The first section of the chapter emphasizes three factors that reinforce a commitment to military force as the dominant means: the realist structure of global politics; the multi-actor, non-unitary nature of global politics; and the impact that fear has in reinforcing the idea that force and sometimes violence are the best approach for achieving one's national objectives or advancing one's national security.

The second section of the chapter brings forward additional elements or ways of thinking that might undermine a dominant idea and open the door to a preference for negotiations and concessions as the best policy means available. These include: leadership from within the warring parties that embraces the idea of negotiations as a more effective policy tool; external mediation; an unexpected event or technological change; tit-for-tat interactions that build toward talking or even a mutually agreeable outcome; and changing threat environments. At the end of the chapter, I briefly note how these factors played out in the two periods when negotiations were ascendant, parts of the 1970s and parts of the 1990s, with the Oslo process.

I am not suggesting that only one idea about the best means available to policymakers is present at any moment. Instead, multiple ideas may be present but one is often dominant. In the Arab–Israeli case, even though the preference for threatening and using force is usually the dominant idea, that does not mean that the belief in the value of negotiations and concessions is wholly absent. It may often sit as a lesser or secondary approach, held by a minority of countries and organizations. The notion of non-unitary actors – leaders from within the same country or organization pushing contradictory policies – is consistent with the idea that different leaders or organizations may have different beliefs at the very same moment in time.

Why the idea of the effectiveness of military force is hard to dislodge

The idea that military force is the best policy instrument is reinforced by three elements in contemporary international affairs. First, in terms of the structure of global politics, many parties hold a broadly realist view of the world: conflict and self-reliance are the norm, and one can never let one's guard down to seriously pursue negotiations. The world is a dangerous place, where states can take nothing for granted. Risks and threats are everywhere. Second, the global political environment is noisy, with many actors advancing many policies, interacting simultaneously. Those interested in negotiations are competing with and sometimes drowned out by opponents of talks and supporters of military force and violence. If I hand you a peace plan just as one of my co-nationals is attacking you verbally and another is after you with forceful means, the possibility declines that you will recognize my plan as a genuine olive branch. States, societies, and national movements rarely function as a unitary actor with one voice in the cacophonous international arena. Third, people who feel threatened are more likely to turn to forceful and aggressive policies and reject negotiated pathways. Fear inhibits diplomacy.

It is a realist world

In a realist world, conflict is standard. This notion harkens back, as so many modern authors have observed, to Thomas Hobbes, a seventeenth-century English philosopher. The state of nature is a state of war. The default, zero-sum environment has been one of conflict. The basic attitude is that 'the enemy is expected to be hostile'.[1] The issue at hand is the Arab–Israeli *conflict*, with wars, uprisings, and major military operations starting in 1947–1948, 1956, 1967, 1969, 1973, 1978, 1982, 1987, 1996, 2000, 2006, 2008, 2012, and 2014, not to mention clashes that took place before Israeli statehood in 1948. The major forceful paradigms for achieving core objectives of Israeli survival and Palestinian self-determination, Israeli deterrence, and Palestinian armed struggle, reflect and reinforce the dominance of the idea of force as the best means to achieve given ends, and the seeing of evidence of any type as proof of hostility. While there have been monumental peaceful breakthroughs, the central markers of the relationship between Israel and the Arab states are two wars: 1948 and 1967. Moves toward peace are deviations from the norm.

We see this understanding reflected in much scholarly work. Alexander Wendt, a key figure in the rise of social constructivist thinking in international relations in the 1990s, asks whether the general environment is conflictual or not, and suggests what follows on the basis of that initial factor:

> The greater the degree of conflict in a system, the more the states will fear each other and defend egoistic identities by engaging in relative gains thinking and resisting the factors that might undermine it. In a Hobbesian war of all against all, mutual fear is so great that factors promoting anything but negative identification with the other will find little room to emerge.... The ability of states to create new worlds in the future depends on the old ones they created in the past.[2]

It almost sounds tautological when he asserts that states that have started to get along or are friendly are more likely to see a concession for what it is, while states in midst of conflict are more likely to assume it is a trick. Zeev Maoz and Allison Astorino make a similar point: 'the best predictor of the foreign policy behavior of a state is the type of behavior directed at it by other states'.[3] For example, the second intifada (2000–2005) reduced even further Israeli–Palestinian interactions in Jerusalem: 'Terror attacks and the subsequent militarization of daily life in the city created mutual mistrust, and each community's self-isolation within its own boundaries'.[4] Force and violence lead to mistrust and self-isolation, which, in turn, likely mean more force and violence, and few openings for talks or cooperation.

Herbert Kelman, a prominent social psychologist, discusses another variant of this same idea, negative interdependence. He explains that, over time, both parties, the Israelis and Palestinians, have become deeply convinced that the assertion of their own identity comes at the expense of the other's identity. One cannot have Israeli *and* Palestinian identity, nationalism, and self-determination but rather Israeli *or* Palestinian identity, nationalism, and self-determination: 'each group's success in identity building depends on the other's failure in that task'. It is seen as a zero-sum conflict. The result has been 'the mutual denial of each other's national identity (and hence denial of the right to a national state)'.[5] If the other side has no genuine national identity, concessions become superfluous. Why concede to a fraudulent national movement?

There are many actors

The political environment has many actors and many contradictory policies all happening at the same time.[6] At many times during a conflict, there will be conflicting signals in both rhetorical and empirical terms. At a minimum, the Arab–Israeli conflict has included Egypt, Israel, Jordan, Lebanon, the Palestinian national movement, and Syria, not to mention the superpowers and other governments in the Middle East. And each country or movement itself may not speak with one voice, such as the Palestinian organizations Fatah and Hamas or major Israeli political parties like Labor and Likud. Political and military leaders may see things differently. There is a flood of information – both words and actions – from many directions. The same side, especially if we accept the non-unitary nature of 'Israel' and 'the Palestinians', will say multiple things, some of which seem to open the door to tentative diplomatic steps and others of which have a forceful, aggressive, or warlike character. The same leader may speak differently to different audiences. Some actions may be violent while others are less so, or even potentially cooperative. It thus becomes incumbent upon each side to interpret these signals in a charitable or hostile manner, and some leaders are better than others at differentiating between different opponents.[7] Without a 'Valid Spokesman', to quote

I. William Zartman, a prominent mediation expert, even getting negotiations started will be a difficult.[8] For example, in assessing the immediate aftermath of the 1967 war, Avi Raz illustrates many of the dynamics that demonstrate why it is so hard to move from a conflictual environment and emphasis on the idea that force prevails to negotiations and territorial concessions. It nicely exemplifies the idea of many, competing voices. Raz's revisionist account is focused on Israel, Jordan, and the Palestinians in an environment in which there were many voices, not unitary actors, and multiple signals open to varied interpretations.

According to Raz, Palestinian leaders in the West Bank who wanted to talk were not always the traditional leaders who had had ties with the Jordanian government before 1967. After the war, during which the West Bank had shifted from Jordanian to Israeli control, it was hard for Israel to determine who was an authoritative voice. Israel rejected efforts for West Bank Palestinian leaders to convene to determine the best post-war Palestinian approach to relations with Israel. Some Palestinians favoured turning to Jordan, but others did not. Steps both sides thought would leave the door open to compromise were taken as otherwise. When Palestinians offered the 1947 partition as a starting point, they saw it as a concession toward the acceptance of Israel, while Israel saw it as an irredentist effort to take back territory that had been part of Israel from 1948 onward. (Israel at the end of the 1948 war was approximately 40 per cent larger in area than Israel as mapped out in the United Nations' partition plan of 1947.) When, after the June 1967 war, Israel annexed tens of square kilometres in and around East Jerusalem, Palestinians, as well as Jordan's King Hussein, took it as a sign that Israel was not interested in a larger negotiated settlement since there could not, in their eyes, be a resolution without Jerusalem.[9]

Raz makes clear the Israeli government had anything but a single approach to the West Bank. There were many different views, including some who did not want to part with the West Bank. One early indication was that the 19 June 1967 cabinet decision to address the newly occupied territories did not mention the West Bank as a negotiable territory, but rather only territories that might be negotiated with Egypt and Syria, namely the Sinai Peninsula and the Golan Heights. Absent a consensus, the cabinet left out the West Bank.[10] Israel stalled for time.[11] Raz observed: 'This was a love story: the Israelis fell in love with the Arab lands they occupied in the war'.[12]

Bear in mind that even if I am correct that many peace offers or diplomatic proposals are genuine and could facilitate a political opening, and that many players would like to pursue resolution and reconciliation (which involves concessions), a notable minority (or more) are not interested in concessions. They seek total victory and/or see no hope for a compromise resolution in the foreseeable future. For example, in the Israeli–Palestinian conflict, some seek Israel or Palestine, not Israel and Palestine. At the same time as some West Bank Palestinians wanted to talk with Israel in 1967, the Palestine Liberation Organization was pursuing armed struggle against Israel. So it is not just that there are many voices but also the contradictory or clashing content of some of the other voices that matters.

Moreover, for bargaining reasons, a leader open to concessions may want some aggressive noise so that they can claim limited manoeuvrability if negotiations commence. 'I cannot make deeper concessions', that leader might say, 'because, as we all know, I am being pressured by anti-concession, pro-force elements in my own government or society. My hands are tied, so if you want to make a deal, we have to take that into account.' This builds on the idea of two-level games whereby domestic political pressures can constrain international bargaining flexibility.

One last point is that the tendency to see the other side as monolithic further undermines the possibility of negotiations. One side is less likely to see the fissures and attribute the negative, forceful moves to one entity and the concessionary talk to a distinct entity. There is a tendency not to differentiate between elements of a non-unitary adversary.[13] For many Palestinians, the Israeli left and right are not distinct; for many Israelis, Hamas and Fatah are effectively one and the same.

Fear

Being fearful of the other side or feeling threatened by the other makes turning away from threats, force, and aggression and embracing compromise that much harder and that much less likely. Feeling threatened or fearful makes one less open to ideas about conciliation and concessions. Fear could generate a feeling of being threatened, and a threat could lead one to be fearful.[14]

As a result of 'collective fear orientation', it 'becomes difficult to entertain alternative ideas, solutions, or courses of action'. Bar-Tal adds: 'Oversensitized by fear, a society tends to misinterpret cues and information as signs of threat and danger, searching for the smallest indication in this direction, even in situations that signal good intentions'.[15] Habituated fear overwhelms hope. Threat leads to 'cognitive shutdown' rather than any reconsideration of forceful policies and the possibility of pursuing a new, conciliatory pathway.[16] Broadly speaking, 'individuals reciprocate with hostility to perceived negative intentions'.[17]

According to polls of Israelis, as the perception of threat rises, so does support for increasing Israeli military power and rejecting olive branches. When the political scientist Asher Arian asked in a survey how respondents would prevent another war, the majority of people who characterized the threat as low supported initiating peace negotiations (79 per cent), rather than increasing Israeli military power (21 per cent). Israelis who saw the threat as high favoured peace negotiations by a much smaller margin (55 per cent for, 45 per cent against negotiations). In other words, the number who favoured peace talks increased by about 40 per cent as the perceived threat level lessened.[18] Ifat Maoz and Clark McCauley's work suggests something similar.[19] In surveying work on the impact of threats, Leonie Huddy cites an extensive list of scholarly authors supporting the notion that threat 'leads to support for punitive or violent action against threatening groups'.[20] Daniel Bar-Tal and Dikla Antebi specifically measured and flagged the 'siege mentality', 'a mental state in which members of a group hold a central belief that the rest of the world has highly negative behavioral intentions toward them', among Israeli Jews and noted its impact. Israeli Jews who are subject to siege mentality tend to select information that confirms the world has negative intentions and to support hawkish, uncompromising opinions. In 1989, 64 per cent of Israeli Jews agreed that 'All the means are right to secure the existence of the State of Israel'.[21] Based on 2006 data, Jonathan Caverley, a professor at the US Naval War College, found that Israeli Jews who thought the chances of war were lower (thus, those who felt less threatened) were more likely to favour peace talks to avoid war. Those who felt the chances were higher (and thus felt more threatened) were more likely to favour using 'military might'.[22] In studying the impact of Palestinian rocket attacks or the threat of rocket attacks on southern Israel, Anna Getmansky and Thomas Zeitzoff found that such threats increase the vote share of right-wing parties by two to six percentage points. More broadly, they note this could be a mechanism for the endurance of some conflicts: 'voters who are threatened with violence elect candidates who are less willing to make concessions'.[23]

Khalil Shikaki, the most prominent Palestinian pollster, found similar results among Palestinians. Threat perception is negatively correlated with the willingness to compromise and positively correlated with support for violence.[24] David Jaeger and his colleagues found that the short-term radicalization caused by Palestinian fatalities at Israeli hands dissipates. But those Palestinians who were teenagers during the first intifada have more radical preferences, while those who came of age during the Oslo years tack more moderate.[25]

The media can play a role as well, as more recent research on emotions makes clear. 'Evocative' coverage with fear-inducing cues magnify the impact of threatening information.[26] Information alone is not the only factor; the emotional context in which the media delivers that information also matters.

People who feel threatened see more future threats and act more aggressively. They do not want to make concessions. So, given a world in which the sides already feel threatened, they will lean toward aggression at the expense of backing off and pathways for de-escalation. Prolonged experiences of fear create more of the same, including the 'overestimation of dangers and threats' and increasing 'expectations of threat and danger'.[27] This is all magnified in the Arab–Israeli arena, because, as Janice Gross Stein noted, tight geographical space and a history of warfare tend to increase the perception of a threatening environment.[28]

A dynamic view: how come breakthroughs happen?

Despite all the factors mentioned above, how might actors move from reliance on military force to the idea that negotiations and concessions will help advance their goals? What could open the door to alternative pathways? I suggest five elements that might lead to a change in course:

(1) leadership from within the warring parties
(2) external mediation
(3) an unexpected event (*deus ex machina*)
(4) tit-for-tat cooperation, in the tradition of Robert Axelrod's *The Evolution of Cooperation*
(5) or a changing threat environment.

These five categories are not meant to be mutually exclusive. They may all have a role to play in order for diplomatic tracks to have a chance of breaking the dominant preference for military force among Arabs and Israelis.

The Arab–Israeli conflict has witnessed two periods when the effectiveness of negotiations emerged as the dominant idea or at least an even competitor with the idea of relying largely on military force. Negotiations grew in importance in the mid- to late 1970s with the resulting 1979 Egypt–Israel peace treaty and then again in the 1990s during the Madrid and Oslo years. At the end of the chapter, I briefly come back to both these moments to think about how these different factors might work to explain either example.

Leadership

A change in leaders or a significant shift in the perspective of an incumbent leader may lead to a major shift in policy. Political leaders can provide a different kind of information or different emotional valance (e.g. hope or trust) to break the force-based cycle.[29] Leaders may be affected by structural constraints like the distribution of military power in the Middle East or great-power alliances (e.g. during the Cold War), but they have room to act within these structural parameters and, in some sense, to reshape over time any structural obstacles or impediments.[30] When Anwar Sadat, Yitzhak Rabin (in the 1990s), and

Mahmoud Abbas came into office, for example, they each brought a new way of thinking and dealing with the conflict. Sadat had the biggest impact, Abbas probably the least. Note also that two of the three, Sadat and Rabin, were assassinated by one of their own people, a reaction that suggests the depth of the impact they had made with their (proposed) change of course.

Personal impressions matter too. If leaders impress each other as sincere, there is more evidence to believe a country will behave in the way its leaders say it will, for example in a proposed peace agreement.[31] Leaders can further signal sincerity by engaging in secret diplomatic talks. If I tell you a concession but only in secret, I must mean that concession (I'm not bluffing) if you could hurt my political standing back home by revealing it. If I did not mean it, I would not tell you and take the risk of you leaking it and thereby harming me politically. Concessions presented in secret talks are a costly form of signalling.[32] In October 1962, when the Cuban Missile Crisis was heading toward a direct US–Soviet confrontation, John F. Kennedy, the US president, asked Dean Rusk, his secretary of state, to convey a secret diplomatic proposal to U Thant, United Nations secretary general, via Andrew Cordier. Richard N. Lebow and Janice Gross Stein observed that Kennedy's proposal 'entailed some risk of a leak, a risk the president presumably would only have assumed if he was serious about the stratagem'.[33]

Leaders also may try to use proposals as moments to create broader diplomatic openings. But the reliance on military force and constant talk of security needs tend to obscure these pathways and leave the parties stuck fighting each other. That need not always be, as demonstrated with the opposite type of case, the *successful* negotiations that led to an Egyptian–Israeli treaty in 1979. At key moments, Israeli leaders could have framed Sadat's rhetoric and gestures in a negative and not promising light. Past Begin and Likud rhetoric not only made a negative reaction plausible but actually more likely than a desire to work with Sadat. And some Israeli leaders were sceptical of his initial moves. However, once Sadat visited Israel, Israeli leaders came to see the possibilities, and they pursued them along with Sadat and Jimmy Carter, the US president.

External mediation

The leadership and incentives that bring about a diplomatic opening and a potential turn away from military force may come from outside the conflict as well. Third parties have regularly tried to help solve the Arab–Israeli conflict by providing mediation, incentives and sanctions, and new ideas and proposals. Mediators with extensive resources, like the United States, may function as 'insurer, guarantor, trustee, and benefactor'.[34] They offer economic aid, peacekeepers, political cover, and more.

There are many examples of third-party efforts, including those undertaken by the United Nations, the great powers, and smaller states. Ralph Bunche, acting as a United Nations mediator, skilfully helped orchestrate four armistice agreements to end the 1948 war.[35] The United States was crucial in helping Egypt and Israel sign a peace treaty in 1978–1979.[36] Norway facilitated the 1993 Israeli–Palestinian breakthrough that led to the ultimately unsuccessful Oslo process (1993–2001).

Deus ex machina

Events that are not directly Arab–Israeli events may nonetheless transform the Arab–Israeli conflict. Such 'cataclysmic disruptions' could change the distribution of economic power and military force as well as the perceptions of the warring parties.[37] A global boom or bust or a re-ordering of the great powers in the international system, changes that may have nothing to do with the Arab and Israeli countries, may affect the Arab–Israeli arena as well.³⁸

The most obvious example was the end of the Cold War. In the aftermath of the 1982 Israeli invasion of Lebanon, the Syrian government concluded it needed to ramp up its military and arms programme to catch up with Israel. It could do that only with the help, and subsidized weaponry, of the Soviet Union. But by 1987, the Soviet Union decided it would no longer play that role. Syria was welcome to purchase arms, but the Soviet Union could not and would not foot the bill for an arms race with Israel. Moscow did not have the spare resources. Like the Syrian government, the Palestine Liberation Organization, too, was in a weakened position as the Cold War came to an end. Several factors led to the its policy shifts toward diplomacy in 1988–1993, but one of the important ones was the decline and then disappearance of the Palestinians' main benefactor, the Soviet Union.

Some events inside the conflict may have a similar impact of shaking up the status quo. The 1973 war, for example, changed how Israel and the United States approached the conflict; neither expected the war until the last minute. How the United States managed the aftermath of such events affected the success or failure of subsequent diplomatic efforts.³⁹

Step-by-step cooperation

Scholars and policymakers have suggested that small, positive interactions can build toward greater trust and cooperation. The premise of the failed Oslo process, for example, was that gradual changes could lead to increased trust and snowball into more and more positive, cooperative developments. Confidence-building measures are meant to do just that. Prominent scholarly versions include Robert Axelrod's tit-for-tat diplomacy and Charles Osgood's GRIT, 'Gradual Reduction in Tension'.⁴⁰

A positive, interactive spiral leads to de-escalation and toward conflict resolution. These approaches may not explain the initial move for cooperation but can explain the spread or growth of cooperation. Writing in 1983, Janice Gross Stein also favoured a gradual process with a transitional period and incremental steps, not a comprehensive approach that seeks to solve the entire conflict overnight.[41] Several scholars mentioned earlier in this chapter –Wendt; Maoz and Astorino; and Kelman – have also offered suggestive ideas along these lines. Gradualism may have one more benefit as well: leaders who make gradual changes in policy tend to be more sincere and genuine than leader who make overnight moves, which tend to be more connected to tactical demands. Another way to express the difference is that gradualism signals complex learning while rapid policy shifts signal only simple learning.[42]

Threat environment

Having talked about the ways in which threats, and fear, can reinforce a belief in the dominance of military force, I also want to note the possibility that the threat environment might change in a way that opens up the possibility of ideas favouring negotiations.[43] An environment characterized by low or decreasing threat would reinforce those who believed in the efficacy of negotiations. The end of the Cold War and collapse of the Soviet Union changed the balance of threat in the Middle East, as in many other places. But the threat environment is a tricky and malleable concept that could be manipulated by the actors in the conflict. It might be that those actors committed to the idea of the success of forceful policies stress many dangers and foes, while those actors committed to the idea of the efficacy of negotiations might stress a world with decreasing threats and growing safety.

The Israeli state and the Palestinian national movement both emerged in war and struggle, a threatening environment conducive to reliance on the idea that military force is the best means of conducting foreign policy.

Ascendancy of the non-dominant idea in the 1970s and 1990s

Let me now briefly turn back to the two periods when the idea that negotiations could advance national security and other central interests was most pronounced. Since the start of the Arab–Israeli conflict, the idea that negotiations and concessions rather than the threat and use of force and the denigration of talks could advance core state interests was most prominent in the 1970s and the 1990s. In the 1970s, it led to a peace treaty, the first one between an Arab state (Egypt) and Israel. In the 1990s, it led to second peace treaty, between Israel and Jordan, and prolonged Israeli–Palestinian negotiations, albeit they ultimately failed to resolve the conflict.

Arab and Israeli *leaders* played an important role in both cases, including Menachem Begin, Yitzhak Rabin, and especially Anwar Sadat in the 1970s and then Yasser Arafat, Shimon Peres, and Rabin in the 1990s. *External mediators*, whether from the United States or Norway, were central to the breakthroughs. Without third parties, it is unlikely that either Camp David (1978) or Oslo (1993) would have taken place. Unexpected *external events* were especially influential in the 1990s, first with the end of the Cold War (and the collapse of the Soviet Union) and then with the US triumph in the first Gulf War and the subsequent call to address the Arab–Israeli conflict.

Both in the 1970s and 1990s, a gradual, or *step-by-step*, approach was important to at least some of the diplomatic breakthroughs. Ultimately, gradualism became an impediment to the Oslo process when the passage of time without a final agreement resulted in a decrease in trust and confidence and growing antagonism rather than the hoped-for confidence-building. Rather than manifestations of peaceful relations, many Palestinians noted the continued expansion of Israeli settlements and loss of Palestinian land. They experienced the continued growth of Israel's matrix of control, including both internal (to the West Bank) and external checkpoints.[44] The 1994 Hebron massacre, an Israeli settler's attack on Palestinians, had a negative impact on wider perceptions. Israeli Jews focused on repeated Palestinian terrorist attacks. Hamas, opposed to the Oslo process, led a campaign of bombing Israeli buses in major cities like Jerusalem and Tel Aviv. The hoped-for period of confidence-building not only did not materialize but instead became a period of growing hostility and distrust.

Lastly, in terms of the larger *threat environment*, Egypt shifting away from the Soviet camp and toward the US one in the 1970s, and the collapse of the main Arab benefactor, the Soviet Union, were also noteworthy. The end of the Cold War in 1989/1990 and the collapse of the Soviet Union left the Arab side without a patron. Arab parties lost Soviet subsidies and access to Soviet weapons, even as Israel remained allied with and supplied by the most powerful state in the world, the United States.

I have not provided a definitive account of how the dominant idea about the means of foreign policy changes in the Arab–Israeli conflict. Rather, I have emphasized that the idea can and does change and highlighted some of the factors that cumulatively may help lock in a dominant idea – in this case, the preference for military force – or may introduce pathways for the ascendance of a secondary idea, the belief in the greater value of negotiations and concessions.

CONCLUSION

If military force is problematic and often counter-productive, what are the implications for the future of Arab–Israeli relations? The centrality of force to Arab–Israeli relations continues, as one sees reflected in comments and actions surrounding the 2014 war between Israel and Hamas. The shortcomings remain, including the way in which an over-reliance on military force can backfire in terms of an actor's security needs and obstruct possible negotiating opportunities. Israeli and Palestinian policies of recent years have undermined the achievement of fundamental national goals like security, independence, peace, and territorial control.

For international relations, the Arab–Israeli conflict is a useful case study in thinking about the connection between the display, threat, or use of military force and the ability to create peace in world politics. Force has its place in international affairs, but it can often make peace more distant. The strategic transformation of a long-running conflict requires the carving out of some space for alternatives to military force, whether those alternatives are readily apparent or not. That is no guarantee of peace, for, as we have seen time and again, diplomatic pathways are themselves quite complex and challenging. But when the idea that military force is the best option is so dominant, the logic is often that only the continued threat or use of force can compel the other side to surrender, or at least make nearly all the concessions. The Arab–Israeli examples herein are meant to indicate the steep costs of that approach, including the danger of becoming locked in a self-fulfilling prophecy.

I recognize that while much of this book has been about relations between states, including Egypt, Israel, and Syria, this chapter is focused more upon the conflict between a state, Israel, and a non-state actor, the Palestinian national movement (or really the two parts of that movement, Hamas and Fatah). The Palestinian dimension, and that of all organizations or non-state actors, is different from relations between states like Egypt, Israel, and Syria, at least in terms of how we think about what economic and especially military capabilities are available. Non-state actors generally have less power and thus look for ways to magnify the political or symbolic aspects of using military force.

Despite this difference, the lessons of the earlier chapters are nonetheless useful. First, the Palestinian–Israeli conflict is still a part of the larger Arab–Israeli conflict. The two dimensions, Palestinian–Israeli and Arab–Israeli, have long been intertwined and long influenced each other. Second, the Palestinian–Israeli conflict is the most pressing aspect of the Arab–Israeli conflict today and thus merits a significant amount of analytical attention. To ignore the Palestinian–Israeli angle because it involved non-state actors would be to ignore the core of the larger conflictual relationship. The other major, unresolved dimension of the conflict is the relationship between Israel and Syria, but Syria remains consumed by the civil war and its consequences. Syria's Asad government is focused on its own domestic survival, less so the Arab–Israeli conflict. Third, though Fatah and Hamas are non-state actors, they still seek many of the same goals (security, survival, independence) that states seek and they have versions of the same means: foreign-policy instruments related to both force and negotiations. Both Fatah and Hamas partially govern areas, though they lack the full authority and legitimacy of states. They are not sovereign states, but they do partially govern in territories whose status is ambiguous.

The findings

The dominant view among Arabs and Israelis is that the other side understands only the threat and use of force. The use of military force, coercion, and strength is deemed to be the best way to achieve one's security and fundamental political objectives. We saw this approach in documents, the thinking of two well known leaders, and relevant statements. A number of historical examples provide some support: the 1967 war and how it shifted Egyptian and Syrian policy on Israel; Israel's strength in the late 1960s and early 1970s as a factor undermining the Palestinian national movement's military approach; the first intifada, which pushed Israel toward a negotiated resolution of the Palestinian question; two Israeli unilateral territorial withdrawals that supported the 'force works' narrative, from Lebanon (2000) and Gaza (2005); and the conflict between Israel and Hamas in 2008–2009.

Yet one major shortcoming of military force is that it cannot move warring parties from a state of non-belligerence to a state of peace. War and violence may hurt parties and stop fighting, but they cannot lock in the end of fighting or the transition to a more cooperative and even positive-sum relationship. In the case of the Camp David Accords of 1978 and the Egyptian–Israeli peace, it was leadership, mediation, and diplomacy that brought about the transformation of the relationship, moving it from the end of fighting, through ceasefire and interim agreements, to a final peace treaty. In the Israeli–Syrian case, the fighting stopped but diplomacy failed and the two sides never a reached a peace treaty. Military force was not enough.

Furthermore, military force does not always work as intended: using it may worsen the military-political situation rather than bring a state more security. The use of force may lead to an increase in counter-attacks, cause an arms race, bolster a rival's international political standing, undermine support in one's own society for negotiations, strengthen a rival's view that one is hostile, cause casualties and loss of territory, and spur the creation of a wholly new enemy organization. While this bears some resemblance to security dilemma thinking, neither of the two versions of the security dilemma I discuss fit exactly to what we have seen in the Arab–Israeli relationship. We saw these negative consequences and rising *in*security with the cases of Israel and the Gaza Raid and Suez war (1955–1956), Egypt and other actors and the 1967 war, the Israeli invasion of Lebanon in 1982, and the Palestinian side in the second intifada, which started in 2000.

The embodiment of a commitment to military force in ideas and institutions helped scuttle potential diplomatic opportunities. First, the belief in the likely success of forceful policies is coupled with the denigration of negotiating options. Diplomatic concessions are seen as a sign of weakness and thus avoided. So, conceptually, many leaders are hesitant to pursue talks and to consider making concessions. Second, the commitment to military force is manifest in governmental and organizational institutions. These institutions, in terms of both the ideas they advance and their standard operating procedures, make negotiating breakthroughs less likely. There have been real opportunities that have been missed, as illustrated by the 1974 statement from the Palestine Liberation Organization, the Arab Peace Initiative, and the Gaza disengagement.

We should bear in mind that dominant ideas are not permanent. Yes, some factors do reinforce a dominant idea that the

Conclusion

threat and use of force are the preferred foreign-policy tool, but other factors open up pathways by which what has usually been the secondary idea, the import of negotiations and concessions, can emerge as the dominant idea, at least for short periods. The most prominent periods in the Arab–Israeli conflict when the idea of negotiations took on an important role include in the context of Egyptian–Israeli relations in the 1970s and during the start of the Oslo process in the 1990s.

Hamas (the Islamic Resistance Movement) and the State of Israel, 2014

If the importance of understanding the shortcomings and limitations of a reliance on military force and strength was not already apparent, the battle between Hamas and Israel in the summer of 2014 again brought the issue to the fore. Both Hamas and the Israeli government relied on force and coercion to try to advance their aims.

The pathway to war started with the kidnapping of three Israeli teens in the West Bank. Israel immediately blamed Hamas. The Netanyahu government knew early on that the three teens were dead or likely dead but did not publicize this information. Instead, many Israelis and supporters abroad mobilized to call for the lives of the teens to be spared, and, more importantly, the Israeli government used the episode and the idea of an ongoing search as an opportunity to crack down broadly on Hamas in the West Bank. Israel arrested several hundred Hamas figures in the West Bank, including tens (or more) whom Israel had released in a major prisoner swap in 2011. In other words, the Israeli operation went far beyond a direct response to the kidnapping; it was much larger in its military scope.

Palestinian militants started firing rockets from Gaza at Israel. At first, factions other than Hamas, such as Islamic Jihad, fired them. Hamas had been suppressing such fire for 2013 and much of 2014; according to Israel's Shin Bet (the internal security services), rocket attacks were few in number in 2013 compared with the previous decade.[1] Hamas had a special police force to suppress the fire. My thoughts about why Hamas allowed the factions to start firing are speculative. Perhaps the Hamas personnel in Gaza in charge of suppressing rockets stopped doing their jobs and went into hiding for fear the Israeli crackdown would spread from the West Bank to Gaza. Perhaps Hamas wanted to let the other factions fire in order to send a message to Israel in response to Israel's West Bank crackdown on Hamas. As the fighting in Gaza intensified, Hamas itself joined in the rocket fire, whether to respond to Israeli attacks, to appease domestic calls to fight back, or to keep up with the belligerent actions of other Palestinian militants. Maybe Hamas sensed an opportunity to try to break the siege of Gaza and to inflict damage on Israel.

Prior to the war, Hamas had invested in multiple pathways to facilitate the use of force against Israel. It had trained operatives to attack Israel by sea; it had built a large tunnel system for command and control, hiding arms, sneaking into Israel for attacks, smuggling, and commercial activity; it had amassed thousands of rockets and mortars; and it had explored the use of military drones.[2] It utilized all these pathways during the war.

By launching a major military operation in the West Bank in mid-June 2014 and helping push events toward war, the Netanyahu government briefly avoided – and might have intentionally been trying to thwart – a non-military pathway that had come into being in late April 2014, when Hamas and Fatah signed a reconciliation agreement after years of fragmentation with Hamas running Gaza and Fatah running the West Bank. Hamas, negotiating from a position of political and financial weakness, agreed in April to a single Palestinian government for the West Bank and Gaza that did not include any Hamas officials as ministers. The new Palestinian government was sworn in on 2 June. Mahmoud Abbas, the Palestinian president, stated that the new government would abide by the Quartet's conditions to recognize Israel, reject violence, and accept past agreements.[3] Netanyahu reacted by contending that Abbas, by supporting this unity government, 'said yes to terrorism and no to peace'. From April onward, Israel denounced the entire Palestinian unity process, though even its US ally was willing to give the unity government an opportunity to prove itself as a constructive actor. The US State Department pledged to watch 'closely to ensure that it upholds principles that President Abbas reiterated today'.[4]

At a meeting to discuss possible responses to the kidnapping, Israeli ministers raised the very arguments mentioned many times earlier in this book. Minister Naftali Bennett suggested several options, 'some of them quite extreme'. He was disdainful of other ideas. 'The response we are discussing here is weak and borders on disgraceful', Bennett said. 'This was a severe instance of the kidnapping of three kids and their murder in cold blood. *A weak response to such a grave incident guarantees the next kidnapping.*'[5] In short, he echoed the idea that an insufficiently forceful response merely invites more demands and concessions. The defence minister, Moshe Ya'alon, pushed back: '*If we implement what you propose, it will lead to an escalation we won't know how to control, to the point of a war in Gaza*'.[6] Military force, the defence minister reminded, can have to unintended consequences. Ya'alon added: 'Do we really want a war in Gaza now?' Bennett replied: 'We will ultimately be at war in Gaza. It's better that we be the ones to start it.'[7]

Interestingly, one explanation for why Israel did not feel the need to fulfil the 2012 ceasefire terms was that in the months just after that battle, Gaza was relatively quiet, which the Netanyahu administration assumed was due to deterrence; Israel assumed its military strength, not the negotiated agreement, explained the quiet. The reliance on military force – deterrence – obscured and undermined a diplomatic agreement.[8]

In the meantime, over 2,100 Palestinians, including hundreds of children, and about seventy Israelis died. Thousands more people, mostly Palestinians, were wounded. Israeli bombings again did significant damage to Gaza homes, factories, mosques, and infrastructure facilities (e.g. sewage, water, power). To a lesser degree, Israeli structures were also damaged. Evidence of widespread post-traumatic stress disorder (PTSD) among both populations emerged.[9]

To put some names on the results of the choice to use force, the Israeli military killed Dr Bashir al-Hajjar, a professor of nursing at the Islamic University of Gaza who studied stress and war trauma in Gaza nurses. Four Palestinian boys from the Bakr family were killed on a beach by Israeli forces: Ahed, Ismail, Mohammad, and Zakariya.[10] The boys ranged in age from about seven to twelve. A fragment from a Hamas mortar killed Dror Chanin, an Israeli civilian distributing food to Israeli soldiers near Gaza.[11] Henk Zanoli, a Dutch righteous gentile who helped save a Jew during the Holocaust, returned his medal to the Israeli government after six members of his great-niece's husband's family – Muftiyah, Jamil, Omar, Youssef, Bayan, and Shaaban of the Ziadah family – were killed in Gaza.[12] The larger policy decisions impact individual lives, changing families forever.

The United States

While I am most interested in the implications of my research for the warring Arab and Israeli groups, what about the most significant external actor for much of the conflict, the United States? Herein lies a contradiction. US administrations bolster

Conclusion

the dominance of the idea that force is the answer through a strong alliance with Israel while simultaneously pushing diplomatic processes that are meant to raise the profile of negotiations and mutual concessions.

The United States is Israel's stalwart ally. Every administration since that of Richard Nixon has poured billions and billions of dollars of US aid into Israel.[13] Some of that aid was economic but much of it was military, helping Israel expand its arsenal. In 2016, the Obama administration and the government of Israel signed an agreement for $38 billion in US military aid over ten years (2019–2028).[14] Furthermore, Israel is one of the first foreign countries to get access to the latest US military technology. The two countries have continued cooperation on security, counter-terrorism, and intelligence matters. They regularly consult about common strategic issues.

At the United Nations, the United States has long provided Israel with political cover. In a political venue where other countries try to hold Israel accountable for its reliance on military force, the United States wields its veto power at the UN Security Council in a manner meant to support Israel by blocking such measures. US presidents occasionally allow a Security Council resolution critical of Israeli policy to pass, but that is about it.

Many US administrations have spoken out against Israeli settlements, but few have taken any action to penalize Israel or incentivize Israel to curtail the expansionist project. If we think about the settlement project as reliant on military force (e.g. to take land; to suppress violent and non-violent Palestinian opposition to Israel's expansionist policies; to occupy and control the Palestinian population; to depopulate Palestinian areas), the United States is an indirect but willing ally. It has the most leverage over Israel of any single country, but it chooses not to use it to try to stop settlements. Only George H. W. Bush in the early 1990s chose to attach any material or financial consequences to Israeli settlement expansion (a policy that continued in the Clinton years).

The US government has often been relevant in times of direct Arab–Israeli military confrontations, including war. In 1973, the United States airlifted emergency military supplies to Israel during the war. In 1991, the United States worked to protect Israel from Iraqi missiles during the first Gulf War. At other times, the United States urged Israel to stop or restrain its military response against Arab countries or organizations. President Ronald Reagan grew furious with Israeli military actions in Lebanon in 1982. During the second intifada and then subsequent Hamas–Israel clashes, the United States under George W. Bush and Barack H. Obama accepted Israel's right to defend itself but also sometimes called on Israel to act with restraint in its military activities.

At the same time, the United States has been the foremost proponent of a negotiated resolution of the conflict.[15] Since the 1967 war, we have witnessed many US diplomatic efforts such as the Rogers plans, Kissinger's step-by-step diplomacy, the Geneva conference format, Camp David (with the Carter administration), the autonomy talks, the Reagan plan, the Shultz initiative, the Madrid conference, the Oslo process after the hand-off from Norway, Shepherdstown, Camp David (with the Clinton administration), the Bill Clinton parameters, the Roadmap, the Annapolis talks, the Hillary Clinton talks, and the John Kerry talks. Another purpose for US aid has been to entice Egypt, Israel, and other parties to resolve their differences through negotiations and reward them when they do so.

Washington's efforts have sometimes not led to a negotiating process, sometimes led to failed negotiations, and, on one occasion, led to the conclusion of a successful peace treaty (between Egypt and Israel). Critics might push back that on the

Conclusion

Israeli–Palestinian front, Israel's dramatic advantage in economic and military might was built into the process, meaning its policies on the use of force were embedded in the turn to negotiations. As Hilde Henriksen Waage, a professor of history at the University of Oslo, has noted with regard to Arab–Israeli negotiations, there might be process symmetry – all parties having a seat at the table – but that is coupled with power asymmetry, given the wide gap in capabilities between Israel, the strongest participant, and the Arab parties, especially the Palestine Liberation Organization and the Palestinian Authority.[16]

The Trump administration was the first US government to fully endorse the Israeli right wing's policies and territorial ambitions. Trump officials did not endorse a two-state solution, with Donald Trump himself famously saying in February 2017, 'I'm looking at two-state and one-state and I like the one that both parties like'.[17] His officials supported Israeli settlements and refrained from using the term 'occupation' for Israel's presence in the West Bank. In clashes between Hamas and the Israeli military, they saw Israel's use of force only in terms of self-defence.

Under Trump, the United States recognized Israel's claim to Jerusalem and moved the US embassy from Tel Aviv to Jerusalem, receiving nothing substantive in return from Israel. Trump also fully recognized Israel's sovereignty over the Golan Heights, land captured from Syria in 1967, and again received nothing substantive in return from Israel. That the United States received nothing in return might indicate poor bargaining skills or that Washington saw no issues on which Israel could or should plausibly offer a concession, a sharp contrast with previous administrations.

Meanwhile, Trump officials talked about diplomacy but showed complete disdain for the idea of Palestinian national self-determination and adapted US policies accordingly. The

Trump approach rejected the idea of mutual concessions, and instead highlighted the need only for Palestinian ones. The Israelis could advance an agenda of annexation and indefinite suppression of Palestinian national self-determination, and the Trump administration likely would cheer them along at every step. For Trump's US government, an Israeli position based on military force and rejecting negotiations and concessions was praiseworthy.

In sum, as of mid-2019, the US government seemed fully supportive of the Israeli government's thinking, suggesting the biggest external player would do nothing to challenge Israel's continuing reliance on military force to advance its national objectives.

Israel and Palestine: what next?

What does an assessment of ideas about military force and about negotiations mean for the future of Israel and Palestine? I will start with Israel and then turn to the Palestinian national movement. I start with Israel because Israel holds most of the cards. It is by far the more powerful economic and military actor when compared with the Palestinians. Moreover, Israel is backed by the strongest state in the world, the United States. Israel, with Egypt's support, controls the exit and entry of people and goods to Gaza. Israel holds the West Bank and would have to let go for an independent State of Palestine to emerge. The reverse is not true. To state the obvious, one could not say Palestine holds the West Bank and would have to let go for an independent State of Israel to emerge.

I want to assess Israel and its reliance on military force in two ways, depending on what goal we assume about Israel's central objective. First, I evaluate an Israel that seeks to end the conflict with a genuine two-state solution, a policy that would

Conclusion

necessitate ceding the vast majority of the West Bank to a new State of Palestine. Second, I consider an Israel that does not want to cede control of the West Bank.[18]

So let us assume for the moment that the Israeli government, backed by a majority of the Israeli people, wants to end the Israeli–Palestinian conflict, and that that government sees a two-state solution as the best option to do so. The Israeli left favours a two-state solution. But even Israel's long-time, right-wing prime minister Benjamin Netanyahu has also, on occasion, spoken in favour of two states, starting with his 2009 speech accepting the idea, even if, as noted in Chapter 2, I doubt that view represents his or his party's true preference.[19]

Israeli actions in recent years have made such an outcome far less likely because so many of its policies are reliant on military force. On the ground, the occupation of the West Bank, including East Jerusalem, is built upon administrative detention, checkpoints, expulsion, revocation of residency, and home demolitions.[20] These are all coercive tools. It is not that one would expect Israel to drop these tools all in one moment; in part, such a change would turn on the interactions with Palestinian moves. But were Israel genuinely interested in fundamentally transforming the status quo, it would at least press hard for a dramatic break in Israeli–Palestinian relations so as to lessen the need for such measures in the coming years. Before he was assassinated in 1995 when Israeli prime minister, Yitzhak Rabin sought to fight terrorism as if there were no peace process, and pursue peace as if there were no terrorism. That, too, may not work, but at least it gets closer to the importance of avoiding a near exclusive reliance on military force.

And yet in this force-laden environment, the government of Israel has ignored or minimized a number of openings. Recent Israeli governments have not used the Arab Peace Initiative (2002) as a springboard for Israeli–Palestinian peace.[21] Israel fought to build more and more homes in settlements in 2009 and 2010 when the Obama administration was seeking a total freeze on such construction as a way for Israel to demonstrate serious engagement with possible peace talks. It did not do its utmost to make a success of US-mediated negotiations in 2010, when Hillary Clinton was US secretary of state, or in 2013–2014, when it was John Kerry. It has set forth conditions – for example formal Palestinian acceptance of Israel as a Jewish state, or the stationing of Israeli forces in the Jordan Valley even after a two-state division – that preclude an Israeli–Palestinian agreement.[22] It has not publicly stated a detailed Israeli vision for how to resolve the conflict between Israel and Palestine.[23]

Moreover, the embrace of military measures has not brought Israel long-term security. Israel and Hamas fought in 2008–2009, 2012, and 2014, with thousands of Palestinian casualties and massive structural damage in Gaza, but also casualties, some physical damage, fear, and much trauma on the Israeli side as well. Israel–Gaza violence flares up frequently, as we saw again in 2019. Jerusalem has been on edge a number of times, such as the summer of 2014, and was a central location for a wave of Palestinian knifings, vehicular attacks, and other terrorist attacks in 2015–2016.[24] In a visit to Israel in early 2016, I was struck by how many Israeli Jews expressed to me concerns about intercommunal tensions and fear. The feelings of personal insecurity were palpable. Under the leadership of a prime minister who prides himself on his commitment to Israeli security, Israeli insecurity was still significant.

At times, deterrence or forceful policies may seem to work, and there will be periods of relative quiet for Israelis. But the pattern we have seen is that these periods do not last. The continued absence of a Palestinian homeland and the inevitability of Palestinian tactical and technological innovation such as tunnels, mortars, rockets, and kites mean that the

Conclusion

Israeli–Palestinian confrontation continues. Absent a strategic resolution that considers how policies other than military force can improve relations, Israelis do not escape the violent fallout indefinitely.

At the same time, alarming examples of Israeli violence against Palestinians make one wonder how deeply the reliance on force has penetrated Israeli society. For example, I am thinking of the firebombing of the Dawabsheh family in Duma in July 2015 that resulted in three Palestinian dead and the later rejoicing over it by some Israeli Jews; the murder of a Palestinian attacker who was already lying wounded on the ground in Hebron in March 2016; and the beating by undercover Israeli police of a Palestinian worker at a Tel Aviv supermarket in broad daylight.[25] In the Hebron case, most Israeli Jews, including many politicians, defended the Israeli killer.[26] And by highlighting these exceptional examples, I do not mean to lose sight of the day-to-day violence of the occupation.

The kinds of arguments used to justify employing force to fight Palestinians can be, and have been, used against Israeli Jews as well. If territorial withdrawal is not acceptable and if all Palestinians are terrorists, then the same must be true of anyone who supports withdrawal or working with Palestinians, even if they are Israeli Jews; they are consorting with terrorists. The demonization of Israeli leftists is about many things, including the demonization of any kind of opposition to the idea that Israeli policy necessitates reliance on military force. How ironic that two prominent warnings about fascism in Israel came from military generals, then a recent and a former leader of the Israel Defense Forces, the very embodiment of Israel's commitment to military force. In early May 2016, Major-General Yair Golan, the deputy chief of staff of the army, said, 'It's scary to see horrifying developments that took place in Europe begin to unfold here'. He made the comments during a Holocaust Remembrance

Day address.[27] A few weeks later, Ehud Barak, a former prime minister and defence minister and army chief of staff, warned that Israel has been 'infected by the seeds of fascism'.[28] These warnings were not the first ones.[29]

In sum, if we assume the government of Israel has been seeking a negotiated, compromise resolution over the last decade, we see that its reliance on force has coexisted with the exact kinds of pathologies outlined in this book, problems of insecurity and missed diplomatic opportunities. The most charitable explanation would be that Israeli governments are using military force until Hamas and other violent Palestinian actors themselves cease the use of force *and* until the definition of an acceptable two-state solution is redefined, with greater Palestinian concessions and fewer Israeli ones than had been talked about in high-level Israeli–Palestinian negotiations during, say, the Camp David/Taba process (2000–2001) or the Annapolis talks (2007–2008).[30]

A less charitable view would be that these Israeli governments assume that peace will come only when the Palestinian side is defeated. Force creates peace. Period, no concessions. This book has highlighted the problems with this viewpoint.

And then there is a second way to view the Israeli government under Netanyahu from 2009. It has not sought a negotiated peace where both Palestinian *and* Israeli leaders make deep concessions. It has not sought a two-state solution where the State of Palestine has many of the elements of an independent state. Instead, it has sought indefinite Israeli control of the West Bank, control that by definition means the Israeli reliance on military force to ensure the subjugation of a people who believe they have a right to self-determination, the Palestinian people. Many members of recent Israeli governments, be they from Netanyahu's Likud, the Jewish Home party, or other places, openly express disdain for a two-state solution and explicitly call

Conclusion

for continued Israeli control of the West Bank, if not annexation.[31] Hundreds of thousands of Israelis live in the West Bank as Jewish settlers, and the numbers of such settlers, as well as Israeli government investments in the settlements and related infrastructure, continue to grow.

One scholarly or analytical challenge is that it is hard to be sure of the meaning of the negotiating positions of the Israeli government. More specifically, it is hard to differentiate between a government trying to drive a hard bargain (and a harder bargain than other Israeli governments that have set out the details of a possible two-state solution) and a government trying to use specific negotiating points to prevent *any* kind of deal from being possible. Under Netanyahu's premiership since 2009, Israel has suggested that: in any two-state solution, Israel must have a security presence in the Jordan Valley; the Palestinians must recognize Israel as the Jewish State; and the West Bank settlement blocs Israel annexes must include both the settlements of Ariel and Beit El. Even if one sets aside many larger questions, these specific preferences either lead to an agreement on more favourable terms than Israel might once have expected or lead Palestinians to conclude that Israel is simply adding more and more conditions, such that the proposal moves further away from the Palestinian minimum and no solution is ever reached. If the government of Israel and the Palestinian Authority signed an agreement on a two-state solution, that signing would decide this debate. But the absence of an agreement does not offer definitive evidence either way.

Looked at from this vantage point, the problem is twofold. Palestinian nationalism is real, recognized by most of the world community, *and* millions of Palestinians live in the West Bank, Gaza, and Israel. To maintain an Israeli occupation or to pursue partial or full annexation in the face of Palestinian nationalism means a lifelong commitment to military force as the only means by which to suppress Palestinian nationalism and thereby maintain and grow the Israeli presence.[32]

The likely impact is more instability and violence. Even if the goal of using force is to maintain the occupation or push for official Israeli annexation of part or all of the West Bank, calm and quiet seem unlikely long-term outcomes.

Moreover, today, Israel continues to face not only questions across the globe about its legitimacy but also greater support in most countries for the Palestinian cause (though I do not know how deep that support actually goes); it also faces a lack of international recognition of its borders and of its chosen capital, Jerusalem, except by the United States and a handful of small states such as Guatemala. For state members of the international system, both legitimacy and internationally recognized borders within which to operate are basic elements of statehood. So Israel has some of the trappings – the symbols, powerful armed forces, a bustling economy – but is missing key ingredients of legitimacy that an over-reliance on military force has been unable to provide. It is not that these questions are new – though I suspect legitimacy has become more problematic in the post-Oslo years, as it was before Oslo (as evidenced by the United Nations resolution in 1975 that equated Zionism and racism) – but that they remain major challenges for Israel.

If other countries moved to view Israel's indefinite occupation or annexation and a system of unequal rights as legitimate, if all or at least most Arab states sought fully normal relations with Israel, and if Palestinians in the West Bank and Gaza permanently refrained from significant political or violent protest – such as a third intifada – against continued occupation or annexation, such evidence could serve as a counter-example to the central claim of the book. It would suggest that Israel's forceful policy of settlement, annexation, and repression had led to a successful outcome: Israeli status as a legitimate actor in

Conclusion

the international arena. Based on the history of this particular conflict as well as the history of other unresolved claims for national self-determination, I am sceptical that will occur.

Perhaps ties with Saudi Arabia will be one test in terms of force and Israel's national goals. Can Israel maintain its reliance on military force, keep its distance from diplomatic negotiations with the Palestinians, and still move closer to a normal diplomatic relationship with Saudi Arabia or other Gulf Arab countries based on shared, anti-Iranian security interests? Israel and Saudi Arabia have engaged in security cooperation in recent years. Will doing so in any way help Israel address its problems with both global legitimacy and the local conflict with Palestine?

Meanwhile, the Palestinian national movement lacks even more of the basic elements of statehood. It does not have an independent state with recognized borders. Its quasi-state does have international legitimacy in the sense that the majority of countries recognize the State of Palestine but little else in terms of the core elements of statehood.[33] Of late, the reliance on military force has not advanced the Palestinian cause.

For over a decade now, the Palestinian movement has been severely fragmented, with Fatah rule in parts of the West Bank and Hamas rule in much of Gaza. The split also reflects divergent relationships with military force at the highest levels. Fatah is reticent, formally open to a negotiated resolution. Hamas leaders define themselves as the true representatives of the armed struggle against the Israeli occupation. All the recent major confrontations with Israel have been Israel versus Hamas, not Fatah. One has to go back to the second intifada (2000–2005) to find Fatah cadres as a regular part of the forceful confrontations with Israel.

The political result has been two weak players. If united, as is often talked about and agreed upon but never implemented, would the Palestinian national movement be stronger?

Possibly.[34] It is hard to come up with a single national strategy for achieving the goal of independence when the movement is split and the organizations agree on neither the means nor, quite possibly, the ends.

Since 2000, the use of force has not helped the Palestinian cause reach its goal. Hamas and Islamic Jihad have fired rockets and mortars from Gaza into Israel. Hamas has dug tunnels into Israel for launching surprise infiltration and terrorist attacks. Hamas and Israeli soldiers have fought street battles inside Gaza. But the end result has been the continued blockade and isolation of Gaza, not any move toward Palestinian autonomy or independence. Reconstruction and an overall better quality of life for Palestinians in Gaza remain elusive.

Yes, Hamas argued that Israel closed down its Gaza settlements in response to violence instigated by Hamas as well as other groups. But in the meantime, Israel's occupation, itself built upon the exercise of military force, has only deepened in the West Bank; settlements in the West Bank, including East Jerusalem, have expanded virtually non-stop under every Israeli government; and all key resources and access to Gaza are controlled by Israel, with Egypt's help – air, border crossings, buffer zones, sea, water. Palestinian self-determination is a distant prospect. Palestinians in Gaza are sometimes pounded by Israel's military. The Palestinian national movement's fragmentation has been much to the benefit of those Israelis who oppose any kind of national solution to the Palestinian question.

In 2015–2016, a new wave of Palestinian attacks traumatized Israelis. Unlike in the past, most of the attacks did not appear to be orchestrated by organized militants. Rather, individual Palestinians took it upon themselves to stab or run over Israelis. On occasion, the attacks did involve a gun or a bomb. On social media, some Palestinians posted and watched videos of the attacks. Tens of Israelis and hundreds of Palestinians were killed,

Conclusion

most of the latter either in attempted attacks against Israelis or in demonstrations against the occupation.

As noted already, obscured by these strategic decisions are the actual people who pay the price. In an attack in Tel Aviv in June 2016, one of the dead was Professor Michael Feige of Israel's Ben-Gurion University. Among other topics, Feige had critiqued the Israeli settlement movement.[35] 'It is such a cruel fate for a man who devoted his life and career to peace and taught that scholarship has a social purpose, to be felled by indiscriminate hate and terror', noted Sara Hirschhorn, then a lecturer in Israel Studies at Oxford University.[36]

Palestinian independence will not come at the barrel of a gun. The Palestinian use of force has not compelled Israel to withdraw from the vast majority of the West Bank. And it probably never will. But that will not stop at least some Palestinians from trying, whether they call it armed struggle, resistance, or something else.

If force will not get Israel out of the West Bank, and Israel holds the military and territorial advantage, are Palestinians powerless, simply waiting for Israel to change its mind? One thought has been to put pressure on Israel from the outside, thus the Boycott, Divestment, and Sanctions (BDS) movement. The central question is whether the BDS movement could cause Israeli leaders to concede or whether it empowers Israeli opponents of concessions by confirming a deeply rooted Israeli perspective that Israeli Jews must stand strong against a largely anti-Semitic world. Thus far, my impression is that the latter is the case.

Another Palestinian option would be to recognize the futility of force with regard to the West Bank and to woo the Israelis. This runs counter to much Palestinian activity in recent years, whether it is militant (e.g. the second intifada, rockets, tunnels from Gaza into Israel) or political and cultural (e.g. anti-normalization currents, BDS). But what if an unnamed Palestinian, visiting the bereaved family in 2014 as they mourned

Naftali Fraenkel, was correct: 'We believe that only through the hearts of the Jews will our liberation happen'?[37] Or, as Arik Ascherman, then of Rabbis for Human Rights, put it, 'If we are to see the light at the end of the tunnel, we need more people who perceive our common humanity'.[38] Perhaps one academic version of the same sentiment comes from Herbert Kelman, who noted the need for Israelis and Palestinians to develop a transcendent identity that makes room for both nationalisms.[39]

There is a temptation to view such talk as naïve, and it is certainly true that the odds of such talk working may be low. But it is equally if not more naïve to ignore the conflict's historical record and the inherent limitations and shortcomings of military force. Force cannot solve every situation and sometimes force and violence make things much worse.

Or look at it from a different angle: An Israeli says we cannot sign an agreement, certainly one that includes West Bank withdrawal, until Palestinians accept Israel as the Jewish state. Now, in terms of the military balance, there is nothing the Palestinians can do, even if they do not accept Israel as a Jewish state, so this Israeli stipulation is not necessary. A refusal to sign off on Israel's stated identity would not put Israel in jeopardy, given the power differential between the parties. Strength and force helped shape a reality where many Palestinians have come, begrudgingly, to accept a two-state solution that would address some but far from all their historical concerns.

Yet deeper acceptance, and I put Israel's identity in that category, usually comes after a conflict is resolved and the sides interact peacefully for years or perhaps generations. So why would Palestinians even consider some language about accepting Israel as the Jewish state or at least recognizing that the Jewish community has some communal rights in this territory? Because it might be a pathway toward tamping down the fear, opening minds on the other side, and thereby raising the possibility of a

Conclusion

real withdrawal from the West Bank. Palestinians know that for a two-state solution to come about, they have to convince Israel to part with land. But it matters whether they choose to do so with guns or words.

I accept that Palestinian recognition of Israel as a Jewish state is a radical suggestion that could undermine the standing of Palestinian citizens of Israel, the right of return, and other core matters. My assumption, however unfair, is that for Palestinians to shake the Israeli preference for indefinite territorial control may take a radical political step. That said, recognizing the negative impact of policies of force and, as a result, abandoning force do not automatically mean the Palestinian national movement must make major concessions. The future is not simply a Palestinian choice between military force and capitulation on core issues. There is an undefined middle ground of political pathways that might not demand quite this level of Palestinian concession. So whether a radical or mild concession is needed, my central claim is that there are other constructive pathways once force is set aside.

Thus far, I have assumed a two-state solution is still an option. Is it? I'm not so sure. Israel's settlement project has gone on for over fifty years now and hundreds of thousands of Israeli Jews live in the West Bank. Increasingly, the only stable resolution might be Palestinians, whether they live in Gaza, Israel, or the West Bank, having equal rights within a single state. But whether the preferred resolution is one state or two, the fundamental shortcomings of relying on force and coercion will not change.

Arabs, Israelis, and Palestinians have much experience with the use and costs of military force, whether as the initiator or as the target. But given how high those costs have become, I humbly suggest it is time for societal reassessments.

NOTES

Notes to chapter 1

1 Tolan, *The Lemon Tree*, 123.
2 Dayan, 'Moshe Dayan's eulogy for Roi Rutenberg', 19 April 1956.
3 I use the word 'dominant' in order to make a careful distinction between most of the time ('dominant') and all the time (for which I might have used 'exclusive' or 'only'). I intentionally leave room for other ideas that have sometimes surfaced during the conflict, especially a preference for negotiations and concessions. Sometimes the same leader or organization will shift from one idea to another.
4 For example: Bickerton and Klausner, *A History of the Arab–Israeli Conflict*; Hirst, *The Gun and the Olive Branch*; Khouri, *The Arab–Israeli Dilemma*; Lesch, *The Arab–Israeli Conflict*; Morris, *Righteous Victims*; Pappe, *A History of Modern Palestine*; Sachar, *A History of Israel*; Said Aly, Feldman, and Shikaki, *Arabs and Israelis*; Shlaim, *The Iron Wall*; Smith, *Palestine and the Arab–Israeli Conflict*; Tessler, *A History of the Israeli–Palestinian Conflict* (2009).
5 Skocpol, *States and Social Revolutions*, xi.
6 Works I found especially helpful include Legro, *Rethinking the World*; Autesserre, 'Dangerous tales'; Goldstein and Keohane, *Ideas and Foreign Policy*; Krebs, *Narrative and the Making of US National Security*. Krebs and others quote a line from Barry Posen that is meaningful as well: grand strategy is 'a state's theory about how it can best "cause" security for itself'. Posen, *The Sources of Military Doctrine*, 13.
7 Legro, *Rethinking the World*.
8 See also Johnston, 'Thinking about strategic culture'; and Johnston,

Cultural Realism. My goal is not to sort out differences in terminology and the usage of words like 'ideas', 'norms', 'narratives', 'rhetoric', and 'beliefs'.

9   On narratives, see Krebs, *Narrative and the Making of US National Security*. On rhetoric, see Stuckey, *Defining Americans*. On discourses, see Hansen, *Security as Practice*, and McDonald, 'Discourses of climate security'.
10 Finlayson and Martin, '"It ain't what you say..."', 449–450.
11 Wesley, 'Qualitative document analysis'.
12 For examples, see Rowland and Jones, 'Reagan's strategy for the Cold War and the Evil Empire address'; and Jones and Rowland, 'Redefining the proper role of government'. For opposition to relying upon one text, see Milliken, 'The study of discourse in international relations', 233.
13 To use Gerring's terms, the cases straddle his study across units and case study of one unit, depending how one defines the unit here. If the unit is the Arab–Israeli conflict, this book offers selections about one unit. If each government or actor is thought of as a separate unit, it is a study across units. See Gerring, 'What is a case study and what is it good for?' On case studies, see also George and Bennett, *Case Studies and Theory Development*, and Van Evera, *Guide to Methods*.
14 The cases are also of different lengths. For an example of that, see Lawrence, 'Triggering nationalist violence'.
15 Legro, *Rethinking the World*, 16.
16 Coercive diplomacy is a 'strategy with a degree of limited coercion. Carrots may be included, but, by definition, so too are sticks. The sticks can include economic sanctions as well as military force.' When I am writing about diplomacy in this book, I am focusing on persuasive efforts and organized negotiations, not coercive diplomacy. I consider coercive diplomacy more on the forceful side of the ledger, though analytically it falls short of brute force. Jentleson, *Coercive Diplomacy*, 1. See also Art and Cronin, *The United States and Coercive Diplomacy*.
17 Several categories and details are drawn from Gerner et al., 'The creation of CAMEO'" 28; and Schrodt, *CAMEO: Conflict and Mediation Event Observations Event*. See also Priebe, 'Fear and frustration'.
18 Waltz, *Theory of International Politics*, 186.
19 Keohane and Nye, *Power and Interdependence*, 23–24.
20 Lauren, Craig, and George, *Force and Statecraft*, xiii.
21 In this book, then, I disagree with Thrall, *The Only Language They Understand*.

22 Blainey, *The Causes of War*, 112–114, 118. For a useful survey on the question of the change from war to peace and a preferred solution based on economic crises and domestic politics, see Clary, 'The politics of peace'.
23 Kagan, 'America's dangerous aversion to conflict'.
24 On distinctions between power and influence, see Pressman, 'Power without influence'.
25 Jervis, *Perception and Misperception in International Politics*. See also Snyder, '"Prisoner's dilemma"'.
26 Works on balancing and bandwagoning include Labs, 'Do weak states bandwagon?'; Powell, *In the Shadow of Power*; Schroeder, 'Historical reality vs. neo-realist theory', especially 117–124; Schweller, 'Bandwagoning for profit'; Snyder, *Alliance Politics*; Walt, *The Origins of Alliances*; Waltz, *Theory of International Politics*; and Waltz, 'The origins of war in neorealist theory'.
27 Mearsheimer, 'Hans Morgenthau and the Iraq war'.
28 The White House, 'Vice president speaks at VFW 103rd National Convention', 26 August 2002.
29 Lupovici, *The Power of Deterrence*, 55. On the centrality and meaning of Israeli deterrence, see also Freilich, *Israeli National Security*, 23, 166–174.
30 Milliken, 'The study of discourse in international relations', 235, highlights the utility of others' works on a similar topic serving as 'external checks'. Given some important overlap in the works, I see Lupovici's book as a successful external check. Another excellent work is Del Sarto, *Israel Under Siege*.
31 As Frederick the Great, the eighteenth-century Prussian monarch, said, 'diplomacy without armaments is like music without instruments'. Blainey, *The Causes of War*, 108.
32 'Remarks of President Carter, President Anwar al-Sadat of Egypt, and Prime Minister Menahem Begin of Israel at the Egyptian–Israeli peace treaty signing ceremony'; 'Israeli PM Rabin's speech at the signing of the Declaration of Principles (1993)'; 'PLO Chairman Arafat's speech at the signing of the Declaration of Principles (1993)'.
33 There is also a third idea, beyond an emphasis on military force or on negotiations. A country might reject both negotiations and military force and generally isolate itself from international affairs. Yet the idea of isolationism or hiding is less plausible today, especially in the Arab–Israeli realm, because the world is interconnected and even a country like North Korea finds itself with economic and political relations in the international sphere.

Notes to chapter 2

34 I am open to softer language, such as that different ideas make certain policies more or less likely.
35 Milliken, 'The study of discourse in international relations', 236.
36 A concern I do not address is whether a reliance on force makes the securitization of seemingly non-security issues that much easier. Security talk becomes the master rationale for justifying all kinds of policies and ruling others out. See Buzan, Wæver, and de Wilde, *Security*.
37 One exception is cases of total victory such as the Allied victory over Germany and Japan in World War II.
38 Walt, *The Origins of Alliances*.
39 Jervis, *Perception and Misperception in International Politics*.
40 Roe, 'Which security dilemma?'
41 Though his article is on a different topic, Anshel Pfeffer, a *Ha'aretz* reporter, makes this point as well: 'Actually the first two generations of Israelis won already in 1967, or at the latest in 1973, when they proved once and for all that our neighbors could not dislodge us'. Pfeffer, 'Sending our sons into battle'.
42 Freilich, *Israeli National Security*, 337.

Notes to chapter 2

1 McGeough, *Kill Khalid*, 235.
2 Barak quoted in Rifkind, 'A route to resolution'.
3 'Barak: In the Middle East, there is no mercy for the weak'.
4 Gavron, *Almost Dead*, 62, 95.
5 General treatments of Israel's approach include: Atzili and Pearlman, 'Triadic deterrence'; Freilich, *Israeli National Security*; Inbar, *Israel's National Security*; Lustick, 'Abandoning the iron wall'; Maoz, *Defending the Holy Land*; Mor, 'Strategic beliefs and the formation of enduring international rivalries', 315–322; Rodman, 'Israel's national security doctrine'; and Yaniv, *Deterrence Without the Bomb*. Moshe Sharett, Israel's second prime minister, succinctly summarized this school of thought in a 1957 speech – see Caplan, 'The "Sharettist option" revisited', 68–69.
6 Jabotinsky, 'The iron wall'. Jabotinsky rejected the idea of negotiating right away with the Arabs: 'Yet we keep spoiling our own case, by talking about "agreement" which means telling the [British] Mandatory Government that the important thing is not the iron wall, but discussions'.

7 Shimoni, *The Zionist Ideology*, 384. Zeev Maoz concurs that 'iron wall' thinking was the core assumption of the Israeli right and left. Maoz, *Defending the Holy Land*, 9. Maoz also notes Israeli reliance on the sword and calls Israel 'trigger happy' (6, 9, 388, 479, 552, 558).
8 Ben-Gurion also said: 'The Arab states refused to recognize Israel's right to exist, and awaited an opportunity to destroy it. Although peace was Israel's ultimate objective, this would remain unattainable until the Arabs were unequivocably convinced of the futility of their effort.' Bar-Siman-Tov, 'Ben-Gurion and Sharett', 330. See also Shlaim, *The Iron Wall*.
9 Prittie, *Israel*, 171.
10 Stein and Tanter, *Rational Decision-Making*, 181; and Weizman, *On Eagles' Wings*, 213–214.
11 Segev, *1967*, 203, 205, 206, and 208.
12 Avineri, *Israel Without Zionists*, 134, as cited in Hirst, *The Gun and the Olive Branch*, 298.
13 Benn, 'Operation Pillar of Defense'. Aluf Benn, a *Ha'aretz* journalist, called Dayan's original speech 'a seminal text of Israeli nationalism, perhaps the most important of all; a kind of Israeli Gettysburg Address'. See also Shalev, 'Moshe Dayan's enduring Gaza eulogy'.
14 Moshe Brilliant, 'Israel's policy of reprisals', *Harper's Magazine*, March 1955, 180–182, quoted in Hirst, *The Gun and the Olive Branch*, 324.
15 Oron, 'An open letter to Jewish Americans'.
16 Mann, *Incoherent Empire*, 90.
17 Sharon, 'A decisive conclusion is necessary'.
18 Ibish, 'The Sharon doctrine'; Shlaim, '"Man of Peace"?'
19 Shavit, *My Promised Land*, 235.
20 Shilon, 'There are situations that require the use of physical force'.
21 El-Amir, 'Living by the sword'.
22 Israel Defense Forces, *Deterring Terror*, 25. Emphasis in original.
23 Peck, 'The Israeli left needs to rethink its attitude toward settlers'.
24 Lubell, 'Netanyahu says no Palestinian state'. See also David Horovitz, who said that Netanyahu, in a press conference, 'made explicitly clear that he could *never, ever,* countenance a fully sovereign Palestinian state in the West Bank'. Horovitz, 'Netanyahu finally speaks his mind'. Emphasis in original.
25 'Full text of Netanyahu's foreign policy speech at Bar Ilan'.
26 Contrast parts of that list with the Israeli left-wing position that Jerusalem could serve as the capital of Israel and of Palestine; that

Notes to chapter 2

Israel must withdraw from some territory, including the vast majority of the West Bank, in a two-state solution; and that a small number of Palestinian refugees might be able to move to Israel.
27 See Anziska, *Preventing Palestine*.
28 Del Sarto, *Israel Under Siege*, 98.
29 Breznitz, 'Innovation-based industrial policy in emerging economies?'; and Breznitz, 'Collaborative public space in a national innovation system'.
30 Harkabi, 'The Palestinians in the Israel–Arab conflict', 16–17.
31 Cited in Tessler, *A History of the Israeli–Palestinian Conflict* (1994), 409.
32 Harkabi, 'The Palestinians in the Israel–Arab conflict', 18.
33 *Our Palestine (Falastinuna)* [a Fatah publication], September 1964, p. 3, as cited in Hirst, *The Gun and the Olive Branch*, 402.
34 *Our Palestine (Falastinuna)*, September, 1964, p. 3 as cited in Hirst, *The Gun and the Olive Branch*, 402.
35 PFLP inaugural statement, 11 December 1967, as cited in Hirst, *The Gun and the Olive Branch*, 402.
36 Ben Caspit, interview with Marwan Barghouti in *Ma'ariv*, 9 November 2001, reprinted in Smith, *Palestine and the Arab–Israeli Conflict*, 525.
37 Emphasis in original. McGeough, *Kill Khalid*, 104. On Hamas over the decades, including challenges it faced in relying upon military means, see Baconi, *Hamas Contained*.
38 In 2005, a Hamas committee worked on revisions to the charter but they were shelved after the Hamas victory in the 2006 Palestinian parliamentary elections. McGeough, *Kill Khalid*, 412. For an argument that the Hamas charter is outdated, see Charrett, 'Understanding Hamas'. For an argument on the continuing centrality of force to Hamas's policy, see Litvak, '"Martyrdom is Life"'. Whereas Litvak emphasizes Hamas's religious-ideological motivations, Hroub emphasizes Hamas's focus on ending the Israeli occupation and regaining Palestinian land. Hroub, *Hamas: Political Thought and Practice*, 43–44.
39 'Hamas question & answer'.
40 McGeough, *Kill Khalid*, 329, 412. The brackets are in the McGeough text.
41 Zimmerman, 'The origins of the Fedayeen', 112.
42 'Nasser says he'll "get rid" of Israel'.
43 Geyelin, 'Mideast danger'.
44 'Angry Nasser hurls "liar" charge at Bonn'.
45 'Two leaders cast doubt on the talks'. Whether, over the course of his

rule, Nasser started to think there was a political pathway for resolving the Arab–Israeli conflict is an open question, but either way he did not openly and publicly embrace the idea of negotiations over the idea of military force. See Smith, 'They call him El Rayis'; and Yahel, 'Covert diplomacy between Israel and Egypt'.

46 International Crisis Group, 'Gaza's unfinished business', 6.
47 Goren, 'Livni: We will not allow thugs to rule the Middle East'.
48 On 9 December 1987, at the start of the first intifada, the founders of Hamas issued the first communiqué in the name of the Islamic Resistance Movement (Hamas). In August 1988, Hamas issued its charter. Hroub prefers the 1987 date for marking the founding of Hamas. Hroub, *Hamas: Political Thought and Practice*, 39–40.
49 Roy, *Hamas and Civil Society in Gaza*, 24, 71–73. Roy's examples include allowing Islamists to organize, funnelling money to mosques, and maintaining a policy of non-interference.
50 Higgins, 'How Israel helped to spawn Hamas'. Andrew Higgins, a reporter with the *Wall Street Journal*, spoke with several former Israeli officials who interacted with Hamas and its precursors. See also Tharoor, 'How Israel helped create Hamas'.
51 Hroub, *Hamas: Political Thought and Practice*, 35–36. Roy also argues that the embrace of armed struggle was partly a reaction to the PLO's defeat in and exile from Lebanon in 1982. In 1983, Sheikh Yassin created 'two paramilitary wings' (Roy, *Hamas and Civil Society in Gaza*, 24). This detail is further evidence for the security damage done to Israel by its 1982 invasion of Lebanon.
52 See Tenenbaum and Eiran, 'Israeli settlement activity in the West Bank and Gaza'; and Sasley and Sucharov, 'Resettling the West Bank settlers'.
53 Almog, 'Lessons of the Gaza security fence for the West Bank'.
54 Katz, 'Analysis: Shock, awe … and deception'.
55 Sofer, 'Shin Bet: Hamas feels existential threat'.
56 McCarthy, 'Israel rejects ceasefire'.
57 'Gaza portrayed'.
58 Goren, 'Livni: We will not allow thugs to rule the Middle East'.
59 Barzak and Friedman, 'Israel says Gaza assault "war to the bitter end"'.
60 Sofer, 'Shin Bet: Hamas feels existential threat'.
61 Sofer, 'Shin Bet: Hamas feels existential threat'.
62 Federman, 'Analysis: Israel tries to excise bitter memories'.
63 Greeberg, 'Report: IDF divides Gaza Strip'.
64 Makovsky quoted in Myers, 'The new meaning'.

Notes to chapter 2

65 Hersh, 'Syria calling'.
66 Ben-Yishai, 'Preventing a "divine victory"'.
67 Myers, 'The new meaning of an old battle in the Mideast'.
68 Bowen, 'For as long as both sides think they can win'.
69 Segev, 'Who won?' For a similar perspective on the 2014 clash between Hamas and Israel, see Bar'el, 'Shock-and-awe'.
70 Friedman, 'Israel's goals in Gaza?' See also Harel and Issacharoff, 'Postmortem'. They offer qualified support of Friedman's argument.
71 Rabbani, 'Birth pangs of a new Palestine'; and International Crisis Group, 'Ending the war in Gaza', 10.
72 London, 'The Dahiya strategy'.
73 International Crisis Group, 'Gaza's unfinished business'. The IDF's estimate was 1,166 Palestinians killed – see Lappin, 'IDF releases Cast Lead casualty numbers'.
74 International Crisis Group, 'Ending the war in Gaza', 7.
75 The International Crisis Group cited its own interviews, the Gaza education ministry, figures from the United Nations Development Programme, and the Palestinian Bureau of Statistics. International Crisis Group, 'Gaza's unfinished business', 1.
76 International Crisis Group, 'Gaza's unfinished business', 2–3, 7.
77 'IAF hits Hamas ammo stocks, tunnels'; and Barzak and Friedman, 'Israel says Gaza assault "war to the bitter end"'.
78 Watzman, 'No happy endings in Gaza'. See also Daniel Levy of the New America Foundation as quoted in Myers, 'The new meaning of an old battle in the Mideast'.
79 Alpher, 'Now stop starving the Gazans'.
80 'A big shudder on the wing'.
81 Atallah and Levy, 'Rewrite the script'.
82 'Gaza: the rights and wrongs'.
83 Oren and Halevi, 'Palestinians need Israel to win'.
84 Benhorin, 'UN chief to Olmert'.
85 Witte, 'Israel presses on with Gaza strikes'.
86 He wrote several op-eds, including Grossman, 'Fight fire with a cease-fire'.
87 Cited in Gazzar and Lefkovits, 'Tibi protests Israeli "war crime"'.
88 'A big shudder on the wing'.
89 Gordon, 'What is Israel's goal?'
90 Watzman, 'No happy endings in Gaza'.
91 Levy, 'The IAF, bullies of the clear blue skies'.
92 Gordon, 'What is Israel's goal?'

Notes to chapter 2

93 Quoted in Schneider, 'Israel anticipated a stronger Hamas in Gaza war'.
94 International Crisis Group, 'Gaza's unfinished business', 6.
95 Rubin, 'The region: Hamas's strategy'.
96 International Crisis Group, 'Ending the war in Gaza', 12.
97 Associated Press and Deutsche Presse-Agentur, 'Hamas: Gaza will become graveyard'.
98 Quoted in El-Khodary and Bronner, 'Israeli Gaza strike kills more than 225'.
99 'Israel kills at least 225 in Gaza'.
100 Harel and Ravid, 'After IAF strike kills at least 230 in Gaza'. The third intifada never arrived.
101 Harel and Ravid, 'After IAF strike kills at least 230 in Gaza'.
102 'Israel kills at least 225 in Gaza'.
103 Barzak and Keyser, 'Diplomats seek truce as Gaza's civilian toll rises'.
104 Mahdawi, 'Nasrallah condemns Israeli assault'.
105 Burston, 'Gaza 2009'.
106 International Crisis Group, 'Ending the war in Gaza', 17, 18.
107 Ashton, *King Hussein of Jordan*, 117–119.
108 Morris, *Righteous Victims*, 318.
109 Morris, *Righteous Victims*, 318, 327. See also Lesch, *The Arab–Israeli Conflict*, 212; and Tessler, *A History of the Israeli–Palestinian Conflict* (1994), 397.
110 Ashton, *King Hussein of Jordan*, 120.
111 Tessler, *A History of the Israeli–Palestinian Conflict* (1994), 401–402.
112 Tessler, *A History of the Israeli–Palestinian Conflict* (1994), 369.
113 Lesch, *The Arab–Israeli Conflict*, 214.
114 Dessouki, 'The new Arab political order', 336. For Israeli views just after the war that were sceptical that the war would change Arab aims, see Kolatt, 'The chances for peace and the right to a homeland", 74–75; and Avineri, 'The Palestinians and Israel', 134. Avineri contended that the war had undermined the claim that force produces concessions: 'nor did the prowess of the Israeli armed forces cow them into submission. Those Israelis who in the past had been accustomed to assert that the only language the Arabs understand is the language of force, proved to be as wrong as ever.'
115 Sources that come to a similar conclusion include Almog, 'Cumulative deterrence and the war on terrorism', 10–14; Bar-Siman-Tov, 'The Arab–Israeli conflict', 83; Lustick, 'To build and to be built by'; and Shlaim, *The Iron Wall*. For a source that notes

non-military factors as well, see Tira, 'In search of the Holy Grail', 41.
116 Morris, *Righteous Victims*, 345–346.
117 Khouri, *The Arab–Israeli Dilemma*, 313. See also Sela, *The Decline of the Arab–Israeli Conflict*; and Gorenberg, *The Accidental Empire*, 109. Egypt lacked the military means to recapture its territory. See Greffenius, 'Foreign policy stabilization and the Camp David Accords', 218.
118 Anwar Sadat's interview in the newspaper *al-Ahram* (Egypt), 3 July 1975, as cited in Sela, 'Politics, identity and peacemaking', 61.
119 el-Sadat, *In Search of Identity*, 279–280.
120 Insight Team of the London Sunday Times, *The Yom Kippur War*, 62.
121 Sela, *The Decline of the Arab–Israeli Conflict*, 149; see also Ajami, 'The end of pan-Arabism', 368.
122 Sela, *The Decline of the Arab–Israeli Conflict*, 109. On Sadat specifically, see Sela, *The Decline of the Arab–Israeli Conflict*, 135, 141, 149. See also Telhami, *Power and Leadership in International Bargaining*; and Haber, 'Thank you, Egypt'.
123 Bar-Siman-Tov, 'The Arab–Israeli conflict', 84; and Harkabi, *Arab Strategies and Israel's Response*, 20–21. One can read Harkabi struggling to determine whether Arab voices focused on the 1967 territories – and not Israeli existence – are a sign of genuine change or simply a new façade for the same old rejectionism. See Harkabi, *Arab Strategies and Israel's Response*, 62–63.
124 el-Sadat, 'Where Egypt stands', 119, 123.
125 I disagree here with Abadi, 'Egypt's policy towards Israel', 169.
126 Ismail Fahmy, *Negotiating for Peace in the Middle East* (London: Croom Helm, 1983), 282, as cited in Safty, 'Sadat's negotiations with the United States and Israel', 292.
127 el-Shazly, *The Crossing of the Suez*, 27. Sadat wanted limited war according to Stein, *Heroic Diplomacy*, 72.
128 el-Shazly, *The Crossing of the Suez*, 106.
129 Hybel, *The Logic of Surprise in International Conflict*, 39; see also Jervis, Lebow, and Stein, *Psychology and Deterrence*.
130 El-Gamasy, *The October War*, 167–168.
131 See Drysdale and Hinnebusch, *Syria and the Middle East Peace Process*, 108; and Charles Wakebridge, 'The Syrian side of the hill', *Military Review* 56:2 (1976), 27, as cited in Slater, 'Lost opportunities for peace', 93–94.

Notes to chapter 2

132 Bar-Siman-Tov, 'The Arab–Israeli conflict', 86.
133 Pressman, 'Mediation, domestic politics, and the Israeli–Syrian negotiations'.
134 Harkabi, 'The Palestinians in the Israel–Arab conflict', 11.
135 Avineri, 'Introduction', xx, and see also p. xxiii; Mansour, 'Palestine and the search for a new golden age', 97; and Avineri, 'The Palestinians and Israel', 135 and 149. Shamir suggested that 'a considerable number' of West Bank Palestinians favoured recognition of Israel as a 'reality' and the establishment of peace as a direct result of the 1967 war. Shamir, 'The myth of Arab intransigence', 28.
136 Farsoun with Zacharia, *Palestine and the Palestinians*, 202.
137 Buttu, 'The two-state solution', 183.
138 Libya did not support the resolution. For the Fez text, see http://www.mideastweb.org/fahd_fez_plan.htm (accessed 24 January 2020).
139 Farsoun with Zacharia, *Palestine and the Palestinians*, 203.
140 Farsoun with Zacharia, *Palestine and the Palestinians*, 205–206.
141 Pressman, 'Visions in Collision'.
142 Quoted in Tolan, *The Lemon Tree*, 213.
143 Baumgarten, 'The three faces/phases of Palestinian nationalism', 43, and see also 35–36. Carolin Goerzig suggested a similar way of thinking about the intent of the Quartet's conditions for Hamas after Hamas's election in 2006: 'Hamas needs to be weakened in order to moderate it'. Goerzig rejected this approach and contended that 'it is through pressure that negotiation and moderation become precisely less rational'. The Quartet was composed of the European Union, Russia, the United Nations and the United States. Goerzig, 'Engaging Hamas'.
144 Gorenberg, 'The missing Mahatma', 28.
145 'Israel declines to study Rabin tie to beatings'.
146 Gorenberg, 'The missing Mahatma', 27.
147 Another example is the 1973 war, which affected Israeli thinking especially vis-à-vis Egypt. The war 'proved that limited war can be an instrument to force Israel to withdraw and comply with further Arab demands'. Harkabi, *Arab Strategies and Israel's Response*, 19.
148 Tessler, 'The intifada and political discourse in Israel', 50. See also Farsoun with Zacharia, *Palestine and the Palestinians*, 205, 299; and Levinson, '25 years on'.
149 Schiff and Ya'ari, *Intifada*, 79.
150 Peretz, 'Intifadeh', 975.

151 Raz, *The Bride and the Dowry*, 282.
152 Tessler, 'The intifada and political discourse in Israel', 45, 54–55; and Peretz, 'Intifadeh', 976, 979.
153 Aronoff, 'The Labor Party and the intifada', 336.
154 Sachar, *A History of Israel*, 965.
155 Arian, 'Israeli public opinion and the intifada', 280; Aronoff, 'The Labor Party and the intifada', 328; and Tessler, 'The intifada and political discourse in Israel', 44, 61.
156 Tessler, 'The intifada and political discourse in Israel', 49, 51.
157 Arian, 'Israeli public opinion and the intifada', 281; Gorenberg, 'The missing Mahatma', 27; and Schiff and Ya'ari, *Intifada*, 330. Aharoni does not emphasize the Israeli political shift as much, but he accepts the intifada opened the door to negotiations. Aharoni, 'The Palestinian Intifada', 228–229. See also Dowty, 'Despair is not enough', 14.
158 Tessler, 'The intifada and political discourse in Israel', 53–54, 56.
159 Peretz, *Intifada*, 155.
160 Pressman, 'Visions in collision'.
161 Quoted in Noe, 'Nasrallah's turn'. As Noe pointed out, Nasrallah's choice of words was a bit peculiar because rocket attacks were a Hezbollah tactic.
162 McGeough, *Kill Khalid*, 262.
163 'Hamas question & answer'. See also Dajani, 'Lessons from the Gaza disengagement'.
164 Palestinian Center for Policy and Survey Research, 'Public opinion poll # 16'.
165 Shikaki, 'Shikaki: Since Israeli withdrawal from Gaza'.
166 Kessler, 'Unintended consequences pose risks for Mideast policy'.
167 Sela, 'Ya'alon: disengagement empowered Hamas'.
168 In an interview, Netanyahu later essentially recanted his support for two states: 'there cannot be a situation, under any agreement, in which we relinquish security control of the territory west of the River Jordan'. That does not comport with a sovereign Palestinian state. See Horovitz, 'Netanyahu finally speaks his mind'.

Notes to chapter 3

1 Walsh and Hoagland, 'Sadat and Begin sign treaty'.
2 For a similar judgement, see Quandt, 'Camp David and peacemaking in the Middle East', 359.

3 Maoz made a similar argument in *Defending the Holy Land*, 547, 551. Maoz rejected the idea that any of Israel's 'major military encounters ... led to a political outcome that made Israel more secure than it had been before their outbreak' (552–553).
4 'Address by PM Netanyahu special Knesset session marking the 40th anniversary of the Yom Kippur War'. See also Shilon, 'There are situations that require the use of physical force'.
5 See Jakobsen, 'Pushing the limits of military coercion theory', 164–165. Jakobsen cites the following works: Barry M. Blechman and Stephen S. Kaplan, *Force Without War* (Washington, DC: Brookings Institution, 1978), 517; Patrick C. Bratton, 'When is coercion successful? And why can't we agree on it?', *Naval War College Review* 58:3 (2005), 99–120 at 115; Alexander L. George, 'The need for influence theory and actor-specific behavioral models of adversaries', *Comparative Strategy* 22:5 (2003), 463–487; Alexander L. George, David K. Hall, and William E. Simons, *The Limits of Coercive Diplomacy* (Boston: Little, Brown, 1971), 18; and Alexander H. Montgomery, 'Social action, rogue reaction: U.S. post-cold war counterproliferation strategies', unpublished doctoral dissertation (Stanford University, 2005), 153.
6 Kupchan, *How Enemies Become Friends*; and Stute, 'Oz: "Lose–lose situation for Israel"'. Heradstveit suggests that we need to focus on addressing the conflicting *interests* and only after that expect any significant changes in *beliefs* about the adversary. Heradstveit, *The Arab–Israeli Conflict*, 135. See also Miller, 'When and how regions become peaceful'; and Miller, *States, Nations, and the Great Powers*.
7 Nepstad, 'Nonviolent civil resistance and social movements'.
8 Waage, 'The winner takes all'.
9 On the role of the United States, see Saunders, 'We need a larger theory of negotiation', 251.
10 Kriesberg, 'Timing and the initiation of de-escalation moves', 383. After the Accords were agreed upon, one of Carter's first phone calls was to his predecessor, Gerald Ford. Carter, *Keeping Faith*, 401. Sheehan, 'How Kissinger did it', 43.
11 Spiegel, *The Other Arab–Israeli Conflict*, 312.
12 Spiegel, *The Other Arab–Israeli Conflict*, 314.
13 Sheehan, 'How Kissinger did it', 14, 15.
14 Miller, *The Much Too Promised Land*, 40 and 156. See also Mandell, 'Anatomy of a confidence-building regime', 220–221.
15 Quandt, *Peace Process*, 172.

Notes to chapter 3

16 Quandt, *Peace Process*, 173. See also Khouri, *The Arab–Israeli Dilemma*, 385; Chada, *Paradox of Power*, 54; Sheehan, 'How Kissinger did it', 25; and Spiegel, *The Other Arab–Israeli Conflict*, 313.
17 Mandell and Tomlin, 'Mediation in the development of norms to manage conflict', 53.
18 Quandt, *Peace Process*, 164, 166. See also Ford, *A Time to Heal*, 238–241, 277–283, 298–300. The Ford quotation is from p. 299.
19 See https://history.state.gov/historicaldocuments/frus1969-76v26/d226 (accessed 24 January 2020).
20 Miller, *The Much Too Promised Land*, 157.
21 Quandt, *Peace Process*, 189–190. See also Jensehaugen, *Arab–Israeli Diplomacy Under Carter*.
22 Begin did, however, privately promise Moshe Dayan that Israel would not annex the West Bank as a condition of Dayan accepting the job of foreign minister. Stein, *Heroic Diplomacy*, 23.
23 Technically the 1969 platform was of Gahal, a predecessor to Likud. Dishon, *Middle East Record*, 551.
24 See https://en.idi.org.il/israeli-elections-and-parties/elections/1973 (accessed 24 January 2020) (in Hebrew; translations in text by the author), p. 2. See also Torgovnik, 'The election campaign'.
25 See Azkin, 'The Likud'.
26 Shamir, 'Israel: the conceptual approach to peace', 244.
27 Lorch, *Major Knesset Debates 1948–1981, Volume 5*, 1968.
28 Lorch, *Major Knesset Debates 1948–1981, Volume 5*, 1980.
29 For examples, see Begin's comments during Knesset debates on 20 December 1973 and 21 September 1976 in Lorch, *Major Knesset Debates 1948–1981, Volume 5*, 1852, 2043. For more on Begin's views as prime minister, see Pressman, 'Explaining the Carter administration's Israeli–Palestinian solution', 1117–1147.
30 Stein, *Heroic Diplomacy*, 26, 243. See also Anziska, *Preventing Palestine*, 63–65, who notes that once Begin was prime minister, he privately indicated to Carter on 13 July 1977 'a clear willingness to withdraw forces substantially in the Sinai as part of a peace deal with Egypt'.
31 Yaniv and Pascal, 'Doves, hawks, and other birds of a feather'.
32 Stein, *Heroic Diplomacy*, 256.
33 Meital, *Egypt's Struggle for Peace*, 162; Cornut, 'The Moroccan connection'; and Safty, 'Sadat's negotiations with the United States and Israel', 291. See also Anziska, *Preventing Palestine*, 75, and Jensehaugen, *Arab–Israeli Diplomacy*, 84.
34 Stein, *Heroic Diplomacy*, 202, 215, 217.

Notes to chapter 3

35 For other examples among top Egyptians, see the reference to General Gamasy on p. 288 of Safty, 'Sadat's negotiations with the United States and Israel: from Sinai to Camp David'; and Foreign Minister Mohamed Kamel on pp. 476–478 in Safty, 'Sadat's negotiations with the United States and Israel: Camp David and Blair House'.
36 Stein, *Heroic Diplomacy*, 13, 208, 221–223.
37 el-Sadat, *Those I Have Known*, 104, 106, 107.
38 Gwertzman, 'Sadat seeks Israeli invitation'. See also Stein, *Heroic Diplomacy*, 9.
39 Israel State Archives, '"No More War"'.
40 Stein, 'Continuity and change in Egyptian–Israeli relations', 301.
41 Stein, *Heroic Diplomacy*, 64.
42 Farrell, 'Parliament agrees'. See also Stein, *Heroic Diplomacy*, 223.
43 Stein, *Heroic Diplomacy*, 223–224.
44 Sadat's speech to People's Assembly, 9 November 1977, https://sadat.umd.edu/resources/presidential-speeches (accessed 24 January 2020), 43. For similar phrasing, see also 47, 49, and 50–51.
45 Pitch, *Peace* (unpaginated).
46 Farrell, 'Parliament agrees'.
47 Farrell, 'Applause at airport'.
48 Abadi, 'Egypt's policy towards Israel', 170.
49 Stein, *Heroic Diplomacy*, 227–228. See also Stein's own view on 264.
50 Indyk, *Innocent Abroad*, 28, 87, 252, 257; Miller, *The Much Too Promised Land*, 297.
51 On Begin, see Steinberg and Rubinovitz, *Menachem Begin*.
52 Stein, 'Continuity and change in Egyptian--Israeli relations', 302.
53 Stein, *Heroic Diplomacy*, 233.
54 The peace treaty is reproduced in full at http://www.bitterlemons.org/docs/1979.html (accessed 9 January 2020).
55 Stein, *Heroic Diplomacy*, 257; Kelman, 'Acknowledging the other's nationhood', 21; and Telhami, 'From Camp David to Wye', 382. Another important moment was at the Blair House talks in October 1978.
56 Cluverius, interviewed by Charles Stuart Kennedy. See also Stein, *Heroic Diplomacy*, 29.
57 Stein, *Heroic Diplomacy*, 24. Stein agrees on 45, 252.
58 Miller, *The Much Too Promised Land*, 159, 172, 175.
59 Quandt, *Peace Process*, 241. For an account more critical of Carter that concluded he relied on American political power to compel a deal, see Princen, 'Camp David'.

Notes to chapter 3

60 Mandell and Tomlin, 'Mediation in the development of norms to manage conflict', 54.
61 Sobelman, 'Israel approves more Egyptian troops in Sinai'.
62 Bar-Siman-Tov, 'Israel–Egypt peace', 224–226.
63 Quandt, *Peace Process*, 339. See also 327, 330–332, 335–336, 337–338, 373, 375, 376.
64 For a much more detailed discussion of US-mediated Israel–Syria talks, see Pressman, 'Mediation, domestic politics, and the Israeli–Syrian negotiations'.
65 Olmert, 'The time has come to say these things'.
66 Stein, 'Continuity and change in Egyptian–Israeli relations', 303.
67 Rudoren, 'Clinton sees opportunity as well as uncertainty in Middle East'.
68 Dana and Malsin, 'Regime change in Egypt further tangles political ties with Israel'.
69 Dana and Malsin, 'Regime change in Egypt further tangles political ties with Israel'.
70 'Egyptians protest Hebrew in curriculum'.
71 Bar-Siman-Tov, 'Israel–Egypt peace', 221.
72 Lesch, 'Egyptian–Israeli relations', 72, 77.
73 Lesch, 'Egyptian–Israeli relations', 66, 76; and Stein, 'Continuity and change in Egyptian–Israeli relations', 303–304.
74 Gerges, 'Egyptian–Israeli relations turn sour', 74.
75 Lesch, 'Egyptian–Israeli relations', 69.
76 On the general situation in Sinai after Mubarak, see Londoño, 'In Egypt's Sinai desert'.
77 Awartani and Kleiman, 'Economic interactions among participants in the Middle East peace process', 221, 228.
78 Cohen and Rabinovitch, 'Egyptian firm to buy $15 billion of Israeli natural gas'.
79 Stein, 'Continuity and change in Egyptian–Israeli relations', 306.
80 Lesch, 'Egyptian–Israeli relations', 63, 74.
81 Tessler, *A History of the Israeli–Palestinian Conflict* (1994), 590–599.
82 Weizman in the *Yediot Ahronot* newspaper, 2 November 1984, as cited in Lesch, 'Egyptian–Israeli relations', 82.
83 Stein, 'Continuity and change in Egyptian–Israeli relations', 296.
84 Eldar, 'Israel should make peace with Egyptian people'.
85 Kamel, *The Camp David Accords*, 357, 363–368. On p. 374, Kamel notes another official, Nabil El Araby, director of the legal department, who

had a strongly negative reaction to Egyptian concessions regarding how Jerusalem was handled.
86 'Address by Deputy Premier and Foreign Minister Allon'.
87 Witte and Eglash, 'Iron Dome'. See also Fromer, 'The missiles keeping Israel safe'.

Notes to chapter 4

1 While my focus here is often on unintended negative consequences, unintended benefits might also occur from a reliance on military force.
2 Classic discussions include Jervis, *Perception and Misperception in International Politics*, 58–113; Snyder, '"Prisoner's Dilemma"'; and Snyder and Diesing, *Conflict Among Nations*.
3 Baldwin, 'Power analysis and world politics', 181.
4 Escalation is, however, a tricky concept because some actors want events to spin out of control. In particular, in the Arab–Israeli conflict, weaker, non-state actors have, at times, hoped for escalation that would force other Arab actors to join the fight.
5 Sadat made such a claim in his path-breaking speech to the Israeli parliament on 20 November 1977: 'Perhaps the examples taken from ancient and modern history teach us all that missiles, warships and nuclear weapons cannot establish security. Rather, they destroy what peace and security build.' See https://sadat.umd.edu/resources/presidential-speeches (accessed 25 January 2020).
6 'Mahmud Abbas's call for a halt to the militarization of the intifada'. See also Kalman, 'Is Abbas' pen mightier than Arafat's sword?'
7 Schmemann, 'A senior Palestinian official urges end to suicide attacks'.
8 Note that on other issues, Abbas has also made statements that are ahistorical and not conciliatory. For example, see 'Abbas says Jews' behavior, not anti-Semitism, caused the Holocaust'. I believe the fact that as of 2019, Abbas had never faced a re-election campaign also affected his standing.
9 Stern, 'Abbas: I oppose armed struggle, but won't rule out option for future'.
10 'Abbas tells Israeli TV he has no right to live on land he was displaced from'.
11 The interview was conducted in Arabic. Abu Sarah and Gopin, 'Will there be peace if Palestinians lay down their arms'. The original

interview is at https://www.youtube.com/watch?v=KIcFNqEwWho (accessed 9 January 2020).
12 Bar-Siman-Tov, 'Ben-Gurion and Sharett', 332.
13 Shlaim, 'Conflicting approaches to Israel's relations with the Arabs', 184.
14 See Caplan, 'The "Sharettist option" revisited', 69.
15 'A pointless war has led to a moral defeat'. For another example, one that questions Israel's reliance on force to respond to abductions, see Hauser, 'Israel's addiction to military force'.
16 Azulay, 'Diskin: delusional government brought us to this security deterioration'; and Goldberg, 'Ex-Shin Bet chief: Israeli illusions fueled blowup'.
17 Cook, 'Israel must learn the limits of bombing and violence in Palestine'.
18 Segev, 'Cruel and meaningless wars'.
19 Israel Radio, 27 June 2014.
20 Scheindlin, 'How can you possibly oppose this war?' See also Kristof, 'Who's right and wrong in the Middle East?'
21 Quoted in Hubbard, 'Loss of shelter and electricity worsens a crisis for fleeing Gazans'.
22 Kolatt, 'The chances for peace and the right to a homeland', 75.
23 Tal, 'Israel's armistice wars, 1949–1956', 82.
24 Tal, 'Israel's road to the 1956 war', 65. See also Tal, 'The 1956 Sinai War', 144.
25 Tessler, *A History of the Israeli–Palestinian Conflict* (1994), 345. Casualty figures vary in different sources.
26 Oren, 'Escalation to Suez', 357–358.
27 Shlaim, 'Conflicting approaches to Israel's relations with the Arabs', 188. David Tal sees the raid as consistent with other Israeli attacks and thus unexceptional. Tal, 'Israel's road to the 1956 war', 66.
28 Morris, *Israel's Border Wars*, 325.
29 Robert R. Bowie, *Suez 1956: International Crises and the Role of Law* (NY: Oxford University Press, 1974), p. 10 as cited in Tessler, *A History* (1994), 345.
30 Shlaim cites Ehud Ya'ari's analysis of captured Egyptian intelligence documents. Shlaim, 'Conflicting approaches to Israel's relations with the Arabs', 188–189. See also Tal, 'Israel's armistice wars, 1949–1956', 80. In contrast, John Zimmerman argues that, based on public statements, Egypt was fomenting the Fedayeen even before the Gaza Raid. Zimmerman, 'The origins of the Fedayeen in Nasser's *Weltpolitik*', 112.

31 Morris, *Israel's Border Wars*, 331, 333–334; and Bar-On, *The Gates of Gaza*, 11.
32 Morris, *Israel's Border Wars*, 328–329, 330, 422.
33 Heikal, *Nasser: The Cairo Documents*, 41–74; Hamrush, *Gamal Abed al-Nasser*, 39–86; and text of Nasser's announcement of the deal in *Hadith al-Batal al-Za'im Gamal Abd al-Nasser I'la al-U'ma* (Maktab al-Tahrir, n.d.), 390–394, as cited in Laron, *Cutting the Gordian Knot*, 2.
34 Oren, 'Escalation to Suez', 357–358. See also Morris, *Israel's Border Wars*, 427.
35 Ginat, *The Soviet Union and Egypt*, 207, 210.
36 Laron, *Cutting the Gordian Knot*, 41. See also 26–27, 49–51. Ginat argues the opposite, writing that the Czech portion of the arms deal (separate from direct Soviet–Egyptian talks that intensified in the summer of 1955) was cemented weeks before the Gaza Raid. Ginat, *The Soviet Union and Egypt*, 211.
37 Laron, *Cutting the Gordian Knot*, 50–51.
38 Laron, *Cutting the Gordian Knot*, 42. Mohrez Mahmoud El Hussini concurs that Egypt's decisionmaking was driven by mixed concerns about Arab, Israeli, and Western capabilities and pressure. El Hussini, *Soviet–Egyptian Relations*, 54–55.
39 Ra'anan, *The USSR Arms the Third World*, 54. John Zimmerman's account is directly based on Ra'anan's work. Zimmerman, 'The origins of the Fedayeen in Nasser's *Weltpolitik*', 104. Zimmerman agrees that the Baghdad Pact was a catalyst, 108.
40 Tal, 'Israel's road to the 1956 war', 70. Tal's understanding could also fit with the ideas of another critic of the impact of the Gaza Raid, Rami Ginat. Ginat argues that the arms deal was really two deals, one negotiated with the Czechs in February and one later with the Soviets. Thus, in terms of timing, the Gaza Raid could very well have affected Soviet motivation and the quantity of weapons in the second deal. See Ginat, *The Soviet Union and Egypt*.
41 For more on Soviet thinking, see El Hussini, *Soviet–Egyptian Relations*, 57–64. Ginat suggests that Nikita Khrushchev's rise to Soviet premier and his greater openness to ties with neutral countries facilitated the Soviet–Egyptian deal. See Ginat, *The Soviet Union and Egypt*, 207–208.
42 Rid, 'Deterrence beyond the state', 134.
43 On the general point, see Golani, 'The historical place of the Czech–Egyptian arms deal', 804, 808, 823. On Dayan, see Oren, 'Escalation

Notes to chapter 4

to Suez', 354; and Shlaim, 'Conflicting approaches to Israel's relations with the Arabs', 184, 194.

44 Levey, 'Israel's quest for a security guarantee from the United States', 53. See also Shlaim, 'Conflicting approaches to Israel's relations with the Arabs', 189. I am not persuaded by Tal's argument that Ben-Gurion offered this proposal only because he knew it would be defeated and just wanted to use an extreme plan to push the needle of Israeli strategic thinking in his direction and away from Sharett. There are too many examples of Ben-Gurion pushing for significant military attacks on Egypt for me to think he did not intend them as such. See Tal, 'Israel's road to the 1956 war', 68.

45 Levey, 'Israel's quest for a security guarantee from the United States', 56. See also Shlaim, 'Conflicting approaches to Israel's relations with the Arabs', 193; and Tal, 'Israel's road to the 1956 war', 72.

46 Levy and Gochal, 'Democracy and preventive war', 25. Israel's initial response was to secure Western arms to counter-balance the Czech arms deal. Levy and Gochal argue that war was the next policy instrument, especially after Britain and France expressed interest in joining Israel to fight Egypt.

47 Levy and Gochal, 'Democracy and preventive war', 23–34, 42–43.

48 Bar-On, *The Gates of Gaza*, 7–8.

49 On the cabinet decision, see also Shlaim, 'Conflicting approaches to Israel's relations with the Arabs', 195, who uses the date of 5 December. On Ben-Gurion's fear that an Israeli attack would undermine the quest for securing arms and a great-power patron, see Golani, 'The historical place of the Czech–Egyptian arms deal', 820; Shlaim, 'Conflicting approaches to Israel's relations with the Arabs', 194, 196; and Tal, 'Israel's road to the 1956 war', 72. Earlier, Levey argues, at the time of the Gaza Raid (February 1955), Ben-Gurion took the opposite position. Sharett told Ben-Gurion such raids undermined security relations with the United States, but Ben-Gurion argued that retaliatory raids to ensure security were more important than security relations with Washington. Levey, 'Israel's quest for a security guarantee from the United States', 52.

50 Golani, 'The historical place of the Czech–Egyptian arms deal with the Arabs', 822–823.

51 Shlaim, 'Conflicting approaches to Israel's relations with the Arabs', 196. See also Tal, 'The 1956 Sinai War', 145–146.

52 Levey, 'Israel's quest for a security guarantee from the United States', 57.

53 Tal, 'Israel's road to the 1956 war', 74–76.
54 El Hussini, *Soviet–Egyptian Relations*, 70. See also Bar-On, *The Gates of Gaza*, 322–323.
55 Tal, 'The 1956 Sinai War', 147.
56 Morris, *Israel's Border Wars*, 421; and Bar-On, *The Gates of Gaza*, 321. Bar-On (323) considered both Egypt and Israel as the war's victors.
57 Atzili and Pearlman, 'Triadic deterrence'. See also Pearlman and Atzili, *Triadic Coercion*.
58 On counterfactual thinking, see Lebow, 'What's so different about a counterfactual?'; and Grynaviski, 'Contrasts, counterfactuals, and causes'.
59 For a brief history of the 1967 war, see Lesch, *The Arab–Israeli Conflict*. For another example of such a warning from the Soviets, in 1960, see Bar-Joseph, 'Rotem', 554.
60 Popp, 'Stumbling decidedly into the Six-Day War', 287. Popp's work is in sharp contrast to a book on the Soviet role: Ginor and Remez, *Foxbats Over Dimona*.
61 Katz, *Soldier Spies*, 186. Some reports have suggested lower figures. Dayan wrote that he was told on 27 May that Egypt had 80,000 troops in Sinai. Dayan, *Moshe Dayan*, 332. According to Popp, Egypt had only about 50,000 soldiers in Sinai after mobilizing, according to internal US sources. Popp, 'Stumbling decidedly into the Six-Day War'.
62 Sayigh, *Armed Struggle and the Search for State*, 173.
63 Haddad, 'Islamists and the "problem of Israel"'. See also Roberts, 'Radical Islamism and the dilemma of Algerian nationalism', 562; and Toth, 'Islamism in southern Egypt', 548.
64 Zisser, 'The 1982 "Peace for Galilee" War'.
65 *Ha'aretz*, 17 January 1985, as cited in Sobelman, *New Rules of the Game*, 10. See also Wright, 'Another siege: Israel's war on the PLO'.
66 Sobelman, *New Rules of the Game*, 14.
67 Eiran, *Israel and Weak Neighboring States*, 8.
68 Rid, 'Deterrence beyond the state', 135.
69 Sayigh, *Armed Struggle and the Search for State*, 606.
70 McGeough, *Kill Khalid*, 55–56.
71 Eiran, *Israel and Weak Neighboring States*, 8.
72 Zisser, 'The 1982 "Peace for Galilee" War', 206–207.
73 Pressman, 'Explaining the Carter administration's Israeli–Palestinian solution'.
74 For a detailed treatment of the second intifada, see Pressman, 'The second intifada'.

Notes to chapter 4

75 Kaspit, 'Israel is not a state that has an army'.
76 McGeough, *Kill Khalid*, 275.
77 Hroub, 'Hamas after Shaykh Yasin and Rantisi', 26.
78 Hroub, 'Hamas after Shaykh Yasin and Rantisi', 23.
79 Khaled Hroub cites examples of several Hamas leaders – Shaykh Ahmad Yasin, Khalid Mishal, Musa Abu Marzouq – using this phrasing. Hroub, 'Hamas after Shaykh Yasin and Rantisi', 23.
80 International Crisis Group, *Dealing with Hamas*, 16–17.
81 Paraipan, 'The voice of Hamas'.
82 Anderson, 'Palestinians explore united front', p. A1; al-Mughrabi, 'Israelis kill two Palestinian gunmen'; Susser, 'Desperate times, drastic measures'; and Kifner, 'Militants reject policy on attacks in Israel'.
83 For another example published in *Al Quds* newspaper on 20 June 2002, see 'Urgent appeal to stop suicide bombings', http://www.bitterlemons.net/docs/suicide.html (accessed 14 January 2014). Prominent signers of the appeal included Sari Nusseibah, Hanan Ashrawai, and Eyad El-Sarraj.
84 Crenshaw, 'The logic of terrorism'.
85 Moghadam, 'Palestinian suicide terrorism in the second intifada', 77.
86 Bloom, 'Palestinian suicide bombing', 82–83.
87 Shamir and Shikaki, *Palestinian and Israeli Public Opinion*, 162–164.
88 B'Tselem, 'Fatalities before Operation "Cast Lead"'.
89 For an example that mentions 8.5 per cent, see Matar, 'The wall, 10 years on / Part 2: Wall and peace'.
90 B'Tselem, *Arrested Development*.
91 See, for example, the video by Julie Land, 'Al Walaja: the story of a shrinking village'.
92 See Del Sarto, *Israel Under Siege*.
93 Kalman, 'Rajoub begins his run'.
94 On the economic damage, see Kuperman, 'Why the liberal economic model of international peace failed in the Middle East', especially table 1.
95 Chenoweth and Stephan, *Why Civil Resistance Works*.
96 Tolan, *The Lemon Tree*, 197.
97 Raghavan, 'Mohammed Deif, the shadowy figure'.
98 Sheizaf, 'Why do Palestinians continue to support Hamas despite such devastating losses?' See also Eldar, 'Operation Protective Edge continues cycle of violence'.
99 Roth, 'How Hamas Won'.

100 See the definition of coercion in Byman and Waxman, 'Kosovo and the great air power debate', 9. See also Jakobsen, 'Pushing the limits of military coercion theory'; and Mueller, 'Strategies of coercion', 183.
101 Mueller, 'Strategies of coercion', 192–193, 196, 198–199. Mueller defines aerial punishment on 187.
102 Mueller, 'Strategies of coercion', 207.
103 Horowitz and Reiter, 'When does aerial bombing work?'
104 Dekker, 'The complexity of compellence', 462.
105 Another argument is that timing matters too. Longer occupations, for example, lead to greater entrenchment. See Hassner, 'The path to intractability'; and Goddard, Pressman, and Hassner, 'Correspondence: time and the intractability of territorial disputes'.
106 Stein, 'Calculation, miscalculation, and conventional deterrence II', 81; and Pressman, *Warring Friends*, 100–105.
107 Khatib, 'Palestinian labourers work at a cement factory in Gaza Strip'.

Notes to chapter 5

1 My emphasis on ideas and institutions parallels the operationalization of strategic culture as 'decision-making processes and ideas' in Pearlman and Atzili, *Triadic Coercion*, 15.
2 Although I use a broader understanding of 'missed opportunity' than Elie Podeh, he still considered twenty-eight possible cases of negotiations, from 1919 to 2008. He found that three actually did not present a historical opportunity for a breakthrough. Of the twenty-five remaining that *did* present a historical opportunity for a breakthrough, the plausibility of someone seizing on the opportunity was low or non-existent in another eighteen cases. That left seven examples of opportunities that were medium or high in terms of the plausibility of someone seizing the opportunity. Podeh, *Chances for Peace*, 359–362.
3 This is a broader understanding than Podeh, with Gaza disengagement in 2005 as an example of something I consider a missed opportunity, but he does not. For his definition, see Podeh, *Chances for Peace*, 10–15. We both see the Arab peace initiative of 2002 as a missed opportunity.
4 Jervis, *Why Intelligence Fails*, 40.

5 Jervis, *Perception and Misperception in International Politics*, 82.
6 Heradstveit, *The Arab–Israeli Conflict*, 122.
7 Sebenius, 'Avoiding the costs of negotiation', 166. For a US example, see Pressman, 'September statements, October missiles'.
8 To see how his position evolved, one can compare *Arab Strategies and Israel's Response* (1977) to *Israel's Fateful Hour* (1989).
9 Harkabi, *Arab Strategies and Israel's Response*, 39. See also 42–46.
10 Harkabi, *Arab Strategies and Israel's Response*, 45.
11 Harkabi, *Arab Strategies and Israel's Response*, 62.
12 Maoz, *Defending the Holy Land*, 480, 482.
13 Karsh, *Arafat's War*, 4; Karsh, 'After Annapolis'; and Morris, 'Camp David and after'.
14 Ya'alon in an interview with Ari Shavit. Shavit, 'The enemy within'. In that interview, Ya'alon made the same point about unilateral withdrawal from settlements: 'any such departure under terrorism and violence will strengthen the path of terrorism and violence'.
15 Shiloh, 'Netanyahu: Gov't moves blindly as withdrawal threatens security'.
16 'Statement by incoming foreign minister Avigdor Liberman'.
17 See Caplan, 'The "Sharettist option" revisited', 71.
18 Abdel Shafi, 'The Palestinian crisis'.
19 International Crisis Group, 'Tipping point?', 2. See also Rabbani, 'Twenty years of Oslo', 30.
20 Siegman, 'The great Middle East peace process scam'.
21 Emphasis added. Weizman, 'Israel "destroying peace process" with new housing'.
22 Another possible case that might demonstrate how a reliance on force blocks negotiations is Egypt, Israel, and the United States in the run-up to the 1973 war. The 1973 war 'could have been avoided' but Israel ignored Sadat's overtures. Ben-Ami, *Scars of War*, 366. See also Jervis, 'Perceiving and coping with threat', 21; Stein, 'Calculation, miscalculation, and conventional deterrence I: The view from Cairo', 51; Kipnis, *1973*; Ignatius, 'What a war in 1973 can tell us'; and Terris and Tykocinski, 'Inaction inertia in international negotiations'.
23 Another example of this type of fear occurred near the end of the Cold War, when the United States tried to judge Mikhail Gorbachev. See Gates, *From the Shadows*, 375–389 and 443–448, and especially 376.
24 Shavit, 'The enemy within'.
25 Sayigh, *Armed Struggle and the Search for State*, 342–343.
26 Mcintyre, 'The Palestine Liberation Organization', 86.

27 Agha, 'What state for the Palestinians?' See also Rouleau, 'The Palestinian quest'. For a description of how a two-state solution might work – a description that bears striking resemblance to ideas in the 1990s and 2000s – see Khalidi, 'Thinking the unthinkable'.
28 Sinai, 'That oasis seems to be a mirage'. See also Jones, 'Palestinians' mirage and Egyptians' reality', 33.
29 Tanner, 'Geneva role set by Palestinians', 1.
30 'Palestinian guerillas rebuff Sadat–Hussein views on role'. See also Smith, 'Palestinians remain the "key issue" in Mideast'.
31 Tanner, 'Palestinian moderates on Council gain', 3; see also Tanner, 'Geneva role set by Palestinians'.
32 Avineri et al., 'An exchange on Mideast guarantees', 215. For a broad overview of this position, see Karsh, 'Arafat's grand strategy'.
33 Cohen was associate executive director of the American Jewish Congress. Cohen, '"Moderates" in the Palestinian movement'.
34 Harkabi, *Palestinians and Israel*, 202.
35 Harkabi, *Palestinians and Israel*, 203.
36 Tanner, 'Geneva role set by Palestinians'.
37 Baumgarten, 'The Three Faces/Phases of Palestinian Nationalism', 36.
38 See also a detailed chapter on the Arab Peace Initiative in Podeh, *Chances for Peace*, 304–323.
39 For the full text, see 'The Arab Peace Initiative, 2002', https://al-bab.com/documents-section/arab-peace-initiative-2002 (accessed 15 January 2020).
40 This estimate, which does not include security personnel, is based on two B'Tselem charts: 'Statistics: Israeli civilians killed by Palestinians in Israel, before Operation "Cast Lead"', at https://www.btselem.org/statistics/fatalities/before-cast-lead/by-date-of-event/israel/israeli-civilians-killed-by-palestinians; and 'Statistics: Israeli civilians killed by Palestinians in the Occupied Territories, before Operation 'Cast Lead"', at https://www.btselem.org/statistics/fatalities/before-cast-lead/by-date-of-event/wb-gaza/israeli-civilians-killed-by-palestinians, accessed 19 June 2019.
41 Williams and Hockstader, 'Israel storms Arafat offices in West Bank'.
42 'Response of FM Peres to the decisions of the Arab summit in Beirut'.
43 Schneider, 'Saudi Crown Prince lays out peace plan'.
44 'Text of speech by Sharon to Israeli parliament'.
45 The exact wording of that reservation (the tenth of the fourteen) is as follows: '10. The removal of references other than 242 and 338 (1397, the Saudi Initiative and the Arab Initiative adopted in Beirut).

Notes to chapter 5

A settlement based upon the road map will be an autonomous settlement that derives its validity therefrom. The only possible reference should be to Resolutions 242 and 338, and then only as an outline for the conduct of future negotiations on a permanent settlement.' See 'Israel's road map reservations'.

46 Eldar, 'How to ensure success at the Paris peace conference'.
47 Schneider, 'Arab countries unanimously endorse Saudi peace plan'.
48 Quoted in Ahren, 'Why is Israel so afraid of the Arab peace initiative?'
49 Amr, 'Hamas won't oppose Arab peace plan'.
50 Ya'alon, *Israel's Security Policy in a Changing Middle East*, 12.
51 Ahren, 'Why is Israel so afraid of the Arab peace initiative?'
52 Ahren, 'Why is Israel so afraid of the Arab peace initiative?'
53 Podeh, 'Waiting for a call from Netanyahu'.
54 Ahren, 'Why is Israel so afraid of the Arab peace initiative?' One such meeting of foreign ministers took place on 25 July 2007; see 'Joint press conference with Israeli FM Livni, Egyptian FM Gheit and Jordanian FM al-Khatib'.
55 Ahren and Sterman, 'Netanyahu to Abbas, in English'.
56 Jahn, 'Senior Israeli minister endorses Arab peace plan'. See also 'Peri: Adopt Arab Peace Initiative with corrections'.
57 Ahren, 'Why is Israel so afraid of the Arab peace initiative?'
58 Podeh, 'Waiting for a call from Netanyahu'. See also Podeh, *Chances for Peace*, 322.
59 For a similar list, see Mnookin, Eiran, and Gilad, 'Is unilateralism always bad?', 146–149.
60 Pressman, 'Israeli unilateralism and Israeli–Palestinian relations'. See also Roy, 'Praying with their eyes closed', 69, 70. On disengagement generally, see Rynhold and Waxman, 'Ideological change and Israel's disengagement from Gaza'.
61 Shamir and Shikaki, *Palestinian and Israeli Public Opinion*, 101–103.
62 Peters, 'The Gaza disengagement', 43.
63 'PA chairman Abbas phones PM Sharon'.
64 Cited in Regular and Benn, 'Israel rejects claims by Palestinians'.
65 Benn, 'U.S. voices disapproval of PM's warnings on Hamas'.
66 Knowlton, 'Meeting with Abbas, Bush expresses optimism'.
67 'FM Shalom: Gaza pullout could lead to renewal of peace talks'.
68 Regular and Benn, 'Israel rejects claims by Palestinians'.
69 Benn, 'U.S. voices disapproval of PM's warnings on Hamas'.
70 Benn, Harel, and Regular, 'PA: Abbas–Sharon talks delayed'.
71 Benn, Harel, and Regular, 'PA: Abbas–Sharon talks delayed'.

Notes to chapter 5

72 Weymouth (interviewing Sharon), 'A "fateful step"'.
73 'FM Shalom: Gaza pullout could lead to renewal of peace talks'.
74 Regular and Benn, 'Israel rejects claims by Palestinians'.
75 King and Ellingwood, 'Hamas politicians maneuvering in Gaza Strip'.
76 Shikaki, *Willing to Compromise*, 9. Shikaki goes on to say 'Unilateral steps, when taken in the middle of the violence, as was the Israeli disengagement plan, strengthen public confidence in violence' (15).
77 Quoted in Barzak, 'Hamas claims majority of attacks', 6.
78 King and Ellingwood, 'Hamas politicians maneuvering in Gaza Strip'.
79 Shamir, *Public Opinion in the Israeli–Palestinian Conflict*, 33.
80 Peters, 'The Gaza disengagement', 41.
81 Samhouri, *Gaza Economic Predicament One Year After Disengagement*, 5.
82 Harel and Regular, 'West Bank Hamas plans new attacks'.
83 'A Palestinian state will be the fruit of brains, not brawn'.
84 Peters, 'The Gaza disengagement', 38.
85 Wilson, 'Mideast envoy: "Disturbing signs"'. See also Erlanger, 'Israel steps up reprisals'.
86 Bar-Siman-Tov, 'Coping with the Palestinian threat', 265.
87 Roy, 'A Dubai on the Mediterranean'.
88 Wilson, 'Mideast envoy: "Disturbing signs"'.
89 King and Ellingwood, 'Hamas politicians maneuvering in Gaza Strip'; and Bar'el, 'Of course, Egypt is to blame'.
90 Erlanger, 'In unruly Gaza, clans compete in power void'.
91 'State: W. Bank settler population grew'.
92 'PA chairman Abbas telephones Katsav to praise Israeli pullout'.
93 Wilson, 'Mideast envoy: "disturbing signs"'.
94 Myre, 'Israel lowers its flag in the Gaza Strip'.
95 'Gaza bursting at seams without West Bank link'.
96 Knowlton, 'Meeting with Abbas, Bush expresses optimism'.
97 Wilson, 'Mideast envoy: "disturbing signs"'. See also Peters, 'The Gaza disengagement', 42.
98 Samhouri, 'Gaza economic predicament'. See also Roy, 'Praying with their eyes closed'.
99 Peters, 'The Gaza disengagement', 40.
100 'PA chairman Abbas telephones Katsav to praise Israeli pullout'.
101 For a similar claim, see Peters, 'The Gaza disengagement', 42.
102 'Address to the United Nations General Assembly by foreign minister Dayan'.

103 For an in-depth analysis of these speeches, see Pressman, 'History in conflict'.
104 'Palestinian Declaration of Independence and acceptance of Res. 242 and 338 (1988)'.
105 Pressman, 'History in conflict'.
106 Maoz, *Defending the Holy Land*, 388, 481.
107 Pressman, 'Visions in collision'; and Avishai, 'A plan for peace that still could be'.
108 Pressman, 'Mediation, domestic politics, and the Israeli–Syrian negotiations'.
109 Inbar, 'Great power mediation'.
110 The other exception for Sharon was when, in September 1978, he gave Begin, then the prime minister, the green light to evacuate Israel's settlements in Sinai if such an evacuation would be needed as part of a peace agreement with Egypt.
111 Yacobi and Pullan, 'The geopolitics of neighbourhood', 518–519.

Notes to chapter 6

1 Bar-Siman-Tov, *Israel and the Peace Process*, 2.
2 Wendt, 'Collective identity formation and the international state', 389.
3 Maoz and Astorino, 'The cognitive structure of peacemaking', 653.
4 Klein, 'Jerusalem as an Israeli problem', 61. See also Lehrs, 'Jerusalem on the negotiating table'.
5 Kelman, 'The interdependence of Israeli and Palestinian national identities', 589–590.
6 On noise and its negative impact on conciliatory policies, see Larson, *Anatomy of Mistrust*, 30–31, 246. For a similar argument on signalling and non-unitary actors, see Krause, 'The structure of success', 80, 84.
7 According to Heradstveit, leaders who recognize the pluralism of the other side are more open to conciliatory policies, while those who view the other as a unitary actor are less so. Heradstveit, *The Arab–Israeli Conflict*, 133.
8 Zartman, 'The timing of peace initiatives', 10.
9 Raz, *The Bride and the Dowry*, 69, 75, 77, 146, 152, 169, 215, 264.
10 Raz, *The Bride and the Dowry*, 65–66, 70, 183, 199–200, 223.
11 Raz, *The Bride and the Dowry*, 201, 232, 260, 266, 271, 284.
12 Raz, *The Bride and the Dowry*, 267.
13 See also Pearlman and Atzili, *Triadic Coercion*, 176, 244.

Notes to chapter 6

14 When threats cause fear, the fear may linger even after the threats ebb. See Stein, 'Psychological explanations of international decision making', 202–203.
15 Bar-Tal, 'Why does fear override hope in societies engulfed by intractable conflict?', 609. See also Barr, 'Mind the conflict'. For a media version of the fear argument, see Burston, 'The two peoples of the Holy Land'.
16 Huddy, 'Diverse emotional reactions to threat', 5–6.
17 The idea is drawn from P. M. Blau, *Exchange and Power in Social Life* (1964; New York: John Wiley & Sons, 1984), as cited by Bar-Tal and Antebi, 'Siege mentality in Israel', 59.
18 Arian, 'A people apart', 607. See also Gordon and Arian, 'Threat and decision making'.
19 Maoz and McCauley, 'Threat perceptions and feelings'. See also Shamir and Shikaki, *Palestinian and Israeli Public Opinion*, 76–77.
20 Huddy, 'Diverse emotional reactions to threat', 4. See also Heradstveit, *The Arab–Israeli Conflict*, 59.
21 Bar-Tal and Antebi, 'Siege mentality in Israel', 60, 62, 64; and Bar-Tal and Antebi, 'Beliefs about negative intentions', 634, 643. One of the statements these two authors presented to measure responses was: 'Only demonstration of force will deter our enemies from attacking us' (638).
22 Caverley, *Democratic Militarism*, 223–224.
23 The impact is greatest on nationalist rather than religious right-wing parties. Getmansky and Zeitzoff, 'Terrorism and voting'. See also Getmansky and Zeitzoff, 'Rockets and bombs'. There is a large literature on the impact of threat and uncertainty on left/right political leanings. For example, see Bonanno and Jost, 'Conservative shift among high-exposure survivors'.
24 Shikaki, *Willing to Compromise*, 8–9, 15. See also Shamir and Shikaki, *Palestinian and Israeli Public Opinion*, 70, 76, 154.
25 David A. Jaeger et al., 'The struggle for Palestinian hearts and minds: violence and public opinion in the second intifada', *Journal of Public Economics* 96 (2012), 354–368, as cited by Getmansky and Zeitzoff, 'Rockets and bombs'.
26 Gadarian, 'The politics of threat'.
27 Bar-Tal, 'Why does fear override hope in societies engulfed by intractable conflict?', 604, 608.
28 Stein, 'Building politics into psychology', 261.
29 Bar-Tal and Antebi, 'Siege mentality in Israel', 65.

Notes to Conclusion

30 Other scholars have also highlighted agents or leaders in combination with other types of factors to explain political change. See Braumoeller, *The Great Powers and the International System*; Dyson, *The Blair Identity*; Dyson, 'George W. Bush, the Surge, and presidential leadership'; Dyson, 'Images of international politics'; Golan, *Israeli Peacemaking Since 1967*, 209–216; and Ziv, 'Cognitive structure and foreign policy change'.
31 Yarhi-Milo and Hall, 'The personal touch'.
32 Yarhi-Milo, 'Tying hands behind closed doors'.
33 Lebow and Stein, *We All Lost the Cold War*, 127.
34 Stein, 'The alchemy of peacemaking', 548.
35 Stein, 'The alchemy of peacemaking', 536–538.
36 On US mediation in general, see Pressman, 'American engagement and the pathways to Arab–Israeli peace'. On external mediation, see also Golan, *Israeli Peacemaking Since 1967*, 213–214.
37 Stein, 'The alchemy of peacemaking', 532. Stein considered these kinds of 'environmental' factors and leadership.
38 On the importance of shocks, see also Rasler et al., *How Rivalries End*, 185–186. Rasler et al. do not think policy entrepreneurs and third-party intervention 'are essential' (186, 192).
39 Pressman, 'American engagement and the pathways to Arab–Israeli peace'.
40 Axelrod, *The Evolution of Cooperation*; Osgood, *An Alternative to War or Surrender*.
41 Stein, 'The alchemy of peacemaking', 552, 554. See also Rasler et al., *How Rivalries End*, who similarly highlight 'reciprocity'.
42 Ziv, 'Simple vs. complex learning revisited'.
43 For such an example, see Bruton, 'Ethiopia and Eritrea have a common enemy".
44 Halper, 'The 94 percent solution'.

Notes to Conclusion

1 Armstrong, 'The effectiveness of rocket attacks', 116.
2 For an Israeli military analysis of Hamas tactics after the war, see Booth, 'Here's what really happened'.
3 The Middle East Quartet is composed of the European Union, Russia, the United Nations, and the United States. On Abbas, see Beaumont, 'Palestinian unity government of Fatah and Hamas sworn in'.

Notes to Conclusion

4 Beaumont, 'Palestinian unity government of Fatah and Hamas sworn in'.
5 Emphasis added. Ravid, 'Ya'alon proposes new settlement in memory of murdered teens'. He made a similar point a few weeks later: '[W]hen you want to defeat a terror organization, you reach a decisive victory. When we hold peace talks with a terrorist organization we get more terror.' Azulay and Somfalvi, 'It's time to abandon truce talks'.
6 Emphasis added.
7 Ravid, 'Ya'alon proposes new settlement in memory of murdered teens'.
8 Thrall, 'Hamas's chances'.
9 International Middle East Media Center, 'After Israeli attack, 50% Gaza children have PTSD'; and Goldlist-Eichler, '40% of Israeli children'.
10 Barnard, 'Boys drawn to Gaza beach'.
11 Lappin, 'First Israeli death of Gaza operation'.
12 'Dutchman returns Holocaust medal'; and Hass, 'Dutch nonagenarian returns Righteous Among the Nations medal'.
13 The United States has done the same with the government of Egypt, including providing tens of billions of dollars of military aid and promoting extensive military-to-military ties. But in the case of Egypt, the deep ties and major aid all came after – or one might even say because – Egypt no longer fought against Israel.
14 Name redacted, 'U.S. foreign aid to Israel', 5. For an extensive discussion of Israeli–US ties, see Freilich, *Israeli National Security*, 290–308.
15 See Christison, *Perceptions of Palestine*; Elgindy, *Blind Spot*; Kurtzer and Lasensky, *Negotiating Arab–Israeli Peace*; Kurtzer et al., *The Peace Puzzle*; Pressman, 'American engagement and the pathways to Arab–Israeli peace'; and Quandt, *Peace Process*.
16 Waage, 'The winner takes all'; and Waage, 'The "minnow" and the "whale"'. See also Blecher, 'No, the two-state solution isn't dead yet'; and Elgindy, *Blind Spot*.
17 Borger and Beaumont, 'Donald Trump says US not committed'.
18 Pressman, 'Israel's strategic goal'.
19 'Address by PM Netanyahu at Bar-Ilan University'. See also Ravid, 'Netanyahu: Bar-Ilan 2-state speech no longer relevant'.
20 See Halper, 'The 94 percent solution'. See also Halper, 'Dismantling the matrix of control'; and Pressman, 'Horizontal inequality and violent unrest in Jerusalem'.
21 Netanyahu's comments in 2016 did not lead to serious engagement with the Arab Peace Initiative, fourteen years after it surfaced. Ahren, 'Netanyahu tries to turn Arab Peace Initiative'.

Notes to Conclusion

22 See Netanyahu's comment and the interviewer's analysis of that comment in Horovitz, 'Netanyahu finally speaks his mind'.
23 The Israeli right is not in favour of a two-state solution as it was conceived in 2000–2001 or 2007–2008 under previous centrist and left-wing prime ministers. Much of the Israeli right is not in favour of the idea under any framing. In a January 2016 poll, 45 per cent of Israeli Jews supported annexing 'all the territories conquered in the [1967] war that it still holds'. See http://www.peaceindex.org/files/Peace_Index_Data_January_2016-Eng.pdf (accessed 15 January 2020).
24 Pressman, 'Horizontal inequality and violent unrest in Jerusalem'.
25 Hadid, 'Video shows Israeli extremists celebrating'; Lazaroff, 'Soldier arrested for shooting subdued terrorist'; Kubovich, 'Cops who beat Israeli Arab supermarket worker'.
26 Caspit, 'Why Israelis are defending IDF soldier'.
27 'IDF general in bombshell speech'.
28 Baker, 'Shake-up in Israeli politics'.
29 For example, see Gutwein, 'Israel needs a leftist revolution'.
30 Pressman, 'Visions in collision'; and Podeh, *Chances for Peace*, 276–303 and 340–357.
31 Lis, 'Israel must annex West Bank settlements'; and Ahren, 'EU labeling of West Bank goods is a "'red line'".
32 Perkoski and Pressman, 'Israel, Palestine, and the perpetual denial of nationalist claims'.
33 Article I of the Montevideo Convention (1933) – the Convention on Rights and Duties of States – provides four criteria and thus a useful metric for judging the standing of the Palestinian pursuit of statehood: 'a) a permanent population; b) a defined territory; c) government; and d) capacity to enter into relations with the other states'. Analysts vary in their judgement of Palestine on those four criteria.
34 Krause, 'The structure of success'.
35 Feige, *Settling in the Hearts: Jewish Fundamentalism in the Occupied Territories*.
36 Quoted in Sommer, 'In Tel Aviv terror attack'. For another individual example, see Booth and Eglash, 'A Palestinian teen killed an Israeli mom'.
37 'Slain Israeli teen's uncle consoles'.
38 Noted by the author on a personal Facebook page, 8 July 2014.
39 Kelman, 'The interdependence of Israeli and Palestinian national identities'.

REFERENCES

'A big shudder on the wing' (editorial), *Ha'aretz*, 11 January 2009.
'A Palestinian state will be the fruit of brains, not brawn' (editorial), *Daily Star*, 28 September 2005.
'A pointless war has led to a moral defeat for Israel' (editorial), *Guardian*, 18 January 2009.
Abadi, Jacob, 'Egypt's policy towards Israel: the impact of foreign and domestic constraints', *Israel Affairs* 12:1 (2006), 159–176.
'Abbas says Jews' behavior, not anti-Semitism, caused the Holocaust', *Times of Israel*, 1 May 2018.
'Abbas tells Israeli TV he has no right to live on land he was displaced from', *Mondoweiss*, 2 November 2012, https://mondoweiss. net/2012/11/abbas-tells-israeli-tv-he-has-no-right-to-live-on-land-he-was-displaced-from (accessed 25 January 2020).
Abdel Shafi, Haidar, 'The Palestinian crisis: what to do?', trans. Khader Khader, *Al Quds*, 18 November 2001, https://www.mediamonitors. net/the-palestinian-crisis-what-to-do (accessed 14 January 2020).
Abu Sarah, Aziz, and Marc Gopin, 'Will there be peace if Palestinians lay down their arms?', *+972 Magazine*, 30 July 2014, https://www.972mag. com/will-there-be-peace-if-palestinians-lay-down-their-arms/94603/ (accessed 9 January 2020).
'Address by Deputy Premier and Foreign Minister Allon in the United Nations General Assembly', 3 October 1974, https://mfa.gov.il/MFA/ ForeignPolicy/MFADocuments/Yearbook2/Pages/29%20Address% 20 by% 20Deputy%20Premier%20and%20Foreign%20Minister.aspx (accessed 3 January 2020).
'Address by PM Netanyahu at Bar-Ilan University', 14 June 2009, https://

References

mfa.gov.il/MFA/PressRoom/2009/Pages/Address_PM_Netanyahu_Bar-Ilan_University_14-Jun-2009.aspx (accessed 3 January 2020).

'Address by PM Netanyahu special Knesset session marking the 40th anniversary of the Yom Kippur War' (translation), 15 October 2013, https://www.gov.il/en/departments/news/speechkipur151013 (accessed 9 January 2020).

'Address to the United Nations General Assembly by foreign minister Dayan', 9 October 1978, https://mfa.gov.il/MFA/ForeignPolicy/MFADocuments/Yearbook3/Pages/205%20Address%20to%20the%20United%20Nations%20General%20Assembly.aspx (accessed 26 January 2020).

Agha, Hussein J., 'What state for the Palestinians?', *Journal of Palestine Studies* 6:1 (1976), 3–38.

Aharoni, Reuven, 'The Palestinian intifada, 1987–1991', in Bar-On (ed.), *A Never-Ending Conflict*, 211–230.

Ahren, Raphael, 'EU labeling of West Bank goods is a "red line", Israel's top diplomat [Tzipi Hotovely] warns', *Times of Israel*, 27 September 2015, https://www.timesofisrael.com/eu-labeling-of-west-bank-goods-is-a-red-line-israels-top-diplomat-warns/ (accessed 16 January 2020).

Ahren, Raphael, 'Netanyahu tries to turn Arab peace initiative on its head', *Times of Israel*, 1 June 2016.

Ahren, Raphael, 'Why is Israel so afraid of the Arab peace initiative?', *Times of Israel*, 18 June 2013, https://www.timesofisrael.com/why-is-israel-so-afraid-of-the-arab-peace-initiative (accessed 14 January 2020).

Ahren, Raphael, and Adiv Sterman, 'Netanyahu to Abbas, in English: "Give peace a chance"', *Times of Israel*, 5 June 2013, https://www.timesofisrael.com/netanyahu-to-abbas-in-english-give-peace-a-chance (accessed 15 January 2020).

Ajami, Fouad, 'The end of pan-Arabism', *Foreign Affairs* 57:2 (1978/1979), 355–373.

Almog, Doron, 'Cumulative deterrence and the war on terrorism', *Parameters* 34:4 (2004), 4–19.

Almog, Doron, 'Lessons of the Gaza security fence for the West Bank', *Jerusalem Issue Brief* 4:12 (23 December 2004), https://www.jcpa.org/brief/brief004-12.htm (accessed 7 January 2020).

Alpher, Yossi, 'Now stop starving the Gazans', *International Herald Tribune*, 15 January 2009.

El-Amir, Aymin, 'Living by the sword', *Al-Ahram Weekly On-Line*, 15–21 January 2009.

References

Amr, Wafa, 'Hamas won't oppose Arab peace plan, Palestinian says', *Reuters*, 25 March 2007, https://www.reuters.com/article/id USL 25407300 (accessed 14 January 2020).

Anderson, John Ward, 'Palestinians explore united front', *Washington Post*, 14 August 2002, p. A1.

'Angry Nasser hurls 'liar' charge at Bonn', *Los Angeles Times*, 9 March 1965, pp. 1 and 4.

Anziska, Seth, *Preventing Palestine: A Political History from Camp David to Oslo* (Princeton, NJ: Princeton University Press, 2018).

Arian, Asher, 'A people apart: coping with national security problems in Israel', *Journal of Conflict Resolution* 33:4 (December 1989), 605–631.

Arian, Asher, 'Israeli public opinion and the intifada', in Freedman (ed.), *The Intifada*, 269–292.

Armstrong, Michael J., 'The effectiveness of rocket attacks and defenses in Israel', *Journal of Global Security Studies* 3:2 (2018), 113–132.

Aronoff, Myron J., 'The Labor Party and the intifada', in Freedman (ed.), *The Intifada*, 325–342.

Art, Robert J., and Patrick M. Cronin, *The United States and Coercive Diplomacy* (Washington, DC: United States Institute of Peace, 2003).

Ashton, Nigel, *King Hussein of Jordan: A Political Life* (New Haven, CT: Yale University Press, 2008).

Associated Press and Deutsche Presse-Agentur, 'Hamas: Gaza will become graveyard for Israeli troops', *Ha'aretz*, 3 January 2009, https://www.haaretz.com/1.5058089 (accessed 28 January 2020).

Atallah, Amjad, and Daniel Levy, 'Rewrite the script', *Guardian*, 31 December 2008.

Atzili, Boaz, and Wendy Pearlman, 'Triadic deterrence: coercing strength, beaten by weakness', *Security Studies* 21:2 (2012), 301–335.

Autesserre, Séverine, 'Dangerous tales: dominant narratives on the Congo and their unintended consequences', *African Affairs* 111:443 (2012), 202–222.

Avineri, Shlomo, 'Introduction', in Avineri (ed.), *Israel and the Palestinians*.

Avineri, Shlomo (ed.), *Israel and the Palestinians* (New York: St Martin's Press, 1971).

Avineri, Shlomo, 'The Palestinians and Israel', in Avineri (ed.), *Israel and the Palestinians*, 133–164.

Avineri, Shlomo, et al., 'An exchange on Mideast guarantees', *Foreign Policy* 21 (1975–1976), 212–223.

Avishai, Bernard, 'A plan for peace that still could be', *New York Times*, 7

February 2011, https://www.nytimes.com/2011/02/13/magazine/ 13 Israel-t.html (accessed 15 January 2020).

Awartani, Hisham, and Ephraim Kleiman, 'Economic interactions among participants in the Middle East peace process', *Middle East Journal* 51:2 (1997), 215–229.

Axelrod, Robert, *The Evolution of Cooperation* (New York: Basic Books, 1984).

Azkin, Benjamin, 'The Likud', in Asher Arian (ed.), *The Elections in Israel 1977* (Jerusalem: Jerusalem University Press, 1980), 39–57.

Azulay, Moran, 'Diskin: delusional government brought us to this security deterioration', Ynetnews, 5 July 2014, https://www.ynetnews.com/articles/0,7340,L-4538232,00.html (accessed 3 January 2020).

Azulay, Moran, and Attila Somfalvi, 'It's time to abandon truce talks, reach decisive victory over Hamas', Ynetnews, 20 August 2014, https://www.ynetnews.com/articles/0,7340,L-4560499,00.html (accessed 3 January 2020).

Baconi, Tareq, *Hamas Contained: The Rise and Pacification of Palestinian Resistance* (Stanford, CA: Stanford University Press, 2018).

Baker, Luke, 'Shake-up in Israeli politics prompts "seeds of fascism" warning', Reuters, 23 May 2016, https://www.reuters.com/article/us-israel-politics-idUSKCN0YE1I6 (accessed 15 January 2020).

Baldwin, David A., 'Power analysis and world politics: new trends versus old tendencies', *World Politics* 31:2 (1979), 161–194.

'Barak: In the Middle East, there is no mercy for the weak', *Ha'aretz*, 2 June 2010, https://www.haaretz.com/1.5128485 (accessed 24 January 2020).

Bar'el, Zvi, 'Of course, Egypt is to blame', *Ha'aretz*, 18 September 2005, https://www.haaretz.com/1.4848628 (accessed 28 January 2020).

Bar'el, Zvi, 'Shock-and-awe unlikely to work on Hamas, Gazans', *Ha'aretz*, 27 July 2014, https://www.haaretz.com/.premium-shock-and-awe-unlikely-to-work-1.5256995 (accessed 3 January 2020).

Bar-Joseph, Uri, 'Rotem: the forgotten crisis on the road to the 1967 war', *Journal of Contemporary History* 31:3 (1996), 547–566.

Barnard, Anne, 'Boys drawn to Gaza beach, and into center of Mideast strife', *New York Times*, 16 July 2014, https://www.nytimes.com/2014/07/17/world/middleeast/gaza-strip-beach-explosion-kills-children.html (accessed 15 January 2020).

Bar-On, Mordechai (ed.), *A Never-Ending Conflict: A Guide to Israeli Military History* (Westport, CT: Praeger, 2004).

Bar-On, Mordechai, *The Gates of Gaza: Israel's Road to Suez and Back, 1955–1957* (New York: St Martin's Press, 1994).

References

Barr, Shiri, 'Mind the conflict: mindfulness and the (Israeli–Jewish) conflict mindset. Dis-covering psychological barriers to peace', 2011, Capstone Collection, Paper 2503, https://digitalcollections.sit.edu/capstones (accessed 16 January 2020).

Bar-Siman-Tov, Yaacov, 'Ben-Gurion and Sharett: conflict management and great power constraints in Israeli foreign policy', *Middle Eastern Studies* 24:3 (July 1988), 330–356.

Bar-Siman-Tov, Yaacov, 'Coping with the Palestinian threat: adaptation and learning in Israel's strategies toward the Israeli–Palestinian conflict, 1993–2006', in Oren Barak and Gabriel Sheffer (eds), *Existential Threats and Civil-Security Relations* (Lanham, MD: Lexington Books, 2009), 249–272.

Bar-Siman-Tov, Yaacov, *Israel and the Peace Process, 1977–1982: In Search of Legitimacy for Peace* (Albany, NY: SUNY Press, 1994).

Bar-Siman-Tov, Yaacov, 'Israel–Egypt peace: stable peace?', in Arie M. Kacowicz, Yaacov Bar-Siman-Tov, Ole Elgström, and Magnus Jerneck (eds), *Stable Peace Among Nations* (Lanham, MD: Rowman and Littlefield, 2000), 220–238.

Bar-Siman-Tov, Yaacov, 'The Arab–Israeli conflict: learning conflict resolution', *Journal of Peace Research* 31:1 (1994), 75–92.

Bar-Tal, Daniel, 'Why does fear override hope in societies engulfed by intractable conflict, as it does in the Israeli society?', *Political Psychology* 22:3 (2001), 601–627.

Bar-Tal, Daniel, and Dikla Antebi, 'Beliefs about negative intentions of the world: a study of the Israeli siege mentality', *Political Psychology* 13:4 (1992), 633–645.

Bar-Tal, Daniel, and Dikla Antebi, 'Siege mentality in Israel', *Ongoing Production on Social Representations* 1:1 (1992), 49–67.

Barzak, Ibrahim, 'Hamas claims majority of attacks in the past five years', *Jerusalem Post*, 23 August 2005, p. 6.

Barzak, Ibrahim, and Matti Friedman, 'Israel says Gaza assault "war to the bitter end"', boston.com, 29 December 2008.

Barzak, Ibrahim, and Jason Keyser, 'Diplomats seek truce as Gaza's civilian toll rises', boston.com, 5 January 2009.

Baumgarten, Helga, 'The three faces/phases of Palestinian nationalism, 1948–2005', *Journal of Palestine Studies* 34:4 (2005), 25–48.

Beaumont, Peter, 'Palestinian unity government of Fatah and Hamas sworn in', *Guardian*, 2 June 2014, https://www.theguardian.com/world/2014/jun/02/palestinian-unity-government-sworn-in-fatah-hamas (accessed 15 January 2020).

References

Ben-Ami, Shlomo, *Scars of War, Wounds of Peace: The Israeli–Arab Tragedy* (New York: Oxford University Press, 2006).

Benhorin, Yitzhak, 'UN chief to Olmert: end Gaza op immediately', Ynetnews,, 4 January 2009, https://www.ynetnews.com/articles/0,7340,L-3649880,00.html (accessed 28 January 2020).

Benn, Aluf, 'Operation Pillar of Defense is Ehud Barak's test', *Ha'aretz*, 18 November 2012, https://www.haaretz.com/.premium-aluf-benn-throwing-barak-under-the-bus-1.5198774 (accessed 7 January 2020).

Benn, Aluf, 'U.S. voices disapproval of PM's warnings on Hamas', haaretz.com, 18 September 2005.

Benn, Aluf, Amos Harel, and Arnon Regular, 'PA: Abbas-Sharon talks put off for several weeks', *Ha'aretz*, 10 October 2005, https://www.haaretz.com/1.4877419 (accessed 28 January 2020).

Ben-Yishai, Ron, 'Preventing a "divine victory"', Ynetnews, 29 December, 2008, https://www.ynetnews.com/articles/0,7340,L-3646747,00.html (accessed 24 January 2020).

Bickerton, Ian J., and Carla L. Klausner, *A History of the Arab–Israeli Conflict*, 6th edition (Boston, MA: Prentice Hall, 2010).

Blainey, Geoffrey, *The Causes of War*, 3rd edition (New York: Free Press, 1988).

Blecher, Robert, 'No, the two-state solution isn't dead yet – but you're asking the wrong question', *Daily Beast*, 31 May 2012, https://www.thedailybeast.com/no-the-two-state-solution-isnt-dead-yetbut-youre-asking-the-wrong-question (accessed 15 January 2020).

Bloom, Mia, 'Palestinian suicide bombing: public support, market share, and outbidding', *Political Science Quarterly* 119:1 (2004), 61–88.

Bonanno, George A., and John T. Jost, 'Conservative shift among high-exposure survivors of the September 11th terrorist attacks', *Basic and Applied Social Psychology* 28:4 (2006), 311–323.

Booth, William, 'Here's what really happened in the Gaza war (according to the Israelis)', *Washington Post*, 3 September 2014, https://www.washingtonpost.com/blogs/worldviews/wp/2014/09/03/heres-what-really-happened-in-the-gaza-war-according-to-the-israelis (accessed 15 January 2020).

Booth, William, and Ruth Eglash, 'A Palestinian teen killed an Israeli mom. Now their families struggle with why', *Washington Post*, 31 May 2016.

Borger, Julian, and Peter Beaumont, 'Donald Trump says US not committed to two-state Israel–Palestine solution', *Guardian*, 16 February 2017, https://www.theguardian.com/world/2017/feb/15/trump-says-us-not-committed-to-two-state-israel-palestine-solution (accessed 15 January 2020).

Bowen, Jeremy, 'For as long as both sides think they can win, blood will continue to be spilt', *Guardian*, 3 January 2009.

Braumoeller, Bear F., *The Great Powers and the International System: Systemic Theory in Empirical Perspective* (New York: Cambridge University Press, 2012).

Breznitz, Dan, 'Collaborative public space in a national innovation system: a case study of the Israeli military's impact on the software industry', *Industry and Innovation* 12:1 (2005), 31–64.

Breznitz, Dan, 'Innovation-based industrial policy in emerging economies? The case of Israel's IT industry', *Business and Politics* 8:3 (2006), 1–38.

Bruton, Bronwyn, 'Ethiopia and Eritrea have a common enemy', *Foreign Policy*, 12 July 2018, https://foreignpolicy.com/2018/07/12/ethiopia-and-eritrea-have-a-common-enemy-abiy-ahmed-isaias-afwerki-badme-peace-tplf-eprdf (accessed 3 January 2020).

B'Tselem, *Arrested Development: The Long Term Impact of the Separation Barrier* (Jerusalem: Israeli Information Center for Human Rights in the Occupied Territories, October 2012), https://www.btselem.org/download/201210_arrested_development_eng.pdf (accessed 13 January 2020).

B'Tselem, 'Fatalities before Operation "Cast Lead"', Israeli Information Center for Human Rights in the Occupied Territories, n.d., https://www.btselem.org/statistics/fatalities/before-cast-lead/by-date-of-event (accessed 14 January 2020).

Burston, Bradley, 'Gaza 2009 – to win, all Israel has to do is survive', *Ha'aretz*, 2 January 2009.

Burston, Bradley, 'The two peoples of the Holy Land', *Ha'aretz*, 26 June 2014, https://www.haaretz.com/the-two-peoples-of-the-holy-land-1.5252056 (accessed 15 January 2020).

Buttu, Diana, 'The two-state solution: a Palestinian perspective', in Aslam Farouk-Alli (ed.), *The Future of Palestine and Israel: From Colonial Roots to Postcolonial Realities* (Midrand: Institute for Global Dialogue and Johannesburg, Friedrich-Ebert-Stiftung, 2007), 182–191.

Buzan, Barry, Ole Wæver, and Jaap de Wilde, *Security: A New Framework for Analysis* (Boulder, CO: Lynne Rienner, 1998).

Byman, Daniel, and Matthew C. Waxman, 'Kosovo and the great air power debate', *International Security* 24:4 (2000), 5–38.

Caplan, Neil, 'The "Sharettist Option" revisited', in Elie Podeh and Asher

References

Kaufman (eds), *Arab–Jewish Relations: From Conflict to Resolution* (Brighton: Sussex Academic Press, 2006), 64–73.

Carter, Jimmy, *Keeping Faith: Memoirs of a President* (New York: Bantam Books, 1982).

Caspit, Ben, 'Why Israelis are defending IDF soldier who shot Palestinian attacker', al-Monitor, 28 March 2016, https://www.al-monitor.com/pulse/originals/2016/03/israel-public-idf-soldier-new-hero-hebron-palestinian-shot.html (accessed 15 January 2020).

Caverley, Jonathan D., *Democratic Militarism: Voting, Wealth, War* (Cambridge: Cambridge University Press, 2014).

Chada, Maya, *Paradox of Power: The United States in Southwest Asia, 1973–1984* (Santa Barbara, CA: ABC-Clio, 1986).

Charrett, Cata, 'Understanding Hamas', Mondoweiss, 14 July 2014, https://mondoweiss.net/2014/07/understanding-hamas (accessed 3 January 2020).

Chenoweth, Erica, and Maria Stephan, *Why Civil Resistance Works: The Strategic Logic of Nonviolent Conflict* (New York: Columbia University Press, 2011).

Christison, Kathleen, *Perceptions of Palestine: Their Influence on U.S. Middle East Policy* (Berkeley, CA: University of California Press, 1999).

Clary, Christopher O., 'The politics of peace: the end of interstate rivalries', PhD dissertation (Massachusetts Institute of Technology, 2015).

Cluverius, IV, Wat T., interviewed by Charles Stuart Kennedy, 31 May 1990, Association for Diplomatic Studies and Training Foreign Affairs Oral History Project, https://www.loc.gov/item/mfdipbib000213/ (accessed 24 January 2020).

Cohen, Richard, '"Moderates" in the Palestinian movement', *New York Times*, 27 June 1974, p. 45.

Cohen, Tova, and Ari Rabinovitch, 'Egyptian firm to buy $15 billion of Israeli natural gas', Reuters, 19 February 2018, https://www.reuters.com/article/us-israel-egypt-natgas/egyptian-firm-to-buy-15-billion-of-israeli-natural-gas-idUSKCN1G31BK (accessed 9 January 2020).

Cook, Steven A., 'Israel must learn the limits of bombing and violence in Palestine', *US News and World Report*, 5 January 2009, https://www.usnews.com/opinion/articles/2009/01/05/israel-must-learn-the-limits-of-bombing-and-violence-in-palestine (accessed 3 January 2020).

Cornut, Xavier, 'The Moroccan connection', jpost.com, 22 June 2009, https://www.jpost.com/Features/The-Moroccan-connection (accessed 24 January 2020).

References

Crenshaw, Martha, 'The logic of terrorism: terrorist behavior as a product of strategic choice', in Walter Reich (ed.), *Origins of Terrorism: Psychologies, Ideologies, Theologies, States of Mind* (Washington, DC: Woodrow Wilson Center Press, 1998), 7–24.

Dajani, Mohammed, 'Lessons from the Gaza disengagement', *Palestine–Israel Journal* 13:2 (2006), https://www.pij.org/app.php/articles/812/lessons-from-the-gaza-disengagement (accessed 9 January 2020).

Dana, Joseph, and Jared Malsin, 'Regime change in Egypt further tangles political ties with Israel', *The National*, 21 July 2012, https://www.thenational.ae/world/mena/regime-change-in-egypt-further-tangles-political-ties-with-israel-1.366293#full (accessed 9 January 2020).

Dayan, Moshe, *Moshe Dayan: Story of My Life* (New York: William Morrow, 1976).

Dayan, Moshe, 'Moshe Dayan's eulogy for Roi Rutenberg', 19 April 1956, https://www.jewishvirtuallibrary.org/moshe-dayan-s-eulogy-for-roi-rutenberg-april-19-1956 (accessed 6 January 2020).

Dekker, Willem Martijn, 'The complexity of compellence: revisiting the causal logic of denial', *Comparative Strategy* 29:5 (2010), 450–468.

Del Sarto, Raffaella A., *Israel Under Siege: The Politics of Insecurity and the Rise of the Israeli Neo-Revisionist Right* (Washington, DC: Georgetown University Press, 2017).

Dessouki, Ali E. H., 'The new Arab political order: implications for the 1980s', in Malcolm H. Kerr and El Sayed Yassin (eds), *Rich and Poor States in the Middle East: Egypt and the New Arab Order* (Boulder, CO: Westview Press, 1982), 319–347.

Dishon, Daniel, *Middle East Record* (Jerusalem: Israel Universities Press, 1973).

Dowty, Alan, 'Despair is not enough: violence, attitudinal change, and "ripeness" in the Israeli–Palestinian conflict', *Cooperation and Conflict* 41:1 (2006), 5–29.

Drysdale, Alasdair, and Raymond Hinnebusch, *Syria and the Middle East Peace Process* (New York: Council on Foreign Relations Press, 1991).

'Dutchman returns Holocaust medal after family deaths in Gaza', BBC, 15 August 2014, https://www.bbc.co.uk/news/world-europe-28814555 (accessed 15 January 2020).

Dyson, Stephen B., 'George W. Bush, the Surge, and presidential leadership', *Political Science Quarterly* 125:4 (2010–2011), 557–585.

Dyson, Stephen B., 'Images of international politics in Chinese science fiction: Liu Cixin's three-body problem', *New Political Science* 41:3 (2019), 459–475.

References

Dyson, Stephen B., *The Blair Identity: Leadership and Foreign Policy* (Manchester: Manchester University Press, 2009).

'Egyptians protest Hebrew in curriculum', *Jerusalem Post* (on-line), 11 February 2008.

Eiran, Ehud, *Israel and Weak Neighboring States: Lessons from the Israeli Experience in Lebanon* (Ramat Gan: Mitvim – Israeli Institute for Regional Foreign Policies, February 2013), http://mitvim.org.il/images/Israel_and_Weak_Neighboring_States_-_Dr._Ehud_Eiran.pdf (accessed 20 February 2013).

Eldar, Akiva, 'How to ensure success at the Paris peace conference', al-Monitor, 2 June 2016, https://www.al-monitor.com/pulse/originals/2016/06/prophet-jeremiah-netanyahu-liberman-abbas-peace-idf.html#ixzz4ASva1hAJ (accessed 16 January 2020).

Eldar, Akiva, 'Israel should make peace with Egyptian people', *al-Monitor*, 8 July 2013, https://www.al-monitor.com/pulse/originals/2013/07/israel--egypt--normalization.html#ixzz2cjKrHqa7 (accessed 9 January 2020).

Eldar, Akiva, 'Operation Protective Edge continues cycle of violence', *al-Monitor* (21 July 2014), https://www.al-monitor.com/pulse/originals/2014/07/israel-strategic-achievement-defensive-edge-moshe-yaalon.html (accessed 14 January 2020).

Elgindy, Khaled, *Blind Spot: America and the Palestinians, From Balfour to Trump* (Washington, DC: Brookings Institution Press, 2019).

Erlanger, Steven, 'In unruly Gaza, clans compete in power void', *New York Times*, 17 October 2005.

Erlanger, Steven, 'Israel steps up reprisals in West Bank and Gaza, killing 7', *New York Times*, 28 October 2005.

Farrell, William E., 'Applause at airport', *New York Times*, 19 November 1977.

Farrell, William E., 'Parliament agrees', *New York Times*, 16 November 1977.

Farsoun, Samih K., with Christina E. Zacharia, *Palestine and the Palestinians* (Boulder, CO: Westview Press, 1997).

Federman, Josef, 'Analysis: Israel tries to excise bitter memories of Lebanon with Gaza offensive', courant.com, 4 January 2009.

Feige, Michael, *Settling in the Hearts: Jewish Fundamentalism in the Occupied Territories* (Detroit, MI: Wayne State University Press, 2009).

Finlayson, A., and J. Martin, '"It Ain't What You Say...": British political studies and the analysis of speech and rhetoric', *British Politics* 3:4 (2008), 445–464.

References

'FM Shalom: Gaza pullout could lead to renewal of peace talks', haaretz. com, 14 September 2005.

Ford, Gerald R., *A Time to Heal* (New York: Berkley Books, 1979/1980).

Freedman, Robert O. (ed.), *The Intifada: Its Impact on Israel, the Arab World, and the Superpowers* (Miami, FL: Florida International University Press, 1991).

Freilich, Charles D., *Israeli National Security: A New Strategy for an Era of Change* (New York: Oxford University Press, 2018).

Friedman, Thomas, 'Israel's goals in Gaza?', *New York Times*, 14 January 2009.

Fromer, Yoav, 'The missiles keeping Israel safe may do more long-term harm than good', *Washington Post*, 14 July 2014, https://www.washingtonpost.com/posteverything/wp/2014/07/14/the-missiles-keeping-israel-safe-may-do-more-long-term-harm-than-good (accessed 9 January 2020).

'Full text of Netanyahu's foreign policy speech at Bar Ilan', *Ha'aretz*, 14 June 2009, https://www.haaretz.com/1.5064276 (accessed 24 January 2020).

Gadarian, Shana Kushner, 'The politics of threat: how terrorism news shapes foreign policy attitudes', *Journal of Politics* 72:2 (2010), 469–483.

El-Gamasy, Mohamed Abdel Ghani, *The October War: Memoirs of Field Marshal El-Gamasy of Egypt* (Cairo: American University in Cairo Press, 1993).

Gates, Robert M., *From the Shadows* (New York: Simon and Schuster, 1996).

Gavron, Assaf, *Almost Dead*, trans. Assaf Gavron and James Lever (New York: Harper Perennial, 2010).

'Gaza bursting at seams without West Bank link', *Daily Star*, 14 September 2005.

'Gaza portrayed', *Jerusalem Post*, 28 December 2008.

'Gaza: the rights and wrongs', *The Economist*, 30 December 2008.

Gazzar, Brenda, and Etgar Lefkovits, 'Tibi protests Israeli "war crime"', *Jerusalem Post*, 27 December 2008.

George, Alexander, and Andrew Bennett, *Case Studies and Theory Development in the Social Sciences* (Cambridge, MA: MIT Press, 2005).

Gerges, Fawaz A., 'Egyptian–Israeli relations turn sour', *Foreign Affairs* 74:3 (1995), 69–78.

Gerner, Deborah J., et al., 'The creation of CAMEO (Conflict and Mediation Event Observations): an event data framework for a post

Cold War world', Prepared for delivery at the Annual Meeting of the American Political Science Association, 29 August –1 September 2002.

Gerring, John, 'What is a case study and what is it good for?', *American Political Science Review* 98:2 (2004), 341–354.

Getmansky, Anna, and Thomas Zeitzoff, 'Rockets and bombs make Israelis and Palestinians less willing to compromise', *Washington Post*, 16 July 2014, https://www.washingtonpost.com/blogs/monkey-cage/wp/2014/07/16/rockets-and-bombs-make-israelis-and-palestinians-less-willing-to-compromise (accessed 14 January 2020).

Getmansky, Anna, and Thomas Zeitzoff, 'Terrorism and voting: the effect of rocket threat on voting in Israeli elections', *American Political Science Review* 108:3 (2014), 588–604.

Geyelin, Philip, 'Mideast danger: U.S. authorities fear Arab "liberation" war may threaten Israel', *Wall Street Journal*,12 March 1965, p. 1.

Ginat, Rami, *The Soviet Union and Egypt, 1945–1955* (Portland, OR: Frank Cass, 1993).

Ginor, Isabella, and Gideon Remez, *Foxbats Over Dimona: The Soviets' Nuclear Gamble in the Six-Day War* (New Haven, CT: Yale University Press, 2007).

Goddard, Stacie E., Jeremy Pressman, and Ron E. Hassner, 'Correspondence: time and the intractability of territorial disputes', *International Security* 32:3 (2007/2008), 191–201.

Goerzig, Carolin, 'Engaging Hamas: rethinking the Quartet principles', ISS Opinion (European Union Institute for Security Studies, March 2010), https://www.iss.europa.eu/content/engaging-hamas-rethinking-quartet-principles (accessed 24 January 2020).

Golan, Galia, *Israeli Peacemaking Since 1967: Factors Behind the Breakthroughs and Failures* (New York: Routledge, 2015).

Golani, Motti, 'The historical place of the Czech–Egyptian arms deal, fall 1955', *Middle Eastern Studies* 31:4 (1995), 803–827.

Goldberg, J. J., 'Ex-Shin Bet chief: Israeli illusions fueled blowup', Forward. com, 5 July 2014, https://forward.com/opinion/201468/ex-shin-bet-chief-israeli-illusions-fueled-blowup/ (accessed 28 January 2020).

Goldlist-Eichler, Hayah, '40% of Israeli children in Gaza border town of Sderot suffer from anxiety, PTSD', jpost.com, 8 July 2015, https://www.jpost.com/Israel-News/40-percent-of-Israeli-children-in-Gaza-border-town-of-Sderot-suffer-from-anxiety-PTSD-408306 (accessed 15 January 2020).

Goldstein, Judith, and Robert O. Keohane, *Ideas and Foreign Policy:*

References

Beliefs, Institutions, and Political Change (Ithaca, NY: Cornell University Press, 1993).

Gordon, Carol, and Asher Arian, 'Threat and decision making', *Journal of Conflict Resolution* 45:2 (2001), 196–215.

Gordon, Neve, 'What is Israel's goal?', *Palestine Chronicle*, 30 December 2008, http://www.palestinechronicle.com/what-is-israels-goal (accessed 24 January 2020).

Goren, Yuval, 'Livni: We will not allow thugs to rule the Middle East', *Ha'aretz*, 31 December 2008.

Gorenberg, Gershom, *The Accidental Empire* (New York: Times Books, 2006).

Gorenberg, Gershom, 'The missing Mahatma: searching for a Gandhi or a Martin Luther King in the West Bank', *Weekly Standard* 14:28 (6 April 2009), 20–34.

Greeberg, Hanan, 'Report: IDF divides Gaza Strip into 3', Ynetnews, 4 January 2009, https://www.ynetnews.com/articles/0,7340,L-3649928,00.html (accessed 24 January 2020).

Greffenius, Steven F., 'Foreign policy stabilization and the Camp David Accords: opportunities and obstacles to the institutionalization of peace', in Jerel A. Rosati, Joe D. Hagan, and Martin W. Sampson (eds), *Foreign Policy Restructuring: How Governments Respond to Global Change* (Columbia, SC: University of South Carolina Press, 1995), 203–220.

Grossman, David, 'Fight fire with a cease-fire', *New York Times*, 30 December 2008, https://www.nytimes.com/2008/12/31/opinion/31grossman.html (accessed 7 January 2020).

Grynaviski, Eric, 'Contrasts, counterfactuals, and causes', *European Journal of International Relations* 19:4 (2013), 823–846.

Gutwein, Daniel, 'Israel needs a leftist revolution to stop the fascism', *Ha'aretz*, 9 November 2010.

Gwertzman, Bernard, 'Sadat seeks Israeli invitation to make address in Parliament; Begin agrees, will ask U.S. help', *New York Times*, 15 November 1977.

Haber, Eitan, 'Thank you, Egypt', Ynetnews.com, 19 November 2007, https://www.ynetnews.com/articles/0,7340,L-3473031,00.html (accessed 24 January 2020).

Haddad, Yvonne, 'Islamists and the "problem of Israel": the 1967 Awakening', *Middle East Journal* 46:2 (1992), 266–285.

Hadid, Diaa, 'Video shows Israeli extremists celebrating Palestinian child's death', *New York Times*, 24 December 2015, https://www.nytimes.

References

com/2015/12/25/world/middleeast/ali-dawabsheh-arson-death-israel-wedding-video.html (accessed 15 January 2020).

Halper, Jeff, 'Dismantling the matrix of control', *Middle East Report Online*, 11 September 2009, https://merip.org/2009/09/dismantling-the-matrix-of-control (accessed 3 January 2020).

Halper, Jeff, 'The 94 percent solution: a matrix of control', *Middle East Report* 216 (autumn 2000), https://merip.org/2000/09/the-94-percent-solution (accessed 3 January 2020).

'Hamas question & answer', Al-Qassam, 10 December 2006, http://www.alqassam.ps/english/index.php?action=showinet&inid=2 (accessed 23 October 2008).

Hamrush, Mujtma, *Gamal Abed al-Nasser* (Cairo: Maktabat Madboli, 1983).

Hansen, Lene, *Security as Practice* (London: Routledge, 2006).

Harel, Amos, and Avi Issacharoff, 'Postmortem', *Ha'aretz*, 23 January 2009.

Harel, Amos, and Barak Ravid, 'After IAF strike kills at least 230 in Gaza, Hamas chief vows third intifada has come', *Ha'aretz*, 28 December 2008.

Harel, Amos, and Arnon Regular, 'West Bank Hamas plans new attacks in spite of "lull"', *Ha'aretz*, 28 September 2005.

Harkabi, Yehoshafat, *Arab Strategies and Israel's Response* (New York: Free Press, 1977).

Harkabi, Yehoshafat, *Israel's Fateful Hour* (New York: Harper and Row, 1989).

Harkabi, Yehoshafat, *Palestinians and Israel* (New York: Halsted Press of John Wiley & Sons, 1974).

Harkabi, Yehoshafat, 'The Palestinians in the Israel–Arab conflict', in Avineri (ed.), *Israel and the Palestinians*, 1–21.

Hass, Amira, 'Dutch nonagenarian returns Righteous Among the Nations medal after six relatives killed in Gaza', *Ha'aretz*, 15 August 2014, https://www.haaretz.com/.premium-man-returns-medal-4-saving-wwii-jew-1.5259511 (accessed 15 January 2020).

Hassner, Ron E., 'The path to intractability: time and the entrenchment of territorial disputes', *International Security* 31:3 (2006/2007), 107–138.

Hauser, Emily L., 'Israel's addiction to military force, it's only response in times of crisis', *Ha'aretz*, 26 June 2014, https://www.haaretz.com/opinion/.premium-israels-addiction-to-force-1.5253540 (accessed 9 January 2020).

Heikal, Mohamed, *Nasser: The Cairo Documents* (London, 1971).

References

Heradstveit, Daniel, *The Arab–Israeli Conflict: Psychological Obstacles to Peace*, 2nd edition (Oslo: Universitetsforlaget, 1981).

Hersh, Seymour, 'Syria calling', *New Yorker*, 6 April 2009, https://www.newyorker.com/magazine/2009/04/06/syria-calling (accessed 7 January 2020).

Higgins, Andrew, 'How Israel helped to spawn Hamas', *Wall Street Journal*, 24 January 2009.

Hirst, David, *The Gun and the Olive Branch: The Roots of Violence in the Middle East*, 3rd edition (New York: Thunder's Mouth Press/Nation Books, 2003).

Horovitz, David, 'Netanyahu finally speaks his mind', *Times of Israel*, 13 July 2014, https://www.timesofisrael.com/netanyahu-finally-speaks-his-mind (accessed 7 January 2020).

Horowitz, Michael, and Daniel Reiter, 'When does aerial bombing work? Quantitative empirical tests, 1917–1999', *Journal of Conflict Resolution* 45:2 (2001), 147–173.

Hroub, Khaled, 'Hamas after Shaykh Yasin and Rantisi', *Journal of Palestine Studies* 33:4 (2004), 21–38.

Hroub, Khaled, *Hamas: Political Thought and Practice* (Washington, DC: Institute for Palestine Studies, 2000).

Hubbard, Ben, 'Loss of shelter and electricity worsens a crisis for fleeing Gazans', *New York Times*, 30 July 2014, https://www.nytimes.com/2014/07/30/world/middleeast/loss-of-shelter-and-electricity-worsens-a-crisis-for-fleeing-gazans.html (accessed 9 January 2020).

Huddy, Leonie, 'Diverse emotional reactions to threat', Paper presented at the annual meeting of the American Political Science Association, Toronto, 3–6 September 2009.

El Hussini, Mohrez Mahmoud, *Soviet–Egyptian Relations, 1945–1985* (New York: St Martin's Press, 1987).

Hybel, Alex Roberto, *The Logic of Surprise in International Conflict* (Lexington, MA: Lexington Books, 1986).

'IAF hits Hamas ammo stocks, tunnels', *Jerusalem Post*, 29 December 2008.

Ibish, Hussein, 'The Sharon doctrine: the mixed legacy of an Israeli unilateralist', *Foreign Affairs*, 11 January 2014, https://www.foreignaffairs.com/articles/middle-east/2014-01-11/sharon-doctrine#/ cid=soc-twitter-at-snapshot-the_sharon_doctrine-000000 (accessed 7 January 2020).

'IDF general in bombshell speech: Israel today shows signs of 1930s Germany', jpost.com, 4 May 2016, https://www.jpost.com/Israel-News/Politics-And-Diplomacy/IDF-general-in-bombshell- speech-

Israel-today-shows-signs-of-1930s-Germany-453142 (accessed 3 January 2020).

Ignatius, David, 'What a war in 1973 can tell us about handling Iran in 2013', *Washington Post*, 3 October 2013, https://www.washingtonpost.com/opinions/david-ignatius-what-a-war-in-1973-can-tell-us-about-iran-in-2013/ 2013/10/03/4d004788-2afb-11e3-8ade-a1f23cda135e_story.html (accessed 3 January 2020).

Inbar, Efraim, 'Great power mediation: the USA and the May 1983 Israeli–Lebanese agreement', *Journal of Peace Research* 28:1 (1991), 71–84.

Inbar, Efraim, *Israel's National Security: Issues and Challenges Since the Yom Kippur War* (London: Routledge, 2008).

Indyk, Martin, *Innocent Abroad: An Intimate Account of American Peace Diplomacy in the Middle East* (New York: Simon and Schuster, 2009).

Insight Team of the London Sunday Times, *The Yom Kippur War* (Garden City, NY: Doubleday, 1974).

International Crisis Group, *Dealing with Hamas* (International Crisis Group, 2004), https://www.crisisgroup.org/middle-east-north-africa/eastern-mediterranean/israelpalestine/dealing-hamas (accessed 14 January 2020).

International Crisis Group, 'Ending the war in Gaza', Policy briefing, Middle East briefing no. 26, 5 January 2009.

International Crisis Group, 'Gaza's unfinished business', *Middle East Report* no. 85, 23 April 2009.

International Crisis Group, 'Tipping point? Palestinians and the search for a new strategy', *Middle East Report* no. 95, 26 April 2010.

International Middle East Media Center (IMEMC), 'After Israeli attack, 50% Gaza children have PTSD, 70% have regular nightmare', 25 July 2015, https://www.juancole.com/2015/07/israeli-children-nightmares.html, (accessed 15 January 2020).

'Israel declines to study Rabin tie to beatings', *New York Times*, 12 July 1990, p. A8.

Israel Defense Forces, *Deterring Terror: How Israel Confronts the Next Generation of Threats*, trans. Susan Rosenberg (Cambridge, MA: Belfer Center, 2016).

'Israel kills at least 225 in Gaza', *Jordan Times*, 28 December 2008.

'Israel's road map reservations', *Ha'aretz*, 27 May 2003, https://www.haaretz.com/1.5471994 (accessed 14 January 2020).

Israel State Archives, '"No more war": the peace plan of the Israeli government and President Sadat's journey to Jerusalem, November 1977; documents on the background to Sadat's visit and the Israeli

References

government's reaction', http://www.archives.gov.il/ArchiveGov_Eng/Publications/ElectronicPirsum/SadatVisit (accessed 25 September 2013).

'Israeli PM Rabin's speech at the signing of the Declaration of Principles (1993)', 13 September 1993, https://ecf.org.il/issues/issue/18 (accessed 24 January 2020).

Jabotinsky, Vladimir, 'The iron wall', 4 November 1923, https://www.jewishvirtuallibrary.org/quot-the-iron-wall-quot (accessed 7 January 2020).

Jahn, George, 'Senior Israeli minister endorses Arab peace plan', *USA Today*, 20 June 2013, https://eu.usatoday.com/story/news/world/2013/06/20/israel-palestinian-netanyahu-eu/2441025 (accessed 15 January 2020).

Jakobsen, Peter V., 'Pushing the limits of military coercion theory', *International Studies Perspectives* 12:2 (2011), 153–170.

Jensehaugen, Jørgen, *Arab–Israeli Diplomacy Under Carter: The US, Israel and the Palestinians* (London: I. B. Tauris, 2018).

Jentleson, Bruce, *Coercive Diplomacy: Scope and Limits in the Contemporary World*, Policy Analysis Brief (Muscatine, IA: Stanley Foundation, December 2006).

Jervis, Robert, 'Perceiving and coping with threat', in Jervis et al. (eds), *Psychology and Deterrence*, 13–33.

Jervis, Robert, *Perception and Misperception in International Politics* (Princeton, NJ: Princeton University Press, 1976).

Jervis, Robert, *Why Intelligence Fails* (Ithaca, NY: Cornell University Press, 2010).

Jervis, Robert, Richard Ned Lebow, and Janice Gross Stein (eds), *Psychology and Deterrence* (Baltimore, MD: Johns Hopkins University Press, 1985).

Johnson, Dominic D. P., and Monica Duffy Toft, 'Grounds for war: the evolution of territorial conflict', *International Security* 38:3 (2013/2014), 7–38.

Johnston, Alastair Iain, *Cultural Realism: Strategic Culture and Grand Strategy in Chinese History* (Princeton, NJ: Princeton University Press, 1998).

Johnston, Alastair Iain, 'Thinking about strategic culture', *International Security* 19:4 (1995), 32–64.

'Joint press conference with Israeli FM Livni, Egyptian FM Gheit and Jordanian FM al-Khatib', 25 July 2007, https://mfa.gov.il/MFA/PressRoom/2007/Pages/Press%20Conference%20with%20FM%20Livni%

References

20Egyptian%20FM%20Gheit%20and%20Jordanian%20FM% 20%20 al-Khatib%2025-Jul-2007.aspx (accessed 3 January 2020).

Jones, David Pryce, 'Palestinians' mirage and Egyptians' reality', *New York Times*, 14 June 1974, p. 33.

Jones, John M., and Robert C. Rowland, 'Redefining the proper role of government: ultimate definition in Reagan's first inaugural', *Rhetoric and Public Affairs* 18:4 (2015), 691–718.

Kagan, Robert, 'America's dangerous aversion to conflict', *Wall Street Journal*, 5 September 2014.

Kalman, Matthew, 'Is Abbas' pen mightier than Arafat's sword?', *Ha'aretz*, 2 April 2014, https://www.haaretz.com/.premium-can-abbas-pen-beat-arafat-s-sword-1.5243753 (accessed 9 January 2020).

Kalman, Matthew, 'Rajoub begins his run', *Ha'aretz*, 15 May 2014, https://www.haaretz.com/.premium-rajoub-begins-his-run-1.5248408 (accessed 14 January 2020).

Kamel, Mohamed Ibrahim, *The Camp David Accords: A Testimony* (London: KPI, 1986).

Karsh, Efraim, 'After Annapolis: what chance for agreement with Abbas and the PLO?', *Jerusalem Issue Brief* 7:26 (1 January 2008).

Karsh, Efraim, 'Arafat's grand strategy', *Middle East Quarterly*, spring 2004, 3–11.

Karsh, Efraim, *Arafat's War: The Man and His Battle for Israeli Conquest* (New York: Grove Press, 2003).

Kaspit, Ben, 'Israel is not a state that has an army but rather an army that has a state attached to it', *Ma'ariv*, 6 September 2002 (Rosh Hashana supplement), p. 8.

Katz, Samuel M., *Soldier Spies: Israeli Military Intelligence* (Novato, CA: Presidio Press, 1992).

Katz, Yaakov, 'Analysis: Shock, awe ... and deception', *Jerusalem Post*, 28 December 2008.

Kelman, Herbert C., 'Acknowledging the other's nationhood: how to create a momentum for the Israeli–Palestinian negotiations', *Journal of Palestine Studies* 22:1 (1992), 18–38.

Kelman, Herbert C., 'The interdependence of Israeli and Palestinian national identities: the role of the other in existential conflicts', *Journal of Social Issues* 55:3 (1999), 581–600.

Keohane, Robert O., and Joseph S. Nye, *Power and Interdependence: World Politics in Transition* (Boston, MA: Little, Brown, 1977).

Kessler, Glenn, 'Unintended consequences pose risks for Mideast policy', *Washington Post*, 7 January 2009.

Khalidi, Walid, 'Thinking the unthinkable: a sovereign Palestinian state', *Foreign Affairs* 56:4 (1978), 695–713.

Khatib, Abed Rahim, 'Palestinian labourers work at a cement factory in Gaza Strip', 10 February 2014, https://www.gettyimages.in/detail/news-photo/palestinian-labourers-work-at-a-cement-factory-in-rafah-in-news-photo/524956598 (accessed 28 January 2020).

El-Khodary, Taghreed, and Ethan Bronner, 'Israeli Gaza strike kills more than 225', *New York Times*, 28 December 2008.

Khouri, Fred J., *The Arab–Israeli Dilemma*, 3rd edition (Syracuse, NY: Syracuse University Press, 1985).

Kifner, John, 'Militants reject policy on attacks in Israel', *New York Times*, 14 August 2002.

King, Laura, and Ken Ellingwood, 'Hamas politicians maneuvering in Gaza Strip', *Los Angeles Times*, 18 September 2005.

Kipnis, Yigal, *1973: The Road to War* (Charlottesville, VA: Just World Books, 2013).

Klein, Menachem, 'Jerusalem as an Israeli problem – a review of forty years of Israeli rule over Arab Jerusalem', *Israel Studies* 13:2 (2008), 54–72.

Knowlton, Brian, 'Meeting with Abbas, Bush expresses optimism for peace', *New York Times*, 20 October 2005.

Kolatt, Israel, 'The chances for peace and the right to a homeland', in Avineri (ed.), *Israel and the Palestinians*, 74–84.

Krause, Peter, 'The structure of success: how the internal distribution of power drives armed group behavior and national movement effectiveness', *International Security* 38:3 (2013/2014), 72–116.

Krebs, Ronald R., *Narrative and the Making of US National Security* (Cambridge: Cambridge University Press, 2015).

Kriesberg, Louis, 'Timing and the initiation of de-escalation moves', *Negotiation Journal* 3:4 (1987), 375–384.

Kristof, Nicholas, 'Who's right and wrong in the Middle East?', *New York Times*, 19 July 2014, https://www.nytimes.com/2014/07/20/opinion/sunday/nicholas-kristof-whos-right-and-wrong-in-the-middle-east.html (accessed 9 January 2020).

Kubovich, Yaniv, 'Cops who beat Israeli Arab supermarket worker under criminal probe', *Ha'aretz*, 1 June 2016, https://www.haaretz.com/israel-news/.premium-investigation-opened-against-cops-who-beat-israeli-arab-1.5389949 (accessed 15 January 2020).

Kupchan, Charles, *How Enemies Become Friends: The Sources of Stable Peace* (Princeton, NJ: Princeton University Press, 2010).

Kuperman, Ranan D., 'Why the liberal economic model of international peace failed in the Middle East', in Benjamin Miller and Carmela Lutmar (eds), *Regional Peacemaking and Conflict Management: A Comparative Approach* (New York: Routledge, 2016).

Kurtzer, Daniel, and Scott B. Lasensky, *Negotiating Arab–Israeli Peace: American Leadership in the Middle East* (Washington, DC: United States Institute of Peace Press, 2008).

Kurtzer, Daniel, Scott B. Lasensky, William B. Quandt, Steven Spiegel, and Shibley Telhami, *The Peace Puzzle: America's Quest for Arab–Israeli Peace, 1989–2011* (Ithaca, NY: Cornell University Press, 2013).

Labs, Eric J., 'Do weak states bandwagon?', *Security Studies* 1:3 (1992), 383–416.

Land, Julie, 'Al Walaja: the story of a shrinking village', November 2013, https://vimeo.com/80599955 (accessed 14 January 2020).

Lappin, Yaakov, 'First Israeli death of Gaza operation as mortar shell kills man at Erez Crossing', jpost.com, 15 July 2014, https://www.jpost.com/Operation-Protective-Edge/Barrage-of-rockets-fired-from-Gaza- despite-Israels-acceptance-of-ceasefire-362839 (accessed 15 January 2020).

Lappin, Yaakov, 'IDF releases Cast Lead casualty numbers', *Jerusalem Post*, 26 March 2009, https://www.jpost.com/Israel/IDF-releases-Cast-Lead-casualty-numbers (accessed 24 January 2020).

Laron, Guy, *Cutting the Gordian Knot: The Post-WWII Egyptian Quest for Arms and the 1955 Czechoslovak Arms Deal*, Cold War International History Project Working Paper 55 (Washington, DC: Woodrow Wilson International Center for Scholars, February 2007), https://www.wilsoncenter.org/sites/default/files/WP55_WebFinal.pdf (accessed 3 January 2020).

Larson, Deborah Welch, *Anatomy of Mistrust: U.S.–Soviet Relations During the Cold War* (Ithaca, NY: Cornell University Press, 1997).

Lauren, Paul Gordon, Gordon A. Craig, and Alexander L. George, *Force and Statecraft: Diplomatic Challenges of Our Time*, 4th edition (New York: Oxford University Press, 2007).

Lawrence, Adria, 'Triggering nationalist violence: competition and conflict in uprisings against colonial rule', *International Security* 35:2 (2010), 88–122.

Lazaroff, Tovah, 'Soldier arrested for shooting subdued terrorist after Hebron attack', *Jerusalem Post*, 24 March 2016, https://www.jpost.com/Israel-News/VIDEO-IDF-probes-soldier-who-shot-dead-subdued-Palestinian-terrorist-449094 (accessed 15 January 2020).

Lebow, Richard Ned, 'What's so different about a counterfactual?', *World Politics* 52:4 (2000), 550–585.

Lebow, Richard Ned, and Janice Gross Stein, *We All Lost the Cold War* (Princeton, NJ: Princeton University Press, 1994).

Legro, Jeffrey, *Rethinking the World: Great Power Strategies and International Order* (Ithaca, NY: Cornell University Press, 2007).

Lehrs, Lior, 'Jerusalem on the negotiating table: analyzing the Israeli–Palestinian peace talks on Jerusalem (1993–2015)', *Israel Studies* 21:3 (2016), 179–205.

Lesch, Ann Mosely, 'Egyptian–Israeli relations: normalization or special ties', in Ann Mosely Lesch and Mark Tessler (eds), *Israel, Egypt, and the Palestinians: From Camp David to Intifada* (Bloomington, IN: Indiana University Press, 1989), 61–85.

Lesch, David, *The Arab–Israeli Conflict: A History* (New York: Oxford University Press, 2008).

Levey, Zach, 'Israel's quest for a security guarantee from the United States', *British Journal of Middle Eastern Studies* 22:1–2 (1995), 43–63.

Levinson, Chaim, '25 years on: what did Israeli settlers learn from the first Palestinian intifada?', *Ha'aretz*, 1 April 2013, https://www.haaretz.com/jewish/.premium-25-years-on-intifada-lessons-1.5236295 (accessed 8 January 2020).

Levy, Gideon, 'The IAF, bullies of the clear blue skies', *Ha'aretz*, 31 December 2008.

Levy, Jack, and Joseph R. Gochal, 'Democracy and preventive war: Israel and the 1956 Sinai campaign', *Security Studies* 11:2 (2001/2002), 1–49.

Lis, Jonathan, 'Israel must annex West Bank settlements, right-wing MKs tell Netanyahu', *Ha'aretz*, 27 September 2011, https://www.haaretz.com/1.5183863 (accessed 16 January 2020).

Litvak, Meir, '"Martyrdom is Life": *Jihad* and martyrdom in the ideology of Hamas', *Studies in Conflict and Terrorism* 33:8 (2010), 716–734.

London, Yaron, 'The Dahiya strategy', Ynetnews, 6 October 2008, https://www.ynetnews.com/articles/0,7340,L-3605863,00.html (accessed 7 January 2020).

Londoño, Ernesto, 'In Egypt's Sinai desert, Islamic militants gaining new foothold', *Washington Post*, 13 July 2012, https://www.washingtonpost.com/world/middle_east/in-egypts-sinai-desert-islamic-militants-gaining- new-foothold/2012/07/13/gJQAlqeZiW_story.html (accessed 9 January 2020).

Lorch, Netanel, *Major Knesset Debates 1948–1981, Volume 5* (Lanham, MD: University Press of America, 1993).

References

Lubell, Maayan, 'Netanyahu says no Palestinian state as long as he's prime minister', Reuters, 16 March 2015, https://www.reuters.com/article/us-israel-election/netanyahu-says-no-palestinian-state-as-long-as-hes-prime-minister-idUSKBN0MC1I820150316 (accessed 7 January 2020).

Lupovici, Amir, *The Power of Deterrence: Emotions, Identity and American and Israeli Wars of Resolve* (Cambridge: Cambridge University Press, 2016).

Lustick, Ian, 'Abandoning the iron wall: Israel and "the Middle Eastern muck"', *Middle East Policy* 15:3 (2008), 30–56.

Lustick, Ian, 'To build and to be built by: Israel and the hidden logic of the iron wall', *Israel Studies* 1:1 (1996), 196–223.

Mahdawi, Dalila, 'Nasrallah condemns Israeli assault, "Arab collaboration"', *Daily Star*, 29 December 2008.

'Mahmud Abbas's call for a halt to the militarization of the intifada', *Journal of Palestine Studies* 32:2 (2003), 74–78.

Mandell, Brian S., 'Anatomy of a confidence-building regime: Egyptian–Israeli security co-operation, 1973–1979', *International Journal* 45:2 (1990), 202–223.

Mandell, Brian S., and Brian W. Tomlin, 'Mediation in the development of norms to manage conflict: Kissinger in the Middle East', *Journal of Peace Research* 28:1 (1991), 43–55.

Mann, Michael, *Incoherent Empire* (New York: Verso, 2003).

Mansour, Atallah, 'Palestine and the search for a new golden age', in Avineri (ed.), *Israel and the Palestinians*, 85–100.

Maoz, Ifat, and Clark McCauley, 'Threat perceptions and feelings as predictors of Jewish–Israeli support for compromise with Palestinians', *Journal of Peace Research* 46:4 (2009), 525–539.

Maoz, Zeev, *Defending the Holy Land: A Critical Analysis of Israel's Security and Foreign Policy* (Ann Arbor, MI: University of Michigan Press, 2006).

Maoz, Zeev, and Allison Astorino, 'The cognitive structure of peacemaking: Egypt and Israel, 1970–1978', *Political Psychology* 13:4 (1992), 647–662.

Matar, Haggai, 'The wall, 10 years on: Part 2: Wall and peace', *+972 Magazine*, 11 April 2012, http://972mag.com/the-wall-10-years-on-wall-and-peace/41137 (accessed 28 January 2020).

McCarthy, Rory, 'Israel rejects ceasefire move as divisions emerge in leadership', *Guardian*, 31 December 2008.

McDonald, Matt, 'Discourses of climate security', *Political Geography* 33:1 (2013), 42–51.

References

McGeough, Paul, *Kill Khalid: Mossad's Failed Hit... and the Rise of Hamas* (Crows Nest: Allen and Unwin, 2009).

Mcintyre, Ronald R., 'The Palestine Liberation Organization: tactics, strategies and options towards the Geneva Peace Conference', *Journal of Palestine Studies* 4:4 (1975), 65–89.

Mearsheimer, John J., 'Hans Morgenthau and the Iraq war: realism versus neo-conservatism', Open Democracy, 19 May 2005, https://www.opendemocracy.net/en/morgenthau_2522jsp (accessed 3 January 2020).

Meital, Yoram, *Egypt's Struggle for Peace: Continuity and Change, 1967–1977* (Miami, FL: University Press of Florida, 1997).

Miller, Aaron D., *The Much Too Promised Land: America's Elusive Search for Arab–Israeli Peace* (New York: Bantam Books, 2009).

Miller, Benjamin, *States, Nations, and the Great Powers: The Sources of Regional War and Peace* (New York: Cambridge University Press, 2007).

Miller, Benjamin, 'When and how regions become peaceful: potential theoretical pathways to peace', *International Studies Review* 7:2 (2005), 229–267.

Milliken, Jennifer, 'The study of discourse in international relations: a critique of research and methods', *European Journal of International Relations* 5:2 (1999), 225–254.

Mnookin, Robert H., Ehud Eiran, and Shula Gilad, 'Is unilateralism always bad? Negotiation lessons from Israel's 'unilateral' Gaza withdrawal', *Negotiation Journal* 30:2 (2014), 131–156.

Moghadam, Assaf, 'Palestinian suicide terrorism in the second intifada: motivations and organizational aspects', *Studies in Conflict and Terrorism* 26:2 (2003), 65–92.

Mor, Ben D., 'Strategic beliefs and the formation of enduring international rivalries: Israel's national security conception, 1948–56', *International Relations* 18:3 (2004), 309–329.

Morris, Benny, 'Camp David and after: an exchange (1. An interview with Ehud Barak)', *New York Review of Books* 49:10 (13 June 2002), https://www.nybooks.com/articles/2002/06/13/camp-david-and-after-an-exchange-1-an-interview-wi/ (accessed 28 January 2020).

Morris, Benny, *Israel's Border Wars, 1949–1956: Arab Infiltration, Israeli Retaliation, and the Countdown to the Suez War* (New York: Oxford University Press, 1993).

Morris, Benny, *Righteous Victims: A History of the Zionist–Arab Conflict, 1881–1999* (New York: Alfred A. Knopf, 1999).

References

Mueller, Karl, 'Strategies of coercion: denial, punishment, and the future of air power', *Security Studies* 7:3 (1998), 182–228.

al-Mughrabi, Nidal, 'Israelis kill two Palestinian gunmen in Gaza', *Washington Post*, 24 August 2002, p. A18.

Myers, Steven Lee, 'The new meaning of an old battle in the Mideast', *New York Times*, 4 January 2009, https://www.nytimes.com/2009/01/04/weekinreview/04myers.html (accessed 3 January 2020).

Myre, Greg, 'Israel lowers its flag in the Gaza Strip', *New York Times*, 12 September 2005.

Name redacted, 'U.S. foreign aid to Israel', Congressional Research Service report, RL33222, 10 April 2018.

'Nasser says he'll "get rid" of Israel', *Washington Post*, 27 July 1959, p. A6.

Nepstad, Sharon E., 'Nonviolent civil resistance and social movements', *Sociology Compass* 7:7 (2013), 590–598.

Noe, Nicholas, 'Nasrallah's turn', *Palestine Chronicle*, 2 June 2009, http://www.palestinechronicle.com/nasrallahs-turn (accessed 28 January 2020).

Olmert, Ehud, 'The time has come to say these things', *New York Review of Books* 55:19 (4 December 2008), https://www.nybooks.com/articles/2008/12/04/the-time-has-come-to-say-these-things (accessed 24 January 2020).

Oren, Michael B., 'Escalation to Suez: the Egypt–Israel border war, 1949–56', *Journal of Contemporary History* 24:2 (1989), 347–373.

Oren, Michael B., and Yossi Klein Halevi, 'Palestinians need Israel to win', *Wall Street Journal*, 29 December 2008.

Oron, Assaf, 'An open letter to Jewish Americans', 2002, http://www.seruv.org.il/MoreArticles/English/AssafOronEng_1.htm (accessed 18 September 2008).

Osgood, Charles E., *An Alternative to War or Surrender* (Urbana, IL: University of Illinois Press, 1962).

'PA chairman Abbas phones PM Sharon, leaders agree to meet soon', *Ha'aretz*, 23 August 2005.

'PA chairman Abbas telephones Katsav to praise Israeli pullout', *Ha'aretz*, 23 August 2005, https://www.haaretz.com/1.4935301 (accessed 26 January 2020).

Palestinian Center for Policy and Survey Research, 'Public opinion poll # 16', 22 June 2005, https://www.pcpsr.org/en/node/239 (accessed 28 January 2020).

'Palestinian Declaration of Independence and acceptance of Res. 242 and 338 (1988)', 15 November 1988, https://ecf.org.il/issues/issue/12 (accessed 26 January 2020).

References

'Palestinian guerillas rebuff Sadat–Hussein views on role', *New York Times*, 20 July 1974.

Pappe, Ilan, *A History of Modern Palestine: One Land, Two Peoples* (New York: Cambridge University Press, 2004).

Paraipan, Manuela, 'The voice of Hamas', Open Democracy, 5 November 2010, https://www.opendemocracy.net/en/voice-of-hamas (accessed 14 January 2020).

Pearlman, Wendy, and Boaz Atzili, *Triadic Coercion: Israel's Targeting of States That Host Nonstate Actors* (New York: Columbia University Press, 2018).

Peck, Yoav, 'The Israeli left needs to rethink its attitude toward settlers', forward.com (28 March 2016), https://forward.com/opinion/337086/the-israeli-left-needs-to-rethink-its-attitude-toward-settlers (accessed 7 January 2020).

Peretz, Don, 'Intifadeh: the Palestinian uprising', *Foreign Affairs* 66:5 (1988), 964–980.

Peretz, Don, *Intifada: The Palestinian Uprising* (Boulder, CO: Westview Press, 1990).

'Peri: Adopt Arab Peace Initiative with corrections', jpost.com, 1 June 2013, https://www.jpost.com/Diplomacy-and-Politics/Peri-Adopt-Arab-peace-initiative-with-corrections-315098 (accessed 15 January 2020).

Perkoski, Evan, and Jeremy Pressman, 'Israel, Palestine, and the perpetual denial of nationalist claims', 10 October 2019, Political Violence @ a Glance, http://politicalviolenceataglance.org/2019/10/10/israel-palestine-and-the-perpetual-denial-of-nationalist-claims/ (accessed 28 January 2020).

Peters, Joel, 'The Gaza disengagement: five years later', *Israel Journal of Foreign Affairs* 4:3 (2010), 33–44.

Pfeffer, Anshel, 'Sending our sons into battle: the failure of another Israeli generation', *Ha'aretz*, 31 July 2014, https://www.haaretz.com/.premium-the-failure-of-another-israeli-generation-1.5257669 (accessed 6 January 2020).

Pitch, Anthony S., *Peace* (Englewood, NJ: SBS Publishing, 1979).

'PLO Chairman Arafat's speech at the signing of the Declaration of Principles (1993)', 13 September 1993, https://ecf.org.il/issues/issue/18 (accessed 24 January 2020).

Podeh, Elie, *Chances for Peace: Missed Opportunities in the Arab–Israeli Conflict* (Austin, TX: University of Texas Press, 2015).

Podeh, Elie, 'Waiting for a call from Netanyahu', *Ha'aretz*, 13 May 2013,

References

https://www.haaretz.com/opinion/.premium-elie-podeh-waiting-for-a-call-from-netanyahu-1.5242579 (accessed 15 January 2020).

Popp, Roland, 'Stumbling decidedly into the Six-Day War', *Middle East Journal* 60:2 (2006), 281–309.

Posen, Barry, *The Sources of Military Doctrine: France, Britain, and Germany Between the World Wars* (Ithaca, NY: Cornell University Press, 1984).

Powell, Robert, *In the Shadow of Power: States and Strategies in International Politics* (Princeton, NJ: Princeton University Press, 1999).

Pressman, Jeremy 'American engagement and the pathways to Arab–Israeli peace', *Cooperation and Conflict* 49:4 (2014), 536–553.

Pressman, Jeremy, 'Explaining the Carter administration's Israeli–Palestinian solution', *Diplomatic History* 37:5 (2013), 1117–1147.

Pressman, Jeremy, 'History in conflict: Israeli–Palestinian speeches at the United Nations, 1998–2016', *Mediterranean Politics*, 28 March 2019.

Pressman, Jeremy, 'Horizontal inequality and violent unrest in Jerusalem', *Terrorism and Political Violence*, 17 May 2018.

Pressman, Jeremy, 'Israeli unilateralism and Israeli–Palestinian relations, 2001–2006', *International Studies Perspectives* 7:4 (2006), 360–376.

Pressman, Jeremy, 'Israel's strategic goal', Political Violence @ a Glance, 5 August 2014, https://politicalviolenceataglance.org/2014/08/05/israels-strategic-goal (accessed 15 January 2020).

Pressman, Jeremy, 'Mediation, domestic politics, and the Israeli–Syrian negotiations, 1991–2000', *Security Studies* 16:3 (2007), 350–381.

Pressman, Jeremy, 'Power without influence: the Bush administration's foreign policy failure in the Middle East', *International Security* 33:4 (2009), 149–179.

Pressman, Jeremy 'September statements, October missiles, November elections: domestic politics, foreign-policy making, and the Cuban Missile Crisis', *Security Studies* 10:3 (2001), 80–114.

Pressman, Jeremy, 'The second intifada: an early look at the background and causes of Israeli–Palestinian conflict', *Journal of Conflict Studies* 22:2 (2003), 114–141.

Pressman, Jeremy, 'Visions in collision: what happened at Camp David and Taba?', *International Security* 28:2 (2003), 5–43.

Pressman, Jeremy, *Warring Friends: Alliance Restraint in International Politics* (Ithaca, NY: Cornell University Press, 2008).

Priebe, Miranda, 'Fear and frustration: rising state perceptions of threats and opportunities', PhD dissertation (Massachusetts Institute of Technology, 2015).

References

Princen, Tom, 'Camp David: problem-solving or power politics as usual?', *Journal of Peace Research* 28:1 (1991), 57–69.

Prittie, Terence, *Israel: Miracle in the Desert*, revised edition (New York: Frederick A. Praeger, 1968).

Quandt, William B., 'Camp David and peacemaking in the Middle East', *Political Science Quarterly* 101:3 (1986), 357–377.

Quandt, William B., *Peace Process: American Diplomacy and the Arab–Israeli Conflict Since 1967*, revised edition (Washington, DC, and Berkeley, CA: Brookings Institution Press and University of California Press, 2001).

Ra'anan, Uri, *The USSR Arms the Third World: Case Studies in Soviet Foreign Policy* (Cambridge, MA: MIT Press, 1969).

Rabbani, Mouin, 'Birth pangs of a new Palestine', 7 January 2009, https://merip.org/2009/01/birth-pangs-of-a-new-palestine (accessed 7 January 2020).

Rabbani, Mouin, 'Twenty years of Oslo and the future of the two-state paradigm', *Perspectives*, issue 5 (December 2013), 29–32.

Raghavan, Sudarsan, 'Mohammed Deif, the shadowy figure who heads Hamas's military wing', *Washington Post*, 2 August 2014, https://www.washingtonpost.com/world/middle_east/mohammed-deif-the-shadowy-figure-who-heads-hamass-military-wing/2014/08/02/ed68c46e-1a85-11e4-85b6-c1451e622637_story.html (accessed 28 January 2020).

Rasler, Karen, William R. Thompson, and Sumit Ganguly, *How Rivalries End* (Philadelphia, PA: University of Pennsylvania Press, 2013).

Ravid, Barak, 'Netanyahu: Bar-Ilan 2-state speech no longer relevant in today's reality', *Ha'aretz*, 8 March 2015, https://www.haaretz.com/.premium.bar-ilan-speech-no-longer-relevant-1.5333961 (accessed 16 January 2020).

Ravid, Barak, 'Ya'alon proposes new settlement in memory of murdered teens', *Ha'aretz*, 1 July 2014, https://www.haaretz.com/.premium-yaalon-new-settlement-in-memory-of-teens-1.5254048 (accessed 15 January 2020).

Raz, Avi, *The Bride and the Dowry: Israel, Jordan and the Palestinians in the Aftermath of the June 1967 War* (New Haven, CT: Yale University Press, 2012).

Regular, Arnon, and Aluf Benn, 'Israel rejects claims by Palestinians that pullout won't end Gaza occupation', *Ha'aretz*, 4 September 2005.

'Remarks of President Carter, President Anwar al-Sadat of Egypt, and Prime Minister Menahem Begin of Israel at the Egyptian–Israeli peace treaty signing ceremony', 26 March 1979, https://www.presidency.ucsb.edu/documents/remarks-president-carter-president-anwar-al-sadat-egypt-and-prime-minister-menahem-begin (accessed 24 January 2020).

'Response of FM Peres to the decisions of the Arab summit in Beirut', Communicated by the Foreign Ministry spokesperson, 28 March 2002, https://mfa.gov.il/MFA/PressRoom/2002/Pages/Response%20of%20FM%20Peres%20to%20the%20decisions%20of%20the%20Arab.aspx (accessed 15 January 2020).

Rid, Thomas, 'Deterrence beyond the state: the Israeli experience', *Contemporary Security Policy* 33:1 (2012), 124–147.

Rifkind, Gabrielle, 'A route to resolution for Syria and Israel', *Guardian*, 26 February 2010, https://www.theguardian.com/commentisfree/2010/feb/26/syria-israel-golan-heights-middle-east (accessed 7 January 2020).

Roberts, Hugh, 'Radical Islamism and the dilemma of Algerian nationalism: the embattled Arians of Algiers', *Third World Quarterly* 10:2 (1988), 556–589.

Rodman, David, 'Israel's national security doctrine: an appraisal of the past and a vision of the future', *Israel Affairs* 9:4 (2003), 115–140.

Roe, Paul, 'Which security dilemma? Mitigating ethnic conflict: the case of Croatia', *Security Studies* 13:4 (2004), 280–313.

Roth, Ariel Ilan, 'How Hamas won', *Foreign Affairs*, 20 July 2014, https://www.foreignaffairs.com/articles/israel/2014-07-20/how-hamas-won (accessed 14 January 2020).

Rouleau, Eric, 'The Palestinian quest', *Foreign Affairs* 53:2 (January 1975), 264–283.

Rowland, Robert C., and John M. Jones, 'Reagan's strategy for the Cold War and the Evil Empire address', *Rhetoric and Public Affairs* 19:3 (2016), 427–463.

Roy, Sara, 'A Dubai on the Mediterranean', *London Review of Books* 27:21 (3 November 2005).

Roy, Sara, *Hamas and Civil Society in Gaza: Engaging the Islamist Social Sector* (Princeton, NJ: Princeton University Press, 2011).

Roy, Sara, 'Praying with their eyes closed: reflections on the disengagement from Gaza', *Journal of Palestine Studies* 34:4 (2005), 64–74.

Rubin, Barry, 'The region. Hamas's strategy: the rockets or the media', *Jerusalem Post*, 28 December 2008.

Rudoren, Jodi, 'Clinton sees opportunity as well as uncertainty in Middle East', *New York Times*, 16 July 2012, https://www.nytimes.com/2012/

07/17/world/middleeast/hillary-clinton-sees-opportunity-in-middle-east.html (accessed 9 January 2020).

Rynhold, Jonathan, and Dov Waxman, 'Ideological change and Israel's disengagement from Gaza', *Political Science Quarterly* 123:1 (2008), 11–37.

Sachar, Howard, *A History of Israel from the Rise of Zionism to Our Time*, 2nd edition, revised and updated (New York: Alfred A. Knopf, 1996).

el-Sadat, Anwar, *In Search of Identity: An Autobiography* (New York: Harper and Row, 1978).

el-Sadat, Anwar, *Those I Have Known* (London: Jonathan Cape, 1985).

el-Sadat, Anwar, 'Where Egypt stands', *Foreign Affairs* 51:1 (1972), 114–123.

Safty, Adel, 'Sadat's negotiations with the United States and Israel: Camp David and Blair House', *American Journal of Economics and Sociology* 50:4 (1991), 473–484.

Safty, Adel, 'Sadat's negotiations with the United States and Israel: from Sinai to Camp David', *American Journal of Economics and Sociology* 50:3 (1991), 285–298.

Said Aly, Abdel Monem, Shai Feldman, and Khalil Shikaki, *Arabs and Israelis: Conflict and Peacemaking in the Middle East* (Houndmills: Palgrave, 2013).

Samhouri, Mohammed, *Gaza Economic Predicament One Year After Disengagement: What Went Wrong?*, Middle East Brief 12 (Waltham, MA: Crown Center for Middle East Studies, Brandeis University, November 2006).

Sasley, Brent, and Mira Sucharov, 'Resettling the West Bank settlers', *International Journal* 66:4 (2011), 999–1017.

Saunders, Harold H., 'We need a larger theory of negotiation: the importance of pre-negotiating phases', *Negotiation Journal* 1:3 (1985), 249–262.

Sayigh, Yezid, *Armed Struggle and the Search for State: The Palestinian National Movement 1949–1993* (New York: Oxford University Press, 1997).

Scheindlin, Dahlia, 'How can you possibly oppose this war?', +972 Magazine, 19 July 2014, https://www.972mag.com/how-can-you-possibly-oppose-this-war/93924 (accessed 9 January 2020).

Schiff, Ze'ev, and Ehud Ya'ari, *Intifada: The Palestinian Uprising – Israel's Third Front*, trans. Ina Friedman (New York: Simon and Schuster, 1990).

Schmemann, Serge, 'A senior Palestinian official urges end to suicide attacks', *New York Times*, 31 August 2002, p. A2.

References

Schneider, Howard, 'Arab countries unanimously endorse Saudi peace plan', *Washington Post*, 29 March 2002, p. A01.

Schneider, Howard, 'Israel anticipated a stronger Hamas in Gaza war', *Washington Post*, 4 April 2009.

Schneider, Howard, 'Saudi Crown Prince lays out peace plan; Arafat dispute, bombing tarnish effort', *Washington Post*, 28 March 2002, p. A01.

Schrodt, Philip A., *CAMEO: Conflict and Mediation Event Observations Event and Actor Codebook*, Version 1.1b3, March 2012, http://eventdata.parusanalytics.com/data.dir/cameo.html (accessed 6 January 2020).

Schroeder, Paul, 'Historical reality vs. neo-realist theory', *International Security* 19:1 (1994), 108–148.

Schweller, Randall L., 'Bandwagoning for profit: bringing the revisionist state back in', *International* Security 19:1 (1994), 72–107.

Sebenius, James K., 'Avoiding the costs of negotiation: a commentary on "Is unilateralism always bad?"', *Negotiation Journal* 30:2 (2014), 165–168.

Segev, Tom, *1967: Israel, the War, and the Year That Transformed the Middle East*, trans. Jessica Cohen (New York: Henry Holt and Company, 2007).

Segev, Tom, 'Cruel and meaningless wars', *Ha'aretz*, 23 January 2009.

Segev, Tom, 'Who won?', *Ha'aretz*, 23 January 2009.

Sela, Avraham, 'Politics, identity and peacemaking: the Arab discourse on peace with Israel in the 1990s', *Israel Studies* 10:2 (2005), 15–71.

Sela, Avraham, *The Decline of the Arab–Israeli Conflict: Middle East Politics and the Quest for Regional Order* (Albany, NY: State University of New York Press, 1998).

Sela, Neta, 'Ya'alon: disengagement empowered Hamas', Ynetnews, 21 February 2006, https://www.ynetnews.com/articles/0,7340,L-3219419,00.html (accessed 8 January 2020).

Shalev, Chemi, 'Moshe Dayan's enduring Gaza eulogy: this is the fate of our generation', haaretz.com, 20 June 2014, https://www.haaretz.com/.premium-moshe-dayans-enduring-gaza-eulogy-this-is-the-fate-of-our-generation-1.5256151 (accessed 7 January 2020).

Shamir, Jacob, *Public Opinion in the Israeli–Palestinian Conflict*, Peaceworks no. 60 (Washington, DC: United States Institute of Peace, June 2007).

Shamir, Jacob, and Khalil Shikaki, *Palestinian and Israeli Public Opinion: The Public Imperative in the Second Intifada* (Bloomington, IN: Indiana University Press, 2010).

Shamir, Shimon, 'Israel: the conceptual approach to peace', in Daniel Dishon (ed.), *Middle East Record: 1968* (Jerusalem: Israel Universities Press, 1973), 243–245.

Shamir, Shimon, 'The myth of Arab intransigence', in Avineri (ed.), *Israel and the Palestinians*, 22–30.

Sharon, Gilad, 'A decisive conclusion is necessary', *Jerusalem Post*, 18 November 2012, https://www.jpost.com/Opinion/Op-Ed-Contributors/A-decisive-conclusion-is-necessary (accessed 7 January 2020).

Shavit, Ari, *My Promised Land: The Triumph and Tragedy of Israel* (New York: Spiegel and Grau, 2013).

Shavit, Ari, 'The enemy within', haaretz.com, 29 August 2002, https://www.haaretz.com/1.5000032 (accessed 14 January 2020).

el-Shazly, Saad, *The Crossing of the Suez* (San Francisco, CA: American Mideast Research, 1980).

Sheehan, Edward R. F., 'How Kissinger did it: step by step in the Middle East', *Foreign Policy*, 22 (1976), 3–70.

Sheizaf, Noam, 'Why do Palestinians continue to support Hamas despite such devastating losses?', +972 *Magazine*, 22 July 2014, https://www.972mag.com/why-do-palestinians-continue-to-support-hamas-despite-such-devastating-loses/94080 (accessed 14 January 2020).

Shikaki, Khalil, 'Shikaki: Since Israeli withdrawal from Gaza, Palestinians now give top priority to improving living standard, not end to occupation', Council on Foreign Relations, 19 October 2005, https://www.cfr.org/interview/shikaki-israeli-withdrawal-gaza-palestinians-now-give-top-priority-improving-living (accessed 3 January 2020).

Shikaki, Khalil, *Willing to Compromise: Palestinian Public Opinion and the Peace Process* (Washington, DC: US Institute of Peace, January 2006).

Shiloh, Scott, 'Netanyahu: gov't moves blindly as withdrawal threatens security', *Arutz Sheva*, 7 August 2005, http://www.israelnationalnews.com/News/News.aspx/87263 (accessed 16 January 2020).

Shilon, Avi, 'There are situations that require the use of physical force', *Ha'aretz*, 17 July 2014, https://www.haaretz.com/opinion/.premium-the-value-of-physical-force-1.5255725 (accessed 7 January 2020).

Shimoni, Gideon, *The Zionist Ideology* (Hanover, NH: Brandeis University Press, 1995).

Shlaim, Avi, 'Conflicting approaches to Israel's relations with the Arabs: Ben Gurion and Sharett, 1953–1956', *Middle East Journal* 37:2 (1983), 180–201.

Shlaim, Avi, '"Man of Peace"? Ariel Sharon was the champion of violent solutions', *Guardian*, 13 January 2014, https://www.theguardian.com/

commentisfree/2014/jan/13/ariel-sharon-no-man-of-peace-israel (accessed 7 January 2020).

Shlaim, Avi, *The Iron Wall: Israel and the Arab World* (New York: W. W. Norton, 2000).

Siegman, Henry, 'The great Middle East peace process scam', *London Review of Books*, 16 August 2007, https://www.lrb.co.uk/the-paper/v29/n16/henry-siegman/the-great-middle-east-peace-process-scam (accessed 28 January 2020).

Sinai, Anne, 'That oasis seems to be a mirage', *New York Times*, 22 July 1974.

Skocpol, Theda, *States and Social Revolutions* (New York: Cambridge University Press, 1979).

'Slain Israeli teen's uncle consoles murdered Palestinian's father', *Times of Israel*, 6 July 2014, https://www.timesofisrael.com/slain-israeli-teens-uncle-consoles-murdered-palestinians-father/#ixzz36tagcOpj (accessed 15 January 2020).

Slater, Jerome, 'Lost opportunities for peace in the Arab–Israeli conflict: Israel and Syria, 1948–2001', *International Security* 27:1 (2002), 79–106.

Smith, Charles D., *Palestine and the Arab–Israeli Conflict*, 7th edition (Boston, MA: Bedford/St Martin's, 2010).

Smith, Hedrick, 'They call him El Rayis, "The Boss"', *New York Times*, 16 May 1965.

Smith, Terence, 'Palestinians remain the "key issue" in Mideast', *New York Times*, 16 June 1974.

Snyder, Glenn H., *Alliance Politics* (Ithaca, NY: Cornell University Press, 1997).

Snyder, Glenn H., '"Prisoner's dilemma" and "chicken" models in international politics', *International Studies Quarterly* 15:1 (1971), 66–103.

Snyder, Glenn H., and Paul Diesing, *Conflict Among Nations: Bargaining, Decision Making, and System Structure in International Crises* (Princeton, NJ: Princeton University Press, 1977).

Sobelman, Batsheva, 'Israel approves more Egyptian troops in Sinai', *Los Angeles Times*, 16 July 2013, https://www.latimes.com/world/la-xpm-2013-jul-16-la-fg-wn-israel-egypt-sinai-20130716-story.html (accessed 9 January 2020).

Sobelman, Daniel, *New Rules of the Game: Israel and Hizbollah After the Withdrawal From Lebanon*, Memorandum no. 69 (Tel Aviv: Jaffee Center for Strategic Studies, January 2004), https://www.inss.org.il/publication/new-rules-of-the-game-israel-and-hizbollah-after-the-withdrawal-from-lebanon (accessed 28 January 2020).

Sofer, Roni, 'Shin Bet: Hamas feels existential threat', Ynetnews, 4 January 2009, https://www.ynetnews.com/articles/0,7340,L-3650220,00.html (accessed 9 January 2020).

Sommer, Allison Kaplan, 'In Tel Aviv terror attack, scholar of Israeli–Palestinian conflict becomes its victim', Ha'aretz, 9 June 2016, https://www.haaretz.com/israel-news/tel-aviv-terror-scholar-of-conflict-becomes-its-victim-1.5393917 (accessed 15 January 2020).

Spiegel, Steven L., *The Other Arab–Israeli Conflict: Making America's Middle East Policy, From Truman to Reagan* (Chicago, IL: University of Chicago Press, 1985).

'State: W. Bank settler population grew by 12,800 in past year', haaretz.com, 26 August 2005.

'Statement by incoming foreign minister Avigdor Liberman at the ministerial inauguration ceremony', 1 April 2009, https://mfa.gov.il/MFA/PressRoom/2009/Pages/Statement_by_incoming_FM_Avigdor_Liberman_1-Apr-2009.aspx (accessed 20 January 2020).

Stein, Janice Gross, 'Building politics into psychology: the misperception of threat', *Political Psychology* 9:2 (1988), 245–271.

Stein, Janice Gross, 'Calculation, miscalculation, and conventional deterrence I: the view from Cairo', in Jervis et al. (eds), *Psychology and Deterrence*, 34–59.

Stein, Janice Gross, 'Calculation, miscalculation, and conventional deterrence II: the view from Jerusalem', in Jervis et al. (eds), *Psychology and Deterrence*, 60–88.

Stein, Janice Gross, 'Psychological explanations of international decision making and collective behavior', in Walter Carlsnaes, Thomas Risse, and Beth Simmons (eds), *Handbook of International Relations* (London: Sage, 2013), 195–219.

Stein, Janice Gross, 'The alchemy of peacemaking: the prerequisites and corequisites of progress in the Arab–Israel conflict', *International Journal* 38:4 (1983), 531–555.

Stein, Janice Gross, and Raymond Tanter, *Rational Decision-Making: Israel's Security Choices, 1967* (Columbus, OH: Ohio State University Press, 1980).

Stein, Kenneth W., 'Continuity and change in Egyptian–Israeli relations, 1973–1997', *Israel Affairs* 3:3–4 (1997), 296–320.

Stein, Kenneth W., *Heroic Diplomacy: Sadat, Kissinger, Carter, Begin and the Quest for Arab–Israeli Peace* (New York: Routledge, 1999).

Steinberg, Gerald, and Ziv Rubinovitz, *Menachem Begin and the Israel–Egypt Peace Process: Between Ideology and Political Realism* (Bloomington, IN: Indiana University Press, 2019).

Stern, Yoav, 'Abbas: I oppose armed struggle, but won't rule out option for future', *Ha'aretz*, 28 February 2008.

Stuckey, Mary E., *Defining Americans: The Presidency and National Identity* (Lawrence, KS: University Press of Kansas, 2004).

Stute, Dennis, 'Oz: "Lose–lose situation for Israel"', 30 July 2014, Deutsche Welle, https://www.dw.com/en/oz-lose-lose-situation-for-israel/a-17822511 (accessed 9 January 2020).

Susser, Leslie, 'Desperate times, drastic measures', *Jerusalem Report*, 26 August 2002, p. 12.

Tal, David, 'Israel's armistice wars, 1949–1956', in Bar-On (ed.), *A Never-Ending Conflict*, 69–86.

Tal, David, 'Israel's road to the 1956 war', *International Journal of Middle East Studies* 28:1 (1996), 59–81.

Tal, David, 'The 1956 Sinai War: a watershed in the history of the Arab–Israeli conflict', in Simon C. Smith (ed.), *Reassessing Suez 1956: New Perspectives on the Crisis and Its Aftermath* (Burlington, VT: Ashgate, 2008), 133–147.

Tanner, Henry, 'Geneva role set by Palestinians', *New York Times*, 9 June 1974, p. 1.

Tanner, Henry, 'Palestinian moderates on Council gain', *New York Times*, 10 June 1974, p. 3.

Telhami, Shibley, 'From Camp David to Wye: changing assumptions in Arab–Israeli negotiations', *Middle East Journal* 53:3 (1999), 379–392.

Telhami, Shibley, *Power and Leadership in International Bargaining: The Path to the Camp David Accords* (New York: Columbia University Press, 1990).

Tenenbaum, Karen, and Ehud Eiran, 'Israeli settlement activity in the West Bank and Gaza: a brief history', *Negotiation Journal* 21:2 (2005), 171–175.

Terris, Lesley G., and Orit E. Tykocinski, 'Inaction inertia in international negotiations: the consequences of missed opportunities', Paper prepared for the ISSS-ISAC annual conference, 4–6 October 2013, George Washington University, Washington DC.

Tessler, Mark, *A History of the Israeli–Palestinian Conflict*, 1st edition (Bloomington, IN: Indiana University Press, 1994).

Tessler, Mark, *A History of the Israeli–Palestinian Conflict*, 2nd edition (Bloomington, IN: Indiana University Press, 2009).

Tessler, Mark, 'The intifada and political discourse in Israel', *Journal of Palestine Studies* 19:2 (1990), 43–61.

'Text of speech by Sharon to Israeli parliament', 8 April 2002, *New York*

Times, https://www.nytimes.com/2002/04/08/international/middleeast/text-of-speech-by-sharon-to-israeli-parliament.html (accessed 26 January 2020).

Tharoor, Ishaan, 'How Israel helped create Hamas', *Washington Post*, 30 July 2014, https://www.washingtonpost.com/blogs/worldviews/wp/2014/07/30/how-israel-helped-create-hamas (accessed 7 January 2020).

The White House, 'Vice president speaks at VFW 103rd National Convention', 26 August 2002, https://georgewbush-whitehouse.archives.gov/news/releases/2002/08/20020826.html (accessed 6 January 2020).

Thrall, Nathan, 'Hamas's chances', *London Review of Books* 36:16 (21 August 2014), https://www.lrb.co.uk/the-paper/v36/n16/nathan-thrall/hamas-s-chances (accessed 28 January 2020).

Thrall, Nathan, *The Only Language They Understand: Forcing Compromise in Israel and Palestine* (New York: Metropolitan Books, 2017).

Tira, Ron, 'In search of the Holy Grail: can military achievements be translated into political gains?', *Military and Strategic Affairs* 2:2 (2010), 39–58.

Tolan, Sandy, *The Lemon Tree* (New York: Bloomsbury, 2006).

Torgovnik, Efraim, 'The election campaign: party needs and voter concerns', in Asher Arian (ed.), *The Elections in Israel – 1973* (Jerusalem: Jerusalem Academic Press, 1975), 59–95.

Toth, James, 'Islamism in southern Egypt: a case study of a radical religious movement', *International Journal of Middle East Studies* 35:4 (2003), 547–572.

'Two leaders cast doubt on the talks', *The Age*, 18 September 1970, p. 7.

Van Evera, Stephen, *Guide to Methods for Students of Political Science* (Ithaca, NY: Cornell University Press, 1997).

Waage, Hilde Henriksen, 'The "minnow" and the "whale": Norway and the United States in the peace process in the Middle East', *British Journal of Middle Eastern Studies* 34:2 (2007), 157–176.

Waage, Hilde Henriksen, 'The winner takes all: the 1949 Island of Rhodes armistice negotiations revisited', *Middle East Journal* 65:2 (2011), 279–304.

Walsh, Edward, and Jim Hoagland, 'Sadat and Begin sign treaty', *Washington Post*, 27 March 1979, p. A1.

Walt, Stephen M., *The Origins of Alliances* (Ithaca, NY: Cornell University Press, 1987).

Waltz, Kenneth, 'The origins of war in neorealist theory', in Robert I.

Rotberg and Theodore K. Rabb (eds), *The Origin and Prevention of Major Wars* (Cambridge: Cambridge University Press, 1988), 39–52.

Waltz, Kenneth, *Theory of International Politics* (Reading, MA: Addison-Wesley, 1979).

Watzman, Haim, 'No happy endings in Gaza', Jewcy, 30 December 2008, http://www.jewcy.com/post/no_happy_endings_gaza (accessed 7 January 2020).

Weizman, Ezer, *On Eagles' Wings: The Personal Story of the Leading Commander of the Israeli Air Force* (New York: Macmillan, 1977).

Weizman, Steve, 'Israel "destroying peace process" with new housing', Yahoo News, 30 October 2013, https://sg.news.yahoo.com/israel-destroying-peace-process-housing-174935198.html (accessed 14 January 2020).

Wendt, Alexander E., 'Collective identity formation and the international state', *American Political Science Review* 88:2 (1994), 384–396.

Wesley, J. J., 'Qualitative document analysis in political science', in B. Kal, E. Maks, and A. Van Elfrinkhof (eds), *From Text to Political Positions: State-of-the-Art Approaches to Mapping Party Positions* (Amsterdam: Benjamins, 2014).

Weymouth, Lally (interviewing Ariel Sharon), 'A "fateful step"', *Washington Post*, 11 September 2005, p. B01.

Williams, Daniel, and Lee Hockstader, 'Israel storms Arafat offices in West Bank; Sharon vows to isolate "enemy"', *Washington Post*, 29 March 2002, p. A01.

Wilson, Scott, 'Mideast envoy: "disturbing signs"', *Washington Post*, 25 October 2005, p. A18.

Witte, Griff, 'Israel presses on with Gaza strikes', *Washington Post*, 31 December 2008.

Witte, Griff, and Ruth Eglash, 'Iron Dome, Israel's antimissile system changes calculus of fight with Hamas', *Washington Post*, 14 July 2014, https://www.washingtonpost.com/world/middle_east/israel-shoots-down-hamas-drone/2014/07/14/991c46da-0b47-11e4-b8e5-d0de 807 67fc2_story.html (accessed 3 January 2020).

Wright, Robin, 'Another siege: Israel's war on the PLO', *New Yorker*, 2 August 2014, https://www.newyorker.com/news/news-desk/another-summer-another-siege-israels-war-p-l-o (accessed 14 January 2020).

Ya'alon, Moshe, *Israel's Security Policy in a Changing Middle East*, (Washington, DC: Washington Institute for Near East Policy, 14 June 2013), 12, https://www.washingtoninstitute.org/uploads/Documents/other/20130614YaalonTranscriptv2.pdf (accessed 3 January 2020).

References

Yacobi, Haim, and Wendy Pullan, 'The geopolitics of neighbourhood: Jerusalem's colonial space revisited', *Geopolitics* 19:3 (2014), 514–539.

Yahel, Ido, 'Covert diplomacy between Israel and Egypt during Nasser rule, 1952–1970', SAGE open 6:4, 1 October 2016, https://journals.sagepub.com/doi/full/10.1177/2158244016667449 (accessed 7 January 2020).

Yaniv, Avner, *Deterrence Without the Bomb: Politics of Israeli Strategy* (Lexington, MA: Lexington Books, 1987).

Yaniv, Avner, and Fabian Pascal, 'Doves, hawks, and other birds of a feather: the distribution of Israeli parliamentary opinion on the future of the Occupied Territories, 1967–1977', *British Journal of Political Science* 10:2 (1980), 260–267.

Yarhi-Milo, Keren, 'Tying hands behind closed doors: the logic and practice of secret reassurance', *Security Studies* 22:3 (2013), 405–435.

Yarhi-Milo, Keren, and Todd Hall, 'The personal touch: leaders' impressions, costly signaling, and assessments of sincerity in international affairs', *International Studies Quarterly* 56:3 (2012), 560–573.

Zartman, I. William, 'The timing of peace initiatives: hurting stalemates and ripe moments', *Global Review of Ethnopolitics* 1:1 (2001), 8–18.

Zimmerman, John, 'The origins of the Fedayeen in Nasser's *Weltpolitik*: prelude to the Suez War', *Historian* 42:1 (1979), 101–118.

Zisser, Eyal, 'The 1982 "Peace for Galilee" War: looking back in anger – between an option of a war and a war of no option', in Bar-On (ed.), *A Never-Ending Conflict*, 193–210.

Ziv, Guy, 'Cognitive structure and foreign policy change: Israel's decision to talk to the PLO', *International Relations* 25:4 (2011), 426–454.

Ziv, Guy, 'Simple vs. complex learning revisited: Israeli prime ministers and the question of a Palestinian state', *Foreign Policy Analysis* 9:2 (2013), 203–222.

INDEX

Abbas, Mahmoud 49, 102–104, 142, 157–161, 166–167, 182–183, 195
Abu Jihad 39
Abu al-Najjah, Ibrahim 44
Abu Rudeina, Nabil 142
Abu Shanab, Ismail 39, 123
Abu Sharif, Bassam 58
Abu Zuhri, Sami 142–143, 159
Agha, Hussein 147
aid projects 73, 86, 94, 197
al-Baath (newspaper) 31–32
Alpher, Yossi 44
al-Qassam brigades 34
Al Walaja 126
Annan, Kofi 160
Annapolis talks (2007–2008) 2, 66
annexation policy, Israeli 205–206
Antebi, Dikla 180
anti-Semitism 209
appeasement, fear of 136
Arab–Israeli conflict generally 190; historical view of 3
Arab–Israeli war (1973) 17, 53–56, 68, 71, 73, 81, 97, 113–114, 185, 198
Arab League 57, 143, 151, 154, 167

Arab Peace Initiative (API, 2002) 16, 151–155, 167, 201
Arab revolt (1936–1939) 25
Arafat, Yasser 31, 33, 38–39, 62, 83, 123, 144, 146, 150, 166–167, 187
Argov, Shlomo 118–119
arms supplies 108–112
Ascherman, Arik 210
Ashdod 41
Ashkelon 41
Assad, Bashar 42, 153, 190
Assad, Hafez 83, 88, 90
assassination 7, 39, 97, 183, 201
Astorino, Allison 175, 186
Atallah, Amjad 45
Atzili, Boaz 113
autonomy, Palestinian 29–30, 96, 121–122
Avineri, Shlomo 148
Axelrod, Robert 185

backfiring moves 14–15, 18, 106, 189
backing down 128
Baghdad Pact 109
balancing, *internal* and *external* 7
Baldwin, David 99

Index

'bandwagoning' 9
al-Banna, Hassan 34
Barak, Ehud 20, 26, 41, 90, 204
Barakei, Muhammad 46
Barghouti, Marwan 33, 35
Bar-On, Mordechai 111
Bar-Siman-Tov, Yaacov 55
Bar-Tal, Daniel 179–180
Baumgarten, Helga 58, 150
Begin, Menachem 12, 68–69, 72, 76–79, 83–84, 88, 120–121, 140, 183–184, 187
beliefs 22, 31
   about flawed processes of negotiation 135–143
   about instrumentality 4
   changes in 135
   dominant 2, 10, 19
   evaluation of 6
   resilience of 5
Ben-Ami, Shlomo 165
Ben-Gurion, David 24–25, 104–105, 108, 111–114
Bennett, Naftali 195
Bernstein, Peretz 111
Bloom, Mia 124
bombings 42, 130, 132, 196
   see also suicide bombings
Bowen, Jeremy 43
Boycott, Divestment and Sanctions (BDS) movement 209
Brilliant, Moshe 26
Britain 23–24, 111–112, 115
Bunche, Ralph 184
Bush, George H. W. 12, 197–198
Bush, George W. 9, 153, 157, 198

Camp David talks (1978) 13, 72–73, 79, 84–85, 96, 121, 187, 191
Camp David talks (2000) 62, 66, 156

Carter, Jimmy 68–69, 72, 75–76, 80–81, 84–88, 121, 184
case studies, importance of 5
casualties resulting from hostilities 43–46, 51, 66, 101, 108, 196
Caverley, Jonathan 180
ceasefires 40, 73
Chanin, Dror 196
Cheney, Dick 9
Chenoweth, Erica 127
civilians
   deaths of 46
   direct action by 7
   repression or violence towards 7
Clinton, Bill 83, 90, 198
Clinton, Hillary 202
coalitions and counter-coalitions 14
coexistence 11
Cohen, Richard 148
'cold peace' 92–97, 100
Cold War, ending of 185–188
compromise 163–164
   too little or too much 163
concessions, making of 8–11, 18–19, 21–24, 27–32, 36, 43, 49–50, 59, 62–63, 66–67, 72, 77, 84, 87, 90, 98, 100, 103, 105, 113, 115, 129, 138–146, 149–150, 156–157, 164, 167–168, 172–173, 178–179, 183, 190, 192, 199–200, 204, 211
conciliatory moves 11, 19, 133, 136–140, 150
confidence-building measures 185, 188
conflict seen as the norm 174–175
confrontation 52–56, 65–66, 107, 140, 143, 155
constructivist thinking 4
conventional violence and conventional weapons 7–8, 86

Index

Cook, Steven 106
Cordier, Andrew 183
counter-productive moves 11, 16, 18, 99, 103, 108, 131–132, 172, 189
Craig, Gordon 8
Crenshaw, Martha 124
Crusades 34
Cuban Missile Crisis (1962) 183

Dahiya doctrine 43
Dahlan, Mohammed 64
damage caused by military action 43–44
Danon, Danny 154
Dawabsheh family 203
Dayan, Moshe 1, 26, 80, 85, 111–112, 164
Declaration of Independence, Israeli (1948) 164
Declaration of Independence, Palestinian (1988) 166
defensive moves, misperception of 15
Deif, Mohammed 128
Dekker, Willem 130
Del Sarto, Raffaella 30
Democratic Front for the Liberation of Palestine (DFLP) 57, 150
deterrence 9, 21, 25–27, 30, 41–43, 46, 59, 119, 196
deterrence model 138
diplomatic activity 2, 16–19, 45–46, 53, 55, 58, 61, 71–76, 79–81, 91, 98, 108, 114, 121–122, 129, 133–140, 143–144, 150, 163, 169, 189, 192, 197, 204
disengagement plan 16, 64–65
Diskin, Yuval 106
Dulles, John Foster 112

Eban, Abba 83
Economist, The 45
Egypt 21–22, 25–26, 31, 40, 50–56, 65, 67–88, 92–98, 107–108, 111–118
  peace treaty with Israel (1979) 2, 11–13, 16–18, 53, 69, 72–74, 84–87, 94, 97, 166–167, 171, 182–183, 187, 191–192, 198
Eiland, Giora 93
Einstein, Albert 98
Eiran, Ehud 119
El-Amir, Aymin 27
Eldar, Akiva 96
Erdogan, Recep Tayyip 31
Erekat, Saeb 157–158, 160
Eshkol, Levi 25–26
ethnic cleansing 61
European Union 162
expansionism, Israeli 62–67, 82, 197

Fahd plan (1982) 57
Fahmy, Ismail 54, 80, 97
fascism 204
Fatah 32–34, 37, 47, 49, 58, 125, 127, 150, 179, 190–191, 194, 207–208
fear 179–181
  emotional impact of 19
Fedayeen attacks 107–108
Feige, Michael 209
Finlayson, Alan 4
force *see* military force
Ford, Gerald R. 73–74
foreign policy 10, 12, 73, 75, 85, 92, 105, 138, 175, 188, 190–193
formal and informal proposals 136
Fraenkel, Naftali 209–210
Framework for Peace in the Middle East 121
France 31, 86, 111–112, 115

Index

Freilich, Charles 18
Friedman, Thomas 43

Galili, Israel 81
Gandhi, M. 71
Gaza 16, 18, 26–45, 48–51, 54, 59,
    63–66, 70, 91, 108, 116, 128,
    195–196, 202, 208
  Israeli withdrawal from (2005) 22,
    50, 65, 123, 140–144, 148–149,
    155–163, 166, 191
Gaza Raid (1955) 14, 18, 107–110, 114,
    192
Gazit, Shlomo 81
Gemayel, Bashir 100
'Geneva option' 82
George, Alexander 8
geo-strategic factors 63
Getmansky, Anna 180
Golan, Yair 203
Golan Heights 51, 83, 89–91, 168, 178,
    199
Gorbachev, Mikhail 90
Gordon, Neve 46–47
Green Line 60, 167–168
Grossman, David 46
guerrilla warfare 32
Gulf War (1991) 12, 63, 187, 198
Gur, Mordechai 81

Ha'aretz (newspaper) 45–46
Hafez, Abdel 44
Hajjar, Bashir 196
Hamas 21–22, 29, 33–36, 58–59,
    65–67, 93, 100–106, 117, 123–129,
    144, 154–162, 179. 188, 190–196,
    199, 202, 204, 207–208
  Charter (1988) 23, 33–34
  confrontation with Israel
    (2008–2009) 36–49

Hamdan, Osama 48
Haniya, Ismail 48
'hard' power 8
Harkabi, Yehoshafat 138–140, 149
Hawatmeh, Nayef 150
Hebron massacre (1994) 188
hegemony, military 27
Hezbollah 21, 38, 43, 50, 59, 63–64,
    91, 100, 119–122, 130
Hirschhorn, Sara 209
Hobbes, Thomas 274–275
Hroub, Khaled 123
Huddy, Leonie 180
Hussein, King of Jordan 116, 177
Hussein, Saddam 9
Husseini, Rafiq 161

Ibrahim, Izzat 153
ideas 134–137
  changing of 172–173
  dominant 192–193
  hard to dislodge 173–181
  impacts made 4–5, 12–13, 19
  several present at the same time
    173
identity building 175–176
independence, Palestinian 104,
    208–209
'interim' solutions 149
international affairs 12–13, 17
international relations theory 8–9,
    14, 175
intifada
  first (1987–1993) 21–22, 34, 50,
    58–67, 100, 120, 126–127, 150, 191
  second (2000–2005) 14, 18, 33–34,
    39, 50, 64–67, 102–103, 107,
    122–128, 140, 152–158, 175, 192,
    198, 208
Iran 30–31

Index

Iraq 9, 13, 63, 114, 153
Iron Dome defence system 98
Isaiah the prophet 12
Islam 34
  political 33, 37
Islamic Jihad 37, 39, 160, 208
Islamicization 37
Islamism 37, 67, 117–120
Israel, State of
  annexation policy 205–206
  Declaration of Independence (1948) 164
  expansionism 62, 67, 82, 197
  military force used against 59–60, 65–66
  military spending by 93
  recognition of 52, 55, 167, 210–211
  relations with Egypt *see* Egypt
  relations with Gaza *see* Gaza
  relations with Lebanon *see* Lebanon
  warfare engaged in by *see* Arab–Israeli war (1973)
  Six-Day War
  see also more specific headings
Israel Defense Forces (IDF) 26–27, 40–42, 45–46, 49, 64, 108

Jabotinsky, Vladimir 23–25
Jaeger, David 181
Jaffee Center for Strategic Studies 61–62
Jakobsen, Peter 70–71
Jayus 126
Jericho 149
Jerusalem 29, 57–60, 153, 168, 175, 177, 199, 202, 206
  Sadat's visit to (1977) 80–84, 135, 184

Jervis, Robert 135, 138
Jihad 9, 34
Joint Comprehensive Plan of Action (JCPOA) 30
Jordan, State of 2, 11, 51, 57, 166–167, 187

Kaddoumi, Farouq 166
Kagan, Robert 8
Kamel, Mohamed Ibrahim 97
Karameh, battle of (1968) 117
Karsh, Efraim 140
Katsav, Moshe 157
Kelman, Herbert 85, 175, 186, 210
Kennedy, John F. 183
Keohane, Robert 8
Kerry, John 66, 198, 202
Khairi, Bashir 1
Khartoum summit (1967) 52
al-Khatib, Ghassan 161
Khouri, Fred J. 52
kidnapping 193, 195
al-Kidwa, Nasser 166
Kissinger, Henry 69, 72–75
Knesset, the 79–80
Kupchan, Charles 71

'land for peace' principle 29, 80, 87
land swaps 167–168
language of force 7
Laron, Guy 109–110
Lauren, Paul Gordon 8
leadership
  non-unitary 173
  political 182–184, 187
  role of 169–170
League of Arab States *see* Arab League
learning, *simple* and *complex* 186

Index

Lebanon 89, 92, 168
  Israeli invasion of (1982) 14–15, 18, 42, 96, 99–100, 107, 118–122, 131, 192, 198
  Israeli withdrawal from (2000) 22, 63–64, 100, 102, 119, 129–130, 191
Lebow, Richard N. 183
legitimacy 206–207
Legro, Jeffrey 4–5, 136
Lesch, Ann Mosely 96
Levey, Zach 112
Levy, Daniel 45
Levy, David 165
Levy, Gideon 46
liberation of Palestine 32, 34, 37, 57, 143–146
Lieberman, Avigdor 141, 165
Likud 76–78, 84, 183–184
Livni, Tzipi 36, 41–42, 154–155, 165
lose–lose situations 11
Lupovici, Amir 9–10, 30

Maariv (newspaper) 83
al-Mabhouh, Mahmoud 38
Madrid peace conference (1991) 90
Makovsky, David 42
Maoz, Ifat 180
Maoz, Zeev 139, 175
Martin, J. 4
McCauley, Clark 180
mediators 29, 40, 69, 91, 184, 187
Meir, Golda 26, 81, 83
military capability 27, 190
  imbalance in 8, 55, 89–91, 95, 199
military force
  alternatives to 189
  application of 7–8
  effect of 44–46, 66
  historical record of failure 107–128
  questioning the use of 102–106
  reliance on 2–12, 17–38, 47–49, 53–59, 62–67, 70, 73, 79, 81, 93, 98, 100–106, 128, 131, 133–138, 143–144, 150–155, 169–181, 187, 189–192, 189, 191–192, 195–197, 200–205, 210–211
  self-perpetuating quality of 11, 13
  shortcomings of 3, 5–6, 13–18, 23, 54, 47, 67, 70, 91, 99, 106, 191, 193
  used against Israel 59–60, 65–66
  see also threats of use of force
military posture short of actually using force 7
military spending by Israel 93
Miller, Aaron David 74, 85
Milliken, Jennifer 12
Mishal, Khalid 35, 39, 48, 120, 123
missed opportunities 3, 16, 18, 133–136, 144, 155, 168, 171, 192, 204
Moghadam, Assaf 124
Morocco, secret contacts in (1977) 80
Morsi, Mohamed 87
Mubarak, Hosni 93–94
Mueller, Karl 130
Mujama al-Islamiya group 37
Munich Olympics (1972) 117
Muslim Brotherhood 37

Nablus 20, 140
Nachshon, Emmanuel 153–154
Narkiss, Uzi 26
Nasrallah, Sayyid Hassan 64
Nasser, Gamal Abdel 25, 31, 35, 52, 77, 107–118
national identity 176

Index

national interests 2, 79, 116, 127
  see also objectives, national
nationalism 106
  Palestinian 58–60, 121, 205–206, 211
'negative interdependence' (Kelman) 175
negotiations
  allegedly flawed process of 135–143
  belief in 2–3, 5–6, 10–14, 17–18, 21, 26–30, 33–37, 40, 47, 49, 53–54, 62–63, 70, 75, 81–87, 90–92, 120–121, 133–134, 155, 163, 168, 171–173
  continuing role for 11–12, 19, 182
  disadvantages of 10, 16, 136
neo-conservatives 9
Nepstad, Sharon E. 71
Netanyahu, Benjamin 27–30, 66, 69, 106, 140–141, 153–155, 165, 193–196, 201, 204–205
Netherlands, the 114
New York Times 43, 82, 147–148
'nibbling' 139
Nixon, Richard 73–74, 197
Norway 62–63, 184
nuclear weapons 30, 86
Nye, Joseph 8

Obama, Barack 28–30, 197–198, 202
objectives, national 10–12, 18–19, 52, 101, 189, 200
occupied territories 52–53, 57–64, 67, 70, 79, 103, 120, 146, 149, 159
Olmert, Ehud 40–42, 66, 90–91, 154
al-Omari, Ghaith 65
Oren, Michael 109
Organisation of Islamic Cooperation 152

Oron, Assaf 26
Osgood, Charles 185
Oslo process and agreement (1993) 2, 12, 28, 33–34, 37–39, 50, 58, 62, 65, 83, 102–103, 117, 123, 140–145, 149, 167, 171, 173, 184–188, 193
overlap between different tactics 3
Oz, Amos 71

Palestine Liberation Organization (PLO) 15–16, 21, 31–33, 37–40, 50, 57–58, 61–62, 66–67, 99–100, 117–121, 167, 178, 185, 199
  Charter (1968) 23, 31–32, 117
  ten-point programme (1974) 18, 122, 143, 145–151
Palestinian Authority (PA) 38, 143–145, 156–161, 205, 208
Palestinian homeland 35, 82, 202
Palestinian National Council 145, 148
Palmor, Yigal 46
pan-Arabism 113–114
Pape, Robert 130
partition of Palestine, proposed (1947) 32, 55, 177
peace, commitment to 133, 135, 141, 154–155, 164–167, 180
peace dividend 93
peace process 45, 142, 146, 157
peacekeeping forces 51, 74, 115–116
Pearlman, Wendy 113
Peres, Shimon 93, 152–153, 165, 187
Peretz, Amir 98
Peretz, Don 60
Peri, Yaakov 155
Podeh, Elie 155
political action 150, 211

Index

Popular Front for the Liberation of Palestine (PFLP) 1, 32–33, 57
post-traumatic stress disorder (PTSD) 66, 196
pre-emptive strikes 131
protest movements 127
Pullan, Wendy 169–170

Quandt, William 74, 86
Quartet, the 155–156, 160, 195

Ra'anan, Uri 109
Rabin, Yitzhak 12, 25–26, 58–59, 62, 74, 83, 119, 182–183, 187, 201
radicalization 181
Rajoub, Jibril 127–128
al-Rantissi, Abdel 39
Rayyan, Nizar 48
Raz, Avi 177–178
Reagan, Ronald 121, 198
'realist' view of the world 8, 19, 173–174
reciprocity 74
recognition of Israel 52, 55, 167, 210–211
reconciliation
  between opponents 13, 178
  with opponents 149
refugee issue 151, 153
Regev, Mark 161
reprisals and retaliation 105, 111, 141
Revisionist Zionism 23
Riad, Mohamed 97
Rice, Condoleezza 162
Rid, Thomas 110
'Roadmap' proposal (2003) 153–154
rocket attacks 39–41, 47–49, 64, 100, 125, 159–160, 180, 193–194
Roth, Ariel Ilan 129
Roy, Sara 160

Rubin, Barry 49
Rusk, Dean 183
Rutenberg, Roi 1

Sabra refugee camp 100
Sadat, Anwar 12, 53–55, 68–69, 72–76, 79, 88, 129, 182–184, 187
  assassination of 97
  visit to Israel (1977) 80–84, 135, 184
'salami' tactics 148
Salem, Saleh 35
Salim, Sobhi 106
Samu 116
Saudi Arabia 15, 207
Sayegh, Fayez 32
Sayigh, Yezid 120, 146
Scheindlin, Dahlia 106
Schiff, Ze'ev 60
Sderot 41
secret talks 80, 183
secularism 117
security dilemma in Arab–Israeli relations 14–16, 192
security policy 3, 10–14, 18, 86, 100–111, 114–118, 127, 141, 143
Segev, Tom 43, 106
self-determination, Palestinian 40, 102, 126, 147, 150, 199, 204
self-fulfilling prophecies 190
settlements policy 38–39, 58, 62–67, 77, 103, 117–118, 125, 142, 144, 156–161, 169–170, 197–198, 202, 205, 208
Shafi, Haidar Abdel 142
Shahade, Salah 39
Shalit, Gilad 40
Shalom, Silvan 157, 165, 169
Sharett, Moshe 24–25, 102–105, 111, 114, 141

Index

Sharon, Ariel 25–27, 64, 140, 153–154, 156–159, 165
Sharon, Gilad 154
Sharp, Gene 71
Shatila refugee camp 100
Shavit, Ari 27
el-Shazly, Saad 54–55
Shepherdstown talks (2000) 90
Shikaki, Khalil 65, 181
Shilon, Avi 27
Shimoni, Gideon 25
Shin Bet 194
Shlaim, Avi 112
shows of force 9, 27, 115
shuttle diplomacy 74
'siege mentality' 180
Siegman, Henry 142
Sinai Peninsula 35, 51, 54, 68, 72–79, 83–84, 87–88, 93, 115–118, 129, 167, 178
Six-Day War (1967) 15–18, 22, 25, 29, 31, 50–59, 67–68, 71, 77–78, 97, 107, 113–118, 124, 131, 177, 191–192, 199
Skocpol, Theda 3
social constructivist thinking 175
Soviet Union 15, 21, 54–56, 63, 80, 90, 109–110, 115, 120, 185–188
Spain 9
speeches, analysis of 4
statehood, Palestinian 61–62, 126–127, 147–148, 151, 200–291, 207
states and non-state actors, differences between 17–18, 129, 190–191
status quo, the, acceptance of 16, 42, 59–60, 73, 142, 149, 185, 201

Stein, Janice Gross 181, 183, 186
Stein, Kenneth 95–96
Steinitz, Yuval 154
Stephan, Maria 127
Suez Canal 68, 72–75, 129
Suez war (1956) 14, 18, 35, 107, 112–114, 192
suicide bombings 29, 34, 39, 48, 103, 122–125, 152, 161
Sulaiman, Adel 93–94
Syria 13, 15, 18, 21–22, 26, 51–56, 63, 67, 69–70, 73, 79, 88–92, 98, 100, 116, 120–121, 153, 166, 168, 185; civil war (2011) 42, 89, 91, 190

Taba 62, 66, 93
Tal, David 110, 112
terrorism 7, 26, 28, 33, 38–39, 117–120, 141, 150, 152, 158, 188, 201–203
theories in political science, testing of 6–7
threats of use of force 9, 18, 36, 67, 71, 75, 85, 91–92, 101, 106, 130, 138, 179–181, 186, 190–193
Thucydides 8
Tiran Strait 51, 116
Trump, Donald 30, 199–200
Tuhami, Hassan 80, 109
Turkey 31
two-state solution 28–30, 43, 45, 56–58, 61–62, 66, 103–104, 122, 140–143, 147, 151, 154, 167, 199–201, 204–205, 210–211

understanding the other side's needs 11
unexpected consequences 13–15, 118, 195

Index

United Nations 32, 51, 55, 164–165, 184, 197
  Emergency Force 115
United Nations Security Council 57, 187
  Resolution 194 151
  Resolution 242 52–53, 58, 77, 149
  Resolution 338 58, 75
United States 9, 27, 31, 39, 53–54, 73–76, 80, 114–115, 142, 162, 184, 188, 196–200
  Agency for International Development (USAID) 94
  State Department 195

Vance, Cyrus 85
vital interests 130–131

Waage, Hilde Henriksen 198
Waltz, Kenneth 8
warfare 7, 21
  economic cost of 54
'warm peace' 69–71, 92–93, 98
Watzman, Haim 46
weakness, signs of 27, 36, 100, 115, 133, 136, 138, 143–144, 192
Weisglas, Dov 157–158, 160
Weizman, Ezer 25, 81, 96
Welch, David 158
Wendt, Alexander 175, 186

West Bank of the Jordan 1, 14, 24, 37–38, 48, 51, 56–61, 64, 66, 70, 76–79, 82, 148, 177–178, 201, 204–205, 209–211
  wall 125–126
West Bank State (WBS) 147
West Bank Story (film) 136–137
withdrawals, territorial 22, 29, 50, 63–66, 72, 75–79, 84, 93, 119, 123, 129, 140, 143–144, 148–149, 166–167, 191
Wolfensohn, James 160–162

Ya'alon, Moshe 140, 142, 144, 154, 195
Ya'ari, Ehud 60
Yacobi, Haim 169–170
Yadlin, Amos 41
Yaniv, Avner 9
Yasin, Ahmad 123
Yassin, Ahmed 20, 37, 39
Yehiyeh, Abdel Razak 103
Yisrael, Agudat 78

Zahar, Mahmoud 48
Zanoli, Henk 196
Zartman, I. William 177
Ze'evi, Rehavam 26
Zeitzoff, Thomas 180
Zionism 23–24, 27, 34, 142, 206
Zisser, Eyal 118